Civic Engagement in Australian Democracy

Civic Engagement in Australian Democracy

Edited by

Sarah Murray and Lachlan Umbers

ANTHEM PRESS

Anthem Press
An imprint of Wimbledon Publishing Company
www.anthempress.com

This edition first published in UK and USA 2025
by ANTHEM PRESS
75–76 Blackfriars Road, London SE1 8HA, UK
or PO Box 9779, London SW19 7ZG, UK
and
244 Madison Ave #116, New York, NY 10016, USA

British Library Cataloguing-in-Publication Data
A catalogue record for this book is available from the British Library.

Library of Congress Cataloging-in-Publication Data: 2024950818
A catalog record for this book has been requested.

ISBN-13: 978-1-83999-353-4 (Hbk)
ISBN-10: 1-83999-353-7 (Hbk)

This title is also available as an e-book.

CONTENTS

ACKNOWLEDGEMENTS

Putting this collection together was an immensely enjoyable process. We would like to thank all of the contributors to the volume (and the workshop that preceded it) for their excellent substantive contributions, and the care and attention paid to each other's work as peer reviewers.

We would also like to acknowledge the work of Jack Stewart for his excellent research assistance. The project received financial assistance from the University of Western Australia in the form of a travel grant from the UWA Institute for Advanced Studies and funding allocated to our 'Seeking to Strengthen Australian Democracy' Research Pursuit. We gratefully acknowledge both contributions.

For editorial assistance, we thank Golda, Jebaslin and three anonymous reviewers for Anthem Press, whose invaluable advice improved the collection immeasurably.

Sarah Murray and Lachlan Umbers

LIST OF CONTRIBUTORS

Alan Gamlen is a professor in the School of Regulation and Global Governance at the Australian National University. He is an expert on human migration and mobility. Alan's research has received funding from the Australian Research Council, the Royal Society of New Zealand, the UK Leverhulme Trust, the UK Economic and Social Research Council, the New Zealand Bright Futures Fund and the Japan Society for the Promotion of Science, and he has advised international bodies, governments and NGOs on migration policy. His book *Human Geopolitics* earned him the 2020 Distinguished Book Award for Ethnicity and Migration from the International Studies Association.

Andrea Carson is a professor of political communication in the Department of Politics, Media and Philosophy at La Trobe University in Melbourne, Australia, and a 2024 Visiting Academic Associate at the Reuters Institute for the Study of Journalism, Green Templeton College, University of Oxford. She has authored numerous articles and books on political communication, election campaigns and the media, and mis and disinformation. She previously worked as a journalist at *The Age* newspaper and at the ABC in radio and television.

Chika Anyanwu is a professor of media at UNSW. He is an educational leader renowned for reshaping academic institutions into contemporary educational hubs. His research areas encompass digital media policy, creative industries, African political economy, diaspora and migration, with numerous publications and successful research projects.

David Mickler is the dean of Global Africa, the director of the Centre for Australia-Africa Relations and an associate professor in international relations in the Faculty of Humanities at Curtin University. He works at the intersection of International Relations and African Studies as a scholar and practitioner of academic diplomacy. He serves as Deputy Co-Chair of the Australia Africa Universities Network (AAUN) and as Australian Representative to the Indian Ocean Rim Association Academic Group (IORAG), and he is a Future Africa Visiting Fellow at the University of Pretoria in South Africa.

Dominic Dagbanja is an associate professor at Curtin Law School. He is also a researcher specializing in international investment law and its impact on public interest regulation. Dr Dagbanja is a research fellow at Stellenbosch University, South Africa; a fellow of Higher Education Academy, United Kingdom; and a technical consultant at Growth Perspective Ltd., Jamaica.

Farida Fozdar (aka Tilbury) is a professor of anthropology and sociology and the dean of Global Futures (Humanities) at Curtin University. Her research focus is on migration, race and ethnicity, refugee settlement, racism, nationalism, global citizenship and cosmopolitanism. She has published widely with over a hundred and thirty journal articles, chapters, books and policy-relevant reports. Her current Australian Research Council-funded projects explore African migrants' political and economic engagement and the impacts of securitization legislation on Muslim Australian communities.

Ian Murray is a professor based at the Law School at the University of Western Australia and researches at the intersection of not-for-profit law, tax, trusts and corporate governance. He has practical experience in the regulatory and governance issues faced by not-for-profits, having been a not-for-profit board member, including chairperson, for over five years. Ian has published widely on charity tax concessions, charity regulation, native title charities, accumulation of assets by charities, tax administration and resource taxation from the perspectives of tax policy, equity, trusts, property law, corporations law, regulatory theory and political philosophy. His book *Charity Law & Accumulation: Maintaining an Intergenerational Balance* won the ARNOVA 2023 Virginia A Hodgkinson Research Book Award.

Janet Dzator is an applied economist and a director of the Centre for African Research, Engagement and Partnerships at the University of Newcastle, Australia. Her research focuses on the impact of policy on behaviour and development, with interests in energy, health, equity and sustainability. Her work in applied economics appears in national and international peer-reviewed book chapters, top-ranking journals and conference proceedings.

Jill Sheppard is a senior lecturer in politics at the Australian National University and an investigator on the Australian Election Study. Her research focuses on why people participate in politics, what opinions they hold and why, and how both are shaped by political institutions and systems. Methodologically, her interests focus on sampling and fielding population-based surveys, questionnaire design and respondent recruitment and retention. Jill is also an investigator on the World Values Survey and Asian Barometer Survey.

Joo-Cheong Tham is a professor at Melbourne Law School with expertise in labour law and public law. Joo-Cheong's scholarly publications include his books on *Money and Politics: The Democracy We Can't Afford* (2010), *Electoral Democracy: Australian Prospects* (2011), *The Funding of Political Parties: Where Now?* (2012), *Democracy, Social Justice and the*

Role of Trade Unions (2021) and *Global Labor Migrations: New Directions* (2022). He has also led two major reports for International IDEA, *Climate Change and Democracy: Insights from Asia and the Pacific* (2023) and *Digital Campaigning and Political Finance in the Asia and the Pacific Region: A New Age for an Old Problem* (2022). Joo-Cheong is presently working on a report for International IDEA on digital campaigning resources and democracy and a book project on labour law, the climate crisis and democratic solidarity. He is also the National Tertiary Education Union's Victorian Assistant Secretary (Academic Staff) and an inaugural director of the Centre for Public Integrity.

Justin McCaul is a member of the Mbarbarum people of Far North Queensland. He is currently a postdoctoral fellow at the College of Law, Australian National University (ANU), Canberra.

Justin Phillips is a political scientist and a senior lecturer in the School of Social Sciences at the University of Waikato, New Zealand. He studies comparative political communication with a focus on social media utilizing big datasets. Recently published articles have investigated political communication across traditional and social media during US, New Zealand and Australian election campaigns.

Karen Farquarson is a professor of Sociology and the chair of the Anti-Racism Hallmark Research Initiative at the University of Melbourne. Her research focuses on the sociology of 'race', racism and diversity, with a particular emphasis on media and sport contexts. She has authored and co-authored several books and collections, exploring topics such as diversity management in organizations and the politics of belonging.

Kiros Hiruy is a development anthropologist with expertise in regional and international development at Swinburne University. His broad research interest is understanding development and social change at local, regional and international levels. His particular interests include understanding the dynamics of social impact in rural and regional areas, the social impact of non-governmental organizations (NGOs) and diaspora (African) and social change. Kiros' experiences span international and regional development, sustainable farming, training, social research, environmental management and migration and settlement in Africa, Southeast Asia, the Pacific and Australia.

Lachlan Umbers is a senior lecturer and chair of philosophical studies at the University of Western Australia. He works primarily in moral and political philosophy, with a particular focus on issues in democratic theory and climate justice. His work has been published in journals such as the *British Journal of Political Science*, *Perspectives on Politics*, *Philosophical Studies*, *Political Studies* and the *European Journal of Political Theory*. With Jeremy Moss, he is the co-editor of *Climate Justice and Non-State Actors* (2020) and the co-author of *Climate Justice Beyond the State* (2021).

Murray Wesson is an associate professor in the Law School at the University of Western Australia, where he teaches and researches constitutional law, human rights law and legal theory. He has published widely in these areas, especially on the implied freedom of political communication in Australian constitutional law and social and economic rights in South African constitutional law. He is the lead chief investigator on the Australian Research Council Linkage Infrastructure, Equipment and Facilities grant, 'Digitising the Drafting of the Australian Constitution'. Through a collaboration between the Quill Project at the University of Oxford and nine Australian universities, the grant will support the creation of an open-access, online archive that consolidates, corrects and enhances the digital record of the drafting of the Australian Constitution. Murray is an ordinary member of the Council of the Australian Association of Constitutional Law and also the co-convenor of the Western Australian chapter. He is regularly interviewed by the media on issues in his areas of expertise and has made numerous submissions to parliamentary and other enquiries.

Narelle Miragliotta is an associate professor in the School of Humanities, Arts and Social Sciences at Murdoch University. Her research interests include constitutional politics, elections and electoral systems, political parties and other political institutions. Her work has been published in journals including *European Political Science Review*, *Government and Opposition*, *Party Politics*, *Election Law Journal* and *Electoral Studies*.

Nicholas Barry is a senior lecturer in political science at La Trobe University. His research and teaching interests are in the areas of political theory, political institutions and Australian politics. He is currently working on a number of projects relating to contemporary theories of egalitarian justice, the dynamics of constitutional norms and conventions, and the contemporary Australian party system. His work has been published in journals including the *Canadian Journal of Political Science*, *Australian Journal of Political Science*, *Journal of Politics*, *Governance*, *Parliamentary Affairs* and *Journal of Applied Philosophy*.

Nothando Ngwenya is a project officer at Curtin University specializing in the coordination of social science projects at the state and national levels. She holds a master's degree in international development from the University of Western Australia, specializing in development practice. Nothando has a keen interest in the experiences of the African diaspora and is committed to making meaningful contributions to work supporting Africans in Australia.

Paul Kildea is an associate professor in the School of Global and Public Law, in the Faculty of Law & Justice, at the University of New South Wales. He is also the director of the Elections & Referendums Project at the Gilbert + Tobin Centre of Public Law and a co-convenor of the NSW chapter of the Electoral Regulation Research Network. Paul has published widely on referendums, election law and federalism. Paul is currently undertaking research into state and territory referendums, referendum rules and electoral law reform.

Phoebe Hayman is a PhD candidate at La Trobe University. She researches election campaigns, community organizing and campaign organization. Her doctoral thesis examines the 2022 'Teal' campaigns as a case study of shifting norms in political participation.

Ron Levy, Australian National University, is an interdisciplinary researcher writing on public law and political theory – especially deliberative democratic theory. His recent projects explore referendums in deeply divided societies, Indigenous constitutional reform, environmental constitutionalism and the deliberative dimensions of rights practice. Levy's books include *Deliberative Peace Referendums* (2021, with Ian O'Flynn and Hoi Kong), *The Cambridge Handbook of Deliberative Constitutionalism* (2018, with Hoi Kong, Graeme Orr and Jeff King eds) and *The Law of Deliberative Democracy* (2016, with Graeme Orr).

Ryan Cox is an associate lecturer in philosophy at the University of Sydney. He has published widely in the philosophy of mind and action, epistemology, the philosophy of language, ethics and political philosophy. His work has appeared in journals such as the *Journal of Ethics and Social Philosophy*, *Journal of Applied Philosophy*, *Synthese* and *Philosophical Topics*.

Sarah Murray is an expert in constitutional law and electoral law, court innovation and community justice centres and is a professor based at the Law School at the University of Western Australia. She is a former WA Law Reform Commissioner, a Fellow of the Australian Academy of Law and is Co-Chair of the International Society of Public Law AUS-NZ Chapter. She has published widely in Australia and internationally including being the author of *The Remaking of the Courts- Less-Adversarial Practice and the Constitutional Role of the Judiciary in Australia* (Federation Press, 2014) and a co-author of *The Constitution of the Commonwealth of Australia – History, Principle and Interpretation* (CUP, 2015) and *Winterton's Australian Federal Constitutional Law* (Thomson Reuters, 2022).

Sarah Prout Quicke is a population geographer and an associate professor of geography at the University of Western Australia. Her research interests lie at the intersection of sociology and demography and how these shape and are shaped by place. Her research examines population, development and social policy issues in Indigenous Australia and Africa, with a particular focus on Indigenous mobility and migration, education and housing policy and regional development in resource economies.

Zim Nwokora is an associate professor in Politics and Policy at Deakin University, Melbourne. His expertise is in comparative political institutions, especially constitutions, political parties and political finance. His research on these topics has appeared in leading journals in political science and cognate fields, including the *British Journal of Political Science, International Journal of Constitutional Law, Governance, Party Politics, Political Research Quarterly* and *Political Studies*. He is co-author of *Money, Parties, and Democracy: Political Finance between Fat Cats and Big Government*, forthcoming with Oxford University Press, and co-editor of *Constitutional Conventions: Theories, Practices and Dynamics*, forthcoming with Routledge.

Chapter 1

INTRODUCTION

Lachlan Umbers and Sarah Murray

Few would deny the importance of an active citizenry in a democracy. In 2014, for instance, the International Social Survey Programme asked around 50,000 citizens in 34 countries to rank on a scale of 1 to 7 how important it is for citizens to 'always vote in elections'. About 80 per cent gave a ranking of 5 (11.2 per cent), 6 (16.4 per cent) or 7 (51.8 per cent) (ISSP 2016). Many of us, moreover, are deeply impressed by citizens active within the democratic process in other ways. Organising campaigns, attending demonstrations, petitioning government, knocking on doors and so on – such acts seem to exemplify the promise of democracy as 'rule by the people'.

Presumably, such attitudes stem partly from the fact that democracies are nothing more or less than elaborate systems of norms governing the exercise and distribution of political power. Norms persist only where a sufficient proportion of the citizenry both (a) personally adhere to them and (b) have sufficient confidence that *other* citizens also do so (Bicchieri 2017). Those who seek to advance their political objectives through the democratic process (rather than by circumventing it) thereby express allegiance to the norms constitutive of that process. This, in turn, plays a vital role in sustaining such norms and, as such, protects and promotes the democratic form of life most of us value highly.[1]

Moreover, virtually every theoretical account of the nature of democracy emphasises the importance of participation.[2] Carole Pateman (1970, 2012), for instance, holds that participation is nothing less than the fundamental *purpose* of democratic government. For her, it is only by positively engaging with matters of public significance that individuals may come to develop the virtues necessary for a desirable form of collective life. Only in a democracy of the right kind – one in which citizens not merely enjoy extensive *rights* of participation, but wherein such rights are *exercised* – will this be possible. Pateman's, of course, is a particularly expansive view of democracy. But even so-called minimalists, who see democracy as merely a process through which elites acquire power 'by means of a competitive struggle for the people's vote' (Schumpeter 1950, 269), nevertheless have reason to hold that broad participation is essential if democracies are to deliver desirable outcomes. For such figures, the marvel of democracy is that incumbents typically

1. For an argument that such considerations give rise to a duty to participate in elections, see Umbers (2024).
2. There are many other approaches besides the two outlined here, of course.

surrender power peacefully in response to election results – a dynamic that depends crucially upon a sufficient proportion of the citizenry electing to vote and thereby indicating the real balance of public opinion (see esp. Przeworski 1999).

Participation, then, is a subject of perennial importance for those with an interest in the democratic process. But for those of us with interests in Australian democracy, specifically, recent events have brought such issues into sharper focus.

The ways in which Australians participate in the democratic process are rapidly changing. Consider the precipitous rise in early voting. In 2004, for instance, around 10 per cent of voters in the Federal Election cast their ballots prior to election day. In 2022, over 50 per cent did so (Muller 2022). Less than 1 per cent of Australians now belong to a political party (Gauja 2015, 29), while – according to data from the Australian Election Study (AES, hereafter) – the proportion of voters that has 'always voted for the same party in elections' has declined from 72 per cent in 1967 to 37 per cent in 2022 (Cameron and McAllister 2022, 22). The share of the major parties' primary vote in the lower house has fallen from an average of around 90 per cent in the 1950s–1980s to an all-time low of 68.3 per cent in 2022 (Raue 2023, 342). Such developments have had important consequences. For instance, the success of the Teal independents in 2022, the rise of the Greens and the rotating cast of minor parties in the Senate are all partly attributable to the increasing willingness of Australians to look beyond the major parties.

The past decade has also afforded Australians two notable, historically rare, opportunities to participate directly in the lawmaking process. The 2017 same-sex marriage postal survey, for instance, ultimately led to the legal recognition of same-sex marriage, while the 2023 referendum on enshrining an Aboriginal and Torres Strait Islander Voice to Parliament in the Australian Constitution was defeated by a significant margin. Such exercises raise very difficult questions. Many of those in favour of same-sex marriage saw the postal survey as repugnant, insofar as it appeared to invite the public to 'weigh in' on a matter of fundamental civic equality. Nevertheless, it seems undeniable that the survey proved an effective means of bringing about politically contentious policy change. How, then, should we think of the exercise? Does it represent an abrogation of responsibility on the part of the legislature? Or does it demonstrate that direct participation of this form might provide a means of 'cutting through' otherwise intractable disagreement? The Voice referendum raises still more difficult questions around the claims of oppressed minority groups to be afforded special, distinctive avenues of political representation, whether – if such claims are valid – such bodies need to be afforded recognition in the constitution (rather than merely in legislation), the challenging process of bringing about constitutional and legislative change in such areas, and the legitimacy of the Australian democratic process itself, given our history of colonisation and dispossession.

Finally, the global outlook for democracy is troubled. As we write these sentences, democracy is quite literally under siege in Ukraine. Several nascent democracies have collapsed back into forms of authoritarianism in recent times (Diamond 2015). Even in very well-established democracies, there are reasons for concern. Consider the rise of demagogues like Geert Wilders and Marine Le Pen in Europe, the presidency of

Donald Trump and his attempts to thwart the peaceful transfer of power, the chaos and confusion that have reigned in British democracy following the results of the 2016 Brexit referendum, and so on. Turnout has also been in decline for several decades in the majority of democracies around the world (Vowles 2017). Data from the Institute for Democracy and Electoral Assistance shows that participation rates in national-level presidential and parliamentary elections over the period 2011–2021, worldwide, averaged just over 60 per cent of voting-age populations (IDEA 2021).

Yet, from a certain point of view, Australian democracy is bucking the trend. Turnout remains high, averaging 91.49 per cent for elections to the House of Representatives over the period 2013–2022 (AEC 2022). In contrast to their counterparts in the United Kingdom and United States, neither of the major parties has moved significantly towards the far left or right. Leadership instability notwithstanding, the Federal government has not been afflicted by the gridlock that bedevils American democracy (except, perhaps, on climate policy). And, hard-fought though the 2022 election campaign might have been, following the defeat of the incumbent government, power was transferred peacefully and efficiently, with no attempt to question the legitimacy of the results.

However, there are signs of rising dissatisfaction. For instance, turnout in the 2022 election was below 90 per cent for the House of Representatives for the first time since the introduction of compulsory voting in the 1920s. Though, doubtless, there are many causes (some benign – e.g. higher rates of voter registration), it seems likely that some of the decline is driven by the same forces that have driven turnout decline in other democracies. Blais and Rubenson (2013, 107–122), for instance, have shown that declining turnout in American elections is driven, at least in part, by a declining sense of political efficacy. Australians' feelings of political efficacy are also in decline. On the 2022 AES, just 60 per cent of respondents agreed that 'who people vote for can make a big difference', down from 70 per cent in 1996 (Cameron and McAllister 2022, 103). According to one recent estimate, but for compulsory voting, '[…] turnout would be 40 points lower in Australia […] (i.e., it would be 50 per cent instead of 90 per cent)' (Dassonneville et al. 2023, 53).

Data from the AES, moreover, reveals a public increasingly dissatisfied with its political leaders and with how its democracy is working (Cameron and McAllister 2022). In 2022, 54 per cent of respondents agreed that government was largely run 'for a few big interests', with just 12 per cent agreeing that government was run for 'all the people'. Just 14 per cent agreed that politicians 'know what ordinary people think', and only 30 per cent agreed that 'people in government can be trusted'. The same percentage expressed dissatisfaction with democracy itself. In all cases (though to varying degrees), these figures have steadily worsened since 2007 – a concerning trend, which coincides with the potentially troubling implications of the decline in traditional news media and the associated rise of new digital platforms and the opportunities for misinformation (among other things) such platforms entail.[3]

3. We should also, of course, bear in mind the potentially troubling implications of generative artificial intelligence, the actual and likely effects of which on the democratic process are not yet well-understood.

One should not overstate the case. Relative to much of the rest of the world, Australian democracy is favourably positioned. Nevertheless, the future seems very unclear. What does seem certain, however, is that much will depend upon Australians themselves - their willingness to participate in our democracy, the results they seek to realise by doing so and what exactly our institutions do and do not enable them to achieve. The chapters in this volume seek to focus attention on such issues.

We begin with the significance of constitutional conventions in Miragliotta, Nwokora, Barry and Murray's chapter – 'Citizen Guardians? Civic Engagement and Constitutional Conventions'. Such conventions are unwritten norms that help to operationalise the system of representative government mandated by the Australian Constitution. Conventions of this kind typically emerge over time as a by-product of interactions among political elites and are essential for both enabling and constraining the democratic process. Yet, given that such conventions are characteristically unwritten and therefore not enforceable by courts, the sanctions that may attach to their violation are (save for the prospect of losing one's seat at the next election) at the discretion of the *very same* political actors whose conduct they are intended to regulate. Of course, this allows for a degree of flexibility with respect to both the content of such norms and their enforcement. Where circumstances change, the relevant actors can either selectively excuse violations where this is justified or else move towards a more optimal set of norms, discarding outmoded or inefficient rules.

Yet this also entails obvious risks. There are many instances in which officials have both opportunities to violate constitutional norms and the means to effectively evade sanctions. Consider former prime minister Scott Morrison having himself secretly sworn into multiple ministerial portfolios – an obvious breach of the norms of responsible government. The relevant constitutional conventions, here, failed to function as an effective deterrent given Morrison's ability to conceal his actions. Insofar as all norms presuppose a degree of voluntary compliance on the part of the relevant actors, such acts constitute a significant threat to the established constitutional order. How, then, might we safeguard such norms while, at the same time, allowing officials the flexibility necessary to reform or selectively breach them where this is justified?

Miragliotta et al. suggest a path forward. For them, the purpose of political conventions is to help address the principal-agent problem that arises between the citizenry and their elected representatives. To advance the interests of the citizenry, it is essential that elected representatives should enjoy significant authority and discretion. Yet this very fact enables officials to neglect or undermine the citizenry's interests, should they wish to. The role of conventions is to help restrain officials' conduct, in this respect. The challenge is to ensure that there be some effective means of *deterring* officials from violating these norms. The most obvious solution (indeed, the only solution short of codifying such norms in law and thereby sacrificing the benefits associated with their adaptability to circumstance) is to ensure that office-seeking politicians face a non-trivial threat of electoral sanction (i.e. the loss of their seat or at least the diminution of their majority) where they violate such conventions. Yet this presupposes that the electorate is aware of the relevant conventions and is prepared to punish incumbents who violate them. Citizens, they suggest, must become *custodians* of such conventions – a process which, first and foremost, requires the diffusion of *knowledge* about such norms. As the authors acknowledge, this presents a formidable challenge. Yet there are a wide range of potential strategies that might be attempted in this respect. And, given the inherent fragility of such norms and their importance to the democratic system, it is vital that some such attempt be made.

We next consider the issue of voting. Australia is one of very few advanced democracies that legally obliges citizens to vote and enforces such obligations with (moderate) sanctions.[4] Its effects are profound. Turnout would undoubtedly be significantly lower in its absence, and it is very likely that Australian politics would have a very different complexion were the parties required to act as agents of voter mobilisation (as in other democracies). Sheppard's chapter, 'Compulsory Voting in an Era of Democratic Disengagement', both discusses the emergence of compulsory voting and considers – in light of rising dissatisfaction – the ways in which Australian democracy might be reformed so as to allow citizens to *express* that dissatisfaction in a manner consistent with their obligation to participate.

Compulsory voting was introduced for Federal elections in 1924, Sheppard explains, following a steep decline in turnout. The causes of this decline remain somewhat opaque. But the introduction of compulsory voting as a *solution* to this problem is very notable. As Sheppard notes, the parties do not appear to have seriously considered many alternatives (e.g. improving their mobilisation operations). This seems especially remarkable, given that the fine imposed for non-attendance was £2 – equivalent to $290 today. The effects on Australian politics were significant, plausibly contributing to the consolidation of the two major political parties – Liberal and Labor – by the mid-1940s that have dominated Australia's political landscape ever since. Insofar as it diminishes parties' incentives to maintain a large membership base to draw upon at election time for mobilisation efforts, it has probably contributed to declining party membership. It has also plausibly contributed to the centripetal tendencies of the Australian political system, with important effects on the conduct of political debate and, thereby, policy.

As noted above, however, there are signs of dissatisfaction among voters in the Australian political system. The *objects* of this dissatisfaction have frequently been the major parties – indeed, the share of voters that do not identify with either of the major parties (or, indeed, *any* party) has risen markedly since the early 1990s. Dissatisfied voters may typically opt for one of three ways to express their dissatisfaction: vote for a minor party, decline to participate or seek to reform the system itself. Yet Australia's combination of compulsory and preferential voting (for the lower house) undermines the power of the first and penalises the second. Sheppard argues, then, that there is a range of reforms that might potentially be attractive to the major players in Australian democracy that could afford citizens a greater range of opportunities to express dissatisfaction.

4. For an outstanding overview of the evidence concerning compulsory voting's effects, see Singh (2021, 38–56). For an account of its impact on Australian voters, see Dassonneville et al. (2023). For discussion of the significance of compulsory voting for Australian democracy, see Bonotti and Strangio (2021).

Adopting multi-member proportional representation in the lower house, lowering the fine for abstention to a merely symbolic penalty, and expanding access to convenience voting would all afford citizens such opportunities while keeping the general structure of Australian democracy more or less intact. Enhancing opportunities for participation within the parties themselves would also, she suggests, potentially be of significant benefit.

Next, we consider the issue of early voting, the rise of which appears to have been driven largely by reforms introduced in 2010 allowing for pre-poll ballots to be counted as 'ordinary ballots', thereby eliminating the requirement for citizens to submit a formal declaration that they were eligible to vote early under Schedule 2 of the *Commonwealth Electoral Act 1918* (Cth). Since that time, the popularity of pre-polling has exploded, while rates of mail balloting have remained largely constant. This, together with other indications, suggests that very many Australians are now pre-polling for reasons of mere convenience (though this is not strictly permitted under the Act) (Coma and Smith 2023).

Is this a desirable state of affairs? Umbers' chapter, 'Early Voting and the Democratic Ideal', argues in the negative. He begins by rationally reconstructing the most antecedently plausible arguments for allowing universal access to early voting, both of which begin from the observation that the costs of election-day participation can vary greatly between citizens. This raises two kinds of concerns. First, one might hold that significant inequalities in the cost of voting undermine citizens' equality of substantive opportunities to vote. And, second, insofar as there are reasons to suspect that citizens of lower socioeconomic status will characteristically face higher costs of voting on election day, a requirement to do so threatens to worsen the under-participation of such persons in elections. Universal early voting would mitigate both these concerns. Yet both these arguments fail. The latter because empirical studies overwhelmingly suggest that early voting disproportionately mobilises citizens of *higher* socioeconomic status. The former, on the other hand, trades on an ambiguity between two notions of equality of opportunity: a requirement to render the costs of voting approximately equal and a requirement to ensure that no citizen faces an unreasonably high cost of voting. The case for universal early voting rests upon the first interpretation. Yet there are decisive reasons to prefer the second. Equality of opportunity requires us to ensure that the costs of voting are not excessive, but this only requires making early voting accessible to those for whom election-day participation would be unreasonably great.

Umbers then goes on to suggest, further, that there are reasons to think that a system of universal early voting is positively *unjustified*. In casting one's ballot, one forecloses the possibility of engaging in further deliberation as to who one ought to vote for. In voting *early* (for reasons of mere convenience), Umbers argues that citizens express the conviction that there is *no* deliberative contribution one's fellow citizens could potentially have offered that would have merited being afforded any positive weight in one's determinations as to who to vote for. This, Umbers argues, is problematically *disrespectful*, insofar as it implies that one's fellow citizens lack the capacity to recognise and respond to the reasons which bear upon the matters before the electorate. Insofar as we have reason to prefer a set of electoral institutions that express appropriate, respectful attitudes concerning each citizen, we have reason to adopt a more restrictive attitude towards the availability of early voting and to seek to ensure that most citizens vote on election day.

Since federation, Australians have enjoyed several opportunities for direct participation in the lawmaking process. Some have taken the form of constitutional referenda (e.g. the 1999 Republic referendum), the results of which are legally binding under the Australian Constitution. Yet there have also been numerous advisory plebiscites, the results of which are not legally binding. Consider the 2017 same-sex marriage postal survey, for instance. Parliament was not strictly obliged to legislate for the recognition of same-sex marriage; yet, in the face of the fact that over 60 per cent of respondents were in favour, declining to do so would have been politically unthinkable.

What meaning, then, do such plebiscites have in the Australian political system? As Kildea points out in his chapter, 'Merely Advisory or Effectively Binding? The Status of Plebiscite Results in Australia', one potentially fruitful approach to addressing this question is to simply consider the ways in which political representatives have characteristically *responded* to the results of such exercises. Since 1901, there have been 4 plebiscites at the Federal level and 44 at the state and territory level. In only 3 instances has a plebiscite result not been followed. In each of these cases, Kildea shows, this was due either to confusion as to what the public's preferences as expressed in the plebiscite were or intervention by a higher level of government. Thus, it does indeed seem that Parliaments are inclined to treat the results of such advisory plebiscites as binding.

Why might this be the case? Kildea suggests three potential explanations. First, advisory referenda are initiated by governments themselves, which presumably implies a willingness to abide by the result. Second, conforming to such results is characteristically in most parliamentarians' interests. And, finally, many parliamentarians profess allegiance to the idea that the popular will fundamentally ought to be respected. In some sense, in holding a plebiscite, Parliament delegates legitimate authority over the matter at issue to the citizenry. This suggests that advisory plebiscites, then, are instruments of citizen empowerment. Yet they are also, Kildea points out, instruments of elite control. Insofar as governments control whether a plebiscite is to be held or not, they are able to use such devices as a means of furthering their interests.

Perhaps the most notable recent example of citizen participation in the lawmaking process, however, was the unsuccessful referendum on enshrining an Aboriginal and Torres Strait Islander Voice to Parliament in the Australian Constitution, held on 14 October 2023. Indigenous Australians (and those sympathetic to their interests) have long argued that such persons' interests stand in need of better representation in the political process. The idea of an Aboriginal and Torres Strait Islander Voice was first proposed by the Indigenous lawyer and activist Noel Pearson in 2014. The idea was later taken up by the authors of the 2017 *Uluru Statement from the Heart*, which called for '[…] a First Nations Voice enshrined in the Constitution'. Initially met with hostility by the incumbent Liberal government, incoming Prime Minister Anthony Albanese committed to holding a referendum on the issue in his election night speech on 21 May 2022. At the time, there were strong indications that the referendum might succeed. On the 2022 AES, for instance, 80 per cent of respondents supported the establishment of such a body. In the end, however, the referendum was unsuccessful. Just 39.6 per cent of voters cast their ballots in favour of the proposal – well short of the necessary 'double majority'.

Three of the chapters in this volume seek to consider some of the many issues raised by the referendum. Ryan Cox's chapter, 'Reflections on the Voice Referendum', focuses on the arguments offered for and against the proposal, from a philosophical perspective.[5] Cox argues for three propositions. First, though it is certainly the case that some Australians held false or prejudiced beliefs about the proposal, it is plausible that some were opposed to the proposal for the reason that it would have instigated an apparent form of political inequality between Indigenous and non-Indigenous Australians – with the former enjoying special privileges in the political process denied to the latter. Such concerns seem unlikely to withstand philosophical scrutiny. Cox, nevertheless, argues that the 'Yes' campaign failed to develop a sufficiently compelling response and disseminate it effectively to the majority of Australians. This, Cox argues, at least potentially led many Australians to see the proposal as an unjustified means of realising the valuable end of redressing the injustices experienced by Indigenous Australians.

Second, Cox suggests that the major arguments presented for the Voice in the debate preceding the referendum had a range of shortcomings. For instance, appeals to the idea that the Voice would be likely to promote social justice are powerful but nevertheless fail to address concerns raised by opponents (regardless of their substantive merits) that the Voice would have instituted a form of unfairness in the political process. Appeals to the rights of Indigenous Australians to exercise a greater degree of collective control over their political and economic fortunes, on the other hand, may be compelling in their own terms. Yet (as progressive opponents of the Voice observed), it is unclear whether the Voice proposal would have advanced this end, because the proposal was only ever for a body to advise Parliament, whose power to legislate on matters relating to Indigenous Australians would have remained unchanged.

Third, Cox suggests that a more powerful argument for the Voice might potentially have appealed to the value of political legitimacy and, in particular, to the idea of a *legitimacy deficit*. These arise in cases where (a) there exists some injustice and (b) it is sufficiently clear that if the government continues to operate in accordance with established conventions, it is highly unlikely that injustice will be addressed. The manifold injustices confronted by Indigenous Australians are, to a significant degree, a product of the structure of Australian democracy, wherein such persons (for a variety of reasons) are unable to exercise a degree of influence over political decision-making sufficient to protect and promote their interests. The Voice, then, might have constituted a powerful means of *overcoming* that deficit. The value of *this* line of argument is that it effectively reverses the burden of proof in the debate. If – as is very plausible – political legitimacy requires that the coercive power of the state be justified to each citizen subject to its authority, and if there is a deficit in this respect concerning Australia's Indigenous population, and if the Voice constitutes a potential means of remedying that deficit, the onus would have

5. This chapter is a companion piece to Cox (2024), which argued in favour of the Voice by appeal to legitimacy-based considerations.

surely been on opponents of the Voice to provide arguments as to why the proposal should *not* be enacted.

The second chapter to focus on the Voice is Levy and McCaul's 'Understanding the Competing Sovereignty Claims of the Voice Referendum'. Levy and McCaul begin with the concept of a constitutional legitimacy crisis. These arise, they suggest, where different subsets of the population have conflicting views as to the values underlying a shared constitution. Such crises, they suggest, differ from more typical constitutional disputes where, disagreement notwithstanding, the parties may nevertheless be brought reasonably to accept that there is an authoritative means of *resolving* such disputes. Constitutional legitimacy crises pose a more difficult challenge. In such cases, by definition, there will be no uncontroversial means of settling the disagreement. After all, at issue in such disputes is the legitimacy of the very political structures upon which we conventionally rely to *resolve* such disputes. Levy and McCaul suggest that the debate over the Voice points to precisely such a crisis, particularly with respect to the issue of sovereignty. Opponents of the Voice characteristically hold that sovereignty resides exclusively with the extant Australian state. Indigenous persons, by contrast, are more likely to either recognise unceded Indigenous sovereignty or else insist that there may be multiple sovereignties – thereby challenging the notion that the Australian state enjoys an exclusive claim to political authority. Consider, for instance, the oft-repeated claim by opponents of the Voice that assertions of Indigenous sovereignty lack any substantive basis because the High Court has refused to acknowledge such claims. Such arguments fail to truly engage with the opposing perspective for the obvious reason that it is the legitimacy of institutions such as the High Court that some Indigenous Australians wish to call into question.

The Voice debate, then, raises difficult questions concerning the nature and basis of claims to sovereignty. For some Indigenous peoples, sovereignty emanates from a spiritual connection to traditional lands and a wide range of associated cultural traditions. That connection persists in spite of colonial dispossession and its consequences. Thus, for many Indigenous Australians, sovereignty has never been ceded. Indeed, for some Indigenous critics of the Voice, acceptance of the proposal would have amounted to a concession that sovereignty *had* been ceded. The failure to confront the fact that competing conceptions of sovereignty were fundamentally at issue in the referendum process led, Levy and McCaul suggest, to an impoverished public debate.

Levy and McCaul suggest that matters might have been improved had the referendum process been more *deliberative* – i.e. if the parties to the disagreement had been more willing to seek to exchange reasons relevant to the Voice proposal of a kind acceptable to all (reasonable) parties. There are many ways in which this might have been achieved, but one potentially attractive proposal might have involved convening a so-called deliberative mini-public comprising ordinary Australians whose role would have been to collaboratively produce a public information document on the proposal, following dialogue with experts.[6] Such processes have many advantages, and it seems undeniable, in

6. An enormous amount of research has been conducted on minipublics in recent years. For an overview, see e.g. Fishkin (2009).

retrospect, that the government should have provided citizens with an impartial source of unbiased information (in contrast to the highly partisan pamphlets issued to citizens). Deliberative democracy is not a panacea, of course. But, the authors suggest, there are good reasons to think the tools of deliberative democracy, had they been implemented, might well have proven fruitful.

The Voice referendum took place against the backdrop of a radically transformed media landscape, characterised by the rise of so-called new and digital media and the decline of traditional authoritative sources of information – newspapers, television news bulletins and so on. Carson, Hayman and Phillips' chapter 'Australian Civic Engagement: A Case Study of the 2023 Voice to Parliament Referendum' presents a range of important data about the ways in which the 'Yes' and 'No' campaigns made use of digital media platforms in an attempt to persuade voters one way or the other. Carson et al. cite evidence that around 75 per cent of Australians now get most of their news online, rather than from traditional news sources. As such, it is crucial to understand the ways in which information is disseminated and campaigns are waged on these new online platforms. The Voice campaign therefore constitutes an important case study of the ways in which civic engagement is changing in Australia – and, at least potentially, an indication of how future political contests might play out online.

Among many other findings, they show that different platforms seem to be employed by various actors for different purposes. Activity on X (formerly Twitter), for instance, was often associated with major news events (e.g. the release of the referendum question) and was used by – among others – traditional media outlets as a means of disseminating content. One of the leading groups opposing the Voice, Advance Australia, did not maintain a presence on X. On TikTok, by contrast, Advance Australia enjoyed significantly more success than comparable groups in favour of the referendum. Advance, for instance, had 80,000 followers and received 2.6 million likes, as opposed to the 8,182 followers and 197,100 likes gained by Yes23 – likely a reflection of the fact that Advance appears to have better understood and adapted to the particularities of the platform.

Carson, Hayman and Phillips also suggest that the 'No' campaign appears to have understood that referendum politics in Australia is characterised by (among other things) risk-aversion. This, naturally, is advantageous for groups opposed to constitutional change. Groups opposed to the Voice appear to have exploited this highly effectively in their campaign strategies (e.g. giving prominence to Indigenous Australians *opposed* to the Voice, which made it more difficult for Australians to gain a clear impression of the balance of Indigenous opinion on the issue).

The conduct of political campaigns via the media almost invariably gives rise to difficult questions concerning how governments ought to regulate such actors and the platforms upon which they rely. In the United States, this invariably gives rise to constitutional questions, via the First Amendment. Australia, unusually among major democracies, does not have a constitutionally enshrined bill of rights. Nevertheless, the High Court has been willing to hold that certain rights and freedoms are *implied* in the constitution, among which is an implied freedom of political communication (IFPC, hereafter). What remains controversial, however, is how precisely this implication is supposed to work and what follows for the nature and extent of the IFPC. Wesson's chapter, 'The

Unstable Foundations of the Implied Freedom of Political Communication', investigates these issues.

Wesson begins by outlining the constitutional foundations of the IFPC. The argument developed by the Mason court across a number of seminal cases heard in the early 1990s has it that insofar as the constitution requires a system of representative government and representative government necessarily requires political communication among citizens, it follows that the constitution requires freedom of political communication. This seems compelling. Yet representative government is rather a demanding ideal and might be thought to require a range of protections of the kind Australian courts – with their characteristic deference to Parliament – have historically been *very* reluctant to read into the constitution. In 1997, then, the court issued a unanimous decision in the case of *Lange v Australian Broadcasting Corporation* (1997) 189 CLR 520, which sought to clarify both the derivation and extension of the IFPC. Rather than arising out of a more general commitment to representative democracy underlying the constitution, the court instead focused upon specific provisions of the constitution – especially sections 7 and 24, both of which require that representatives must be 'chosen' by the people. Since that time, the court has consistently refused to recognise any further rights or freedoms – with the exception of a right to vote in *Roach v Electoral Commissioner* (2007) 233 CLR 162.

This raises difficult questions. Is there something exceptional about political communication that renders it a uniquely appropriate object for constitutional implication? If so, why? And if not, how to justify the court's continuing to affirm the IFPC, while refusing to imply other democratically significant rights or freedoms? The foundations of the IFPC, thus, appear to be fundamentally *unstable*. Wesson, thus, discusses the various approaches taken by the judges on the court in order to better , understand the status of the IFPC under the constitution.

Wesson outlines three distinct approaches, each associated with a current member of the court. Steward J is sceptical of the very existence of the IFPC partly (though not solely) on the grounds that the ideal of representative democracy, which is supposed to *justify* the IFPC, admits of a wide range of interpretations, and (in his view) it is the role of Parliament to choose among these. A very different view has been advanced by Gageler CJ. Influenced by the work of the American legal theorist John Hart Ely (1980), Gageler has argued that the High Court ought to act as a 'referee', whose role is to ensure that the processes of representative democracy continue to operate so as to enable the Australian people to exercise effective self-government and to guard against legislative overreach in this respect. Finally, Edelman J does not doubt the existence of the IFPC but has insisted that it constitutes a relatively *weak* constraint, to be applied only in the face of sufficiently fundamental threats to the operation of representative and responsible government. In other such cases, it will be for the legislature to determine the limits on political communication. Thus, the foundations of the IFPC, together with its extension, remain both contested and uncertain. In the absence of more determinate constitutional protections, Wesson concludes, legislative action to protect freedom of expression would be highly desirable.

Civil society organisations – whether or not their purposes are overtly political – are widely considered to be important sites of civic engagement in democracies.[7] Yet, for a variety of reasons, the Australian state has imposed an increasingly burdensome set of regulations upon the not-for-profit sector in recent times with the object (notionally, at least) of ensuring greater transparency and accountability. Prior to 2012 and the creation of the Australian Charities and Not-for-profits Commission (ACNC, hereafter), the obligations imposed upon such organisations in Australia were minimal. Since that time, reporting and governance requirements have increased significantly. Organisations wishing to enjoy charitable status must register with the ACNC. This obliges them to, *inter alia*, maintain financial records, provide financial information and comply with a series of governance and conduct standards. This approach, which appears to be largely modelled on the *for*-profit sector, has resulted in a significantly increased administrative burden for those involved in not-for-profit organisations.

Ian and Sarah Murray's chapter, 'Increasing Third-Sector Governance Expectations as a Barrier to Civic Engagement in Australia', argues forcefully that these changes are not 'impact-neutral'. Though a credible regulatory framework is obviously of value, the new *status quo* entails important costs. Burdensome regulatory requirements render participation in such organisations increasingly difficult in a variety of ways. One should therefore expect such regulations to have the effect of suppressing participation. Indeed, Murray and Murray present a range of evidence to suggest that participation in such organisations is in decline in Australia and that increased governance expectations are at least partly responsible.

The results, they argue, are highly problematic. The not-for-profit sector is a vital site of civic engagement, both because such organisations often engage excluded and otherwise neglected parts of the community, and because participation in such bodies is a valuable source of social capital – allowing individuals to form valuable relationships with others and to develop, communicate and refine their political preferences. These, in deliberation with other members of the political community, ought to help inform the conception of the common good towards which our political institutions ought to be oriented. Reduced participation by members of the community in the sector threatens to deprive Australian democracy of the associated benefits. Increased governance expectations have also contributed to an increased *professionalisation* of the sector, which (naturally) threatens to undermine the ability of persons without particular managerial skills to participate. Given the vital role that such organisations play in protecting and promoting democratic values, the over-regulation of the sector risks undermining the quality of Australian civic life.

Australian culture is immeasurably enriched by its multicultural character and many migrant communities. It is widely thought that participation in civic life is an important indicator of successful migrant integration. Fozdar et al.'s chapter, 'Civic Engagement

7. Contributors to this volume have also discussed issues concerning the value of civil society groups as contributors to Australian democracy elsewhere. See Murray, Wesson and Umbers (2024).

among the Australian African Diaspora: National and Transnational Activity', seeks to focus particular attention on the civic life of African Australians. Extant research has tended to suggest that migrant Australians, in general, exhibit civic behaviours (e.g. rates of political participation) that are broadly comparable to non-migrant Australians. Little research has been done, however, on African Australians, specifically. This chapter, then, forms part of a larger research agenda which aims to deepen our understanding of this community.

Over the last two decades, there has been a rapid increase in the number and diversity of African migrants in Australia such that, as of 2021, 3.2 per cent of the population were either born or had at least one parent born in Africa. Of these persons, over 70 per cent were drawn from just five countries – South Africa, Egypt, Zimbabwe, Mauritius and Kenya. African-born migrants comprise a relatively small share of the voting-age population (1.9 per cent). However, on the other hand, they are also around 15 percentage points more likely to be voting citizens than other migrants. Increasing numbers of African migrants are acting as political representatives – e.g. current ACT senator David Pocock and former SA senator Lucy Gichuhi. Fozdar et al. present interesting evidence suggesting that, broadly speaking, such persons also engage in civic behaviours at roughly comparable rates to other Australians, despite the obstacles such persons often confront (e.g. negative media coverage).

Fozdar et al. also highlight that members of the African diaspora are often engaged in civic life transnationally. There is evidence that many African Australians are increasingly identifying as part of a pan-African diaspora. However, many migrant African Australians also remain deeply connected to their countries of origin, continuing to maintain relationships with people in those countries and sometimes continuing to be engaged with political and social issues therein (for instance, some African migrants are involved in fundraising efforts for the benefit of communities in their countries of origin). Even sending remittances – a common aspect of the migrant experience – has an inherently political dimension, insofar as it contributes to building a distinctive identity for members of diaspora communities and helps promote development internationally. The picture that emerges is one in which African Australians are active and purposive political agents, contributing in a range of ways to multiple political communities.

Finally, some of the most dramatic and impressive examples of civic engagement in recent times have centred around the issue of climate change.[8] On 15 March 2019, for instance, an astonishing 1.6 million students across 125 countries went on strike to demand action on climate change (BBC 2019). Yet climate policy in Australia has been divisive for parties of both the left and right, resulting in Australia's response to the climate crisis being, and remaining, manifestly inadequate. Joo-Cheong Tham's chapter, 'Australian Democracy and the Climate Crisis', begins by setting out three puzzling facts. First, evidence suggests that democracies consistently out-perform non-democracies with respect to climate policy. Yet Australia, one of the most robust democracies in

8. For discussion of the normative dimensions of climate activism, see Umbers and Moss (2021, 80–106).

the world, consistently ranks among the *worst* developed countries with respect to climate action. Second, this inaction sits uncomfortably with the fact that Australia is both disproportionately vulnerable to climate change given the particularities of our natural environment and disproportionately responsible, given that we are among the highest per-capita emitters of greenhouse gases internationally. And thirdly, our relative inaction on climate change is hard to square with survey research showing that Australians are broadly *supportive* of a more robust policy response to the issue.

Tham points to numerous factors that help explain Australia's policy failures in this area. The first is short-termism – an unwillingness to adequately prepare for and enact the structural changes necessary to both reduce emissions and adapt to the changing climate over the long run. The second is capture by vested interests. The fossil fuel industry comprises some of the most powerful actors in the Australian economy. Evidence suggests that they have expended significant resources both within Australia and worldwide to undermine the prospects for action on climate change. Their efforts here and elsewhere have met with considerable success. Third, the mechanisms of electoral democracy are in an important sense 'self-referring', wherein politicians are accountable to voters in the present day, though their decisions with respect to climate change will affect many future generations of Australians. This naturally tends towards an overweighting of the interests of the former and an underweighting of the latter. Finally, Tham points to weak multilateralism – the inability of the international system to compel states to adopt a more robust set of climate policies.

Tham also importantly observes, however, that just as Australia's reticence on climate change amounts to a failure (thus far) of our democratic processes to adequately address a pressing policy challenge, so too does climate change threaten democracy itself. It seems overwhelmingly likely that climate change will prove to be highly disruptive in democratic politics in the following decades. For instance, given the likely negative effects of climate change on certain sectors of the economy, climate change appears likely to lead to increased inequality and insecurity (both within Australia and in our region). This will put pressure on Australia's democratic system to which the parties (together with the population at large) will need to respond. It is crucial, then, that efforts be undertaken to renew and revitalise Australian democracy if it is to address the climate crisis. Tham has a number of suggestions, the most significant of which – for our purposes – is the development of a *solidaristic ethos*, whereby the politics of self-interest – arising as it does from both incidental and structural features of Australian democracy – may be countered by the combined efforts of citizens and civil society groups. Civic participation in the democratic process by citizens of many kinds seems certain to be essential if we are to adequately confront this most difficult policy challenge.

References

AEC (Australian Electoral Commission). 2022. 'Voter Turnout – Previous Events'. https://www.aec.gov.au/elections/federal_elections/voter-turnout.htm (accessed 29 August 2022).

BBC (British Broadcasting Corporation). 2019. 'School Strike for Climate: Protests Staged around the World'. https://www.bbc.com/news/world-48392551 (accessed 24 September 2019).

Bicchieri, Cristina. 2017. *Norms in the Wild: How to Diagnose, Measure, and Change Social Norms.* Oxford: Oxford University Press.

Blais, André and Rubenson, Daniel. 2013. 'The Source of Turnout Decline: New Values or New Contexts?' *Comparative Political Studies* 46 (1): 95–117.

Bonotti, Matteo and Strangio, Paul (eds.). 2021. *A Century of Compulsory Voting in Australia: Genesis, Impact, and Future.* Gateway East Singapore: Palgrave-MacMillan.

Cameron, Sarah M. and McAllister, Ian. 2022. *Trends in Australian Political Opinion: Results from the Australian Election Study, 1987–2022.* Canberra: Australian National University.

Coma, Ferran Martinez i and Smith, Rodney. 2023. 'The Rise and Rise of Early Voting'. In *Watershed: The 2022 Australian Federal Election*, edited by Anika Gauja, Marian Sawer and Jill Sheppard, 413–432. Canberra: ANU Press.

Cox, Ryan. 2024. 'Political Legitimacy and the Indigenous Voice to Parliament'. *Journal of Applied Philosophy* 41 (3): 423–441.

Dassonneville, Ruth, Barbosa, Thiago, Blais, André, McAllister, Ian and Turgeon, Mathieu. 2023. *Citizens Under Compulsory Voting: A Three-Country Study.* Edited by R. Michael Alvarez, Emily Beaulieu Bacchus and Charles Stewart III, Cambridge Elements: Elements in Campaigns and Elections. Cambridge: Cambridge University Press.

Diamond, Larry. 2015. 'Facing up to the Democratic Recession'. *Journal of Democracy* 26 (1): 141–155.

Ely, John Hart. 1980. *Democracy and Distrust.* Cambridge, MA: Harvard University Press.

Fishkin, James S. 2009. *When the People Speak.* Oxford: Oxford University Press.

Gauja, Anika. 2015. 'The State of Democracy and Representation in Australia'. *Representation* 51 (1): 23–34.

IDEA (Institute for Democracy and Electoral Assistance). 2021. 'Voter Turnout Database'. IDEA. https://www.idea.int/data-tools/data/voter-turnout (accessed 23 November 2021).

ISSP. 2016. 'ISSP 2014 - Citizenship II: Variable Report'. Germany: GESIS - Leibniz Institute for the Social Sciences.

Muller, Damon A. 2022. 'Trends in Early Voting in Federal Elections'. Australian Parliamentary Library. https://www.aph.gov.au/About_Parliament/Parliamentary_Departments/Parliamentary_Library/FlagPost/2022/May/Early_voting_at_the_2022_federal_election (accessed 17 January 2023).

Murray, Ian, Wesson, Murray and Umbers, Lachlan. 2024. 'Regulating Political Advocacy by Charities Liberally'. *Nonprofit and Voluntary Sector Quarterly* 53 (1): 236–256.

Pateman, Carole. 1970. *Participation and Democratic Theory.* Cambridge: Cambridge University Press.

Pateman, Carole. 2012. 'Participatory Democracy Revisited'. *Perspectives on Politics* 10 (1): 7–19.

Przeworski, Adam. 1999. 'Minimalist Conception of Democracy: A Defense'. In *Democracy's Value*, edited by Ian Shapiro and Casiano Hacker-Cordón. Cambridge: Cambridge University Press.

Raue, Ben. 2023. 'The House of Representatives Results'. In *Watershed: The 2022 Australian Federal Election*, edited by Anika Gauja, Marian Sawer and Jill Sheppard. Canberra: ANU Press.

Schumpeter, Joseph A. 1950. *Capitalism, Socialism, and Democracy: Third Edition.* New York: Harper & Row.

Singh, Shane P. 2021. *Beyond Turnout: How Compulsory Voting Shapes Citizens and Political Parties.* Oxford: Oxford University Press.

Umbers, Lachlan Montgomery. 2024. 'Geoff Brennan on the Ethics and Rationality of Voting'. *History of Economics Review* 88 (1): 20–36.

Umbers, Lachlan Montgomery and Moss, Jeremy. 2021. *Climate Justice Beyond the State*. London: Routledge.

Vowles, Jack. 2017. 'The Big Picture: Turnout at the Macro-Level'. In *The Routledge Handbook of Elections, Voting Behavior and Public Opinion*, edited by Justin Fisher, Edward Fieldhouse, Mark N. Franklin, Rachel Gibson, Marta Cantijoch and Christopher Wlezien. London: Routledge.

Chapter 2

CITIZEN GUARDIANS? CIVIC ENGAGEMENT AND CONSTITUTIONAL CONVENTIONS

Nicholas Barry, Narelle Miragliotta, Sarah Murray and Zim Nwokora

Introduction

A robust constitutional framework is one of the preconditions of a healthy democracy, setting out the essential rules, principles and expectations that regulate and animate the political system. However, not all the rules that matter are set out in a codified, written constitution. Some of these rules are unwritten and take the form of constitutional conventions (or political norms).[1] These conventions give form, meaning and substance to the written constitution. They play a crucial role in regulating democratic processes and elite behaviour, managing disagreements and in remedying constitutional and political stalemates (Azari and Smith 2012; Helmke and Levitsky 2004; Levitsky and Ziblatt 2018; Lieberman et al. 2019). Conceiving of a constitution without the conventions that complement it provides an incomplete picture of the framework of rules undergirding democracy in Australia or, for that matter, any democratic country.

Constitutional conventions are created, interpreted and enforced by public officials. While this arrangement is efficient and practical, and has desirable normative properties, it is not without limitations. This chapter seeks to identify the factors that may be weakening elite adherence to constitutional norms in Australia. It then examines how to address this problem, arguing that citizens have a key role to play as guardians of these norms. We argue that the important work that conventions perform in regulating public officials can be better reflected in, and supported by, the Australian citizenry. However, this requires a reinterpretation of the role of citizens and efforts to boost their capacity to play a greater role in providing critical oversight of those who violate conventions without cause.

More specifically, this chapter makes the case for the 'democratisation of constitutional conventions', defined for our purposes as the diffusion of awareness and knowledge about conventions beyond the political class whose actions these conventions

1. The authors use the terms 'conventions' and 'norms' interchangeably in this chapter. However, both words are used to denote those uncodified rules that emerge specifically from, or regulate the operation of, the constitution.

regulate. We argue that contemporary changes in the media landscape, governmental practices and emergent political polarisation make it necessary to extend the custodianship of norms beyond government officials to be more inclusive of citizens. Doing so will increase the political and electoral costs of norm transgression without weakening the inherent flexibility of these essential constitutional devices.

The Virtues and Vices of Constitutional Conventions

Constitutional conventions are unwritten rules that set out expectations for government processes and conduct by public officials. They are not expressed in the written constitution, though they often shape how it operates in practice. In Westminster systems, such as Australia, constitutional conventions are fundamental to the regulation of executive power, placing limits on how public officials use their discretionary authority (Dicey 1915; Foley 2013). In so doing, constitutional conventions 'structure collective expectations about how disputes will be resolved' (Azari and Smith 2012, 38) and how discretionary power and decision-making authority will be wielded. Constitutional conventions are essential to the delivery of an accountable system of modern representative government (Rosenbluth and Shapiro 2018).

The unwritten nature of constitutional conventions is, however, both a virtue and a vice. The virtues are manifold. First, conventions give form to vital constitutional principles (Boughey and Weeks 2013; Appleby 2018). That is, constitutional conventions provide structure and guidance around those processes and systems on which the constitution is silent, incomplete or redundant. Second, their unwritten format enjoins them with the theoretical and practical flexibility to evolve over time. Essentially, these rules can change and adapt without the delay, complications and challenges that accompany formal rule change. Third, punishment for breaching conventions has the capacity to arrive swiftly. This stands in contrast with cases going before the courts, which generally require lengthy investigatory and judicial processes. Fourth, the authority for upholding the observance of constitutional conventions rests primarily with members of parliament (at least between elections) and cabinet. This expectation that parliamentarians self-regulate reflects and ought to promote the belief that members of parliament (MPs) should take responsibility for their actions and those of their colleagues. It is assumed that in a functioning democracy, where public power is dynamic and alternates between groups, public officials have a mutual interest in upholding compliance because it maintains the constitutional order.

The properties that make conventions valuable also give rise to particular vices. The fact that they are not included in the written constitution means they are not usually enforced by the courts (but for exceptions, see Ahmed et al. 2019), rendering them vulnerable to non-observance by elected officials. These conventions, unlike other rules, are created, interpreted and enforced by the elected officials whom they regulate. Although some important conventions are recorded in official documents, this is not the case for all conventions, and even when they are inscribed in authoritative texts, they may not be accessible beyond the public officials who have primary custodianship over them. Take, for example, cabinet manuals (Barry et al. 2023). Such documents distil various fundamental conventions pertaining to the proper use of executive power in a democracy. Yet, despite the significant work that they do in shaping how the executive functions and the fact that these texts are publicly available, it would be a stretch to describe them as 'accessible'. They are written in curt, technical language by public officials in order to guide ministers and their advisers. They are shared with, but not written for, the general public. Furthermore, in addition to the work that manuals do to encapsulate particular conventions, these texts also include details on other operational and procedural matters. The inclusion of the latter, though important, makes engagement with conventions challenging because a reader seeking to understand the conventions of executive power – what exactly these conventions are and how they fit with other rules – will need to be able to differentiate the sections dealing expressly with conventions from the other content on operational matters.

Quite apart from the inaccessibility of constitutional conventions to the general public, they are challenging to enforce. Violations of conventions can be difficult to detect and to prevent because they rely on public officials being aware of the transgression and being willing to take action to sanction the norm violator by outing unconstitutional actions and demanding remedy. The flexibility of norms is one of their more alluring virtues, but it also means that it is uncertain whether a norm violation will be sanctioned and, if so, what kind of sanction will be imposed. The practice of sanctioning occurs through a political toolkit that is more nebulous than legal punishments and remedies. Political sanctions take diverse forms that include, inter alia:

(1) public shaming, for example, such as when the norm violator is forced to stand before parliament and/or the media to apologise for their transgressions;
(2) a formal motion of censure by the parliament;
(3) the norm violator voluntarily resigns from a leadership role, particularly a ministerial position, or is forced to resign by the party leader (or the party, if they are the leader);
(4) the norm violator is expelled by their party;
(5) the norm violator resigns from parliament; and/or
(6) the norm violator (or their party) suffers an electoral penalty at the next election, with a swing against them resulting in the loss of their seat in parliament or, in the case of the party, the loss of government.

The sanctions listed above are in approximate order of severity from the standpoint of the transgressor. Arguably, the most severe penalty for the transgressor is for the voters to cast them out of office. However, this penalty can only be imposed when an election is held, which might be months or even years following the breach. Under these conditions, there is always the risk that electors might not remember the transgression, fully understand it or care about it enough to change their vote. The other listed sanctions offer more immediate relief because the penalty can be imposed sooner. These more temporally proximate penalties for breaches might also be applied in various combinations depending on the circumstances. For instance, public shaming may be followed by resignation from a leadership role if the apology is unconvincing or weak.[2] Nevertheless, most sanctions involve the electorate only indirectly and as a last resort.

Political sanctions are also meant to have a deterrent effect – the threat of a sanction is supposed to discourage parliamentarians from violating conventions. Political sanctions are meant to be sufficiently onerous so as to discourage elected officials from violating norms. However, in order for a political sanction to act as a compelling deterrent, there needs to be awareness of the pertinent convention or conventions, an understanding of its constitutional and political significance and an expectation that other actors (elected officials or citizens) will be prepared to impose the sanction. It is not just that the transgressor must fear the political consequences of their actions but that those elites who are responsible for meting out punishment must also fear the judgment of the public if they do not take suitable steps to punish the transgressor.

Contemporary Challenges to Constitutional Norms: The Growing Complexity of the Norm Ecosystem

The fact that conventions are breached is certainly not a new phenomenon. Nor does every breach necessarily constitute a problem. Breaches may sometimes be practical, necessary and broadly agreed to by relevant actors. Instead, it is the breaches that undercut constitutional values and those that can induce political and constitutional crises that are a cause for concern. The occurrence of such problematic breaches of conventions, or at least the conditions that make such breaches more or less likely, has increased over time in response to several forces that have reshaped politics, especially in recent decades.

Early concerns about the violation of conventions can be traced back to the emergence of modern party systems in Australia and elsewhere, in the late 1800s. The rise of parties gave rise to a new type of MP who, in being elected as a representative of a political party, was more likely to interpret norms through the prism of partisanship (Harmer 2004). Another period of rapid change began in the 1960s when concerns about compliance with conventions were reignited by the emergence of the modern regulatory state and then later (in the 1980s) by the new public management paradigm that prescribed, among other matters, the outsourcing of public functions away from government responsibility (Barberis 1998). It is during this time, especially, that formal accountability mechanisms were significantly expanded, giving rise to what Bruce Stone has described as 'more complex structures which typically devolve more authority downwards, reduce the number of layers (and hence the capacity for close supervision) and which recognize and encourage a more diverse range of relationships with actors outside the traditional hierarchy' (Stone 1995, 509). This introduced an additional layer of rules which interacted with conventions. It also led to greater formalisation – or 'soft codification' – of some conventions, which were increasingly set

2. Furthermore, it should be noted that the use of these political sanctions does not preclude adjunct legal sanctions from being applied.

out in documents such as cabinet manuals, in order to better protect norms against transgression (Barry et al. 2023).

In the 2000s, heightened anxieties about norm violations occurred against the backdrop of emergent political polarisation. A number of studies traced changes in observance of important norms in Australia (e.g. Mulgan 2012; Flinders 2017; Galligan and Brenton 2015). The electoral success of populist political leaders, such as Donald Trump and Boris Johnson, and their contentious relationship with democratic norms, led to a renewed focus on norm observance (e.g. Postema 2022; Chafetz and Pozen 2018).

Although it is difficult to systematically track the status of conventions and the regularity of their observance in Australian politics and public life, what seems apparent is the growing complexity of the legal and political ecosystem in which conventions must operate. This ecosystem is characterised by an increasingly sophisticated electorate, a decline in the traditional power of mainstream legacy media, the politicisation of the public service and increasing and unpredictable demands of governing, arising from the expansion of the modern state. The confluence of these factors has placed the system of norms under greater strain, creating a stronger imperative for citizens to assume more responsibility for the oversight of these norms.

The Australian population has benefited from increases in tertiary educational opportunities and, while equality of access remains an enduring problem (Wesley 2023), the nation is made up of an increasingly sophisticated citizenry, especially compared with previous generations. Arguably, this has contributed to a greater distrust of politicians and the machinery of government, or at least heightened levels of mistrust. Holloway and Manwaring (2024, 57) have found that there has been a 'long-term decline in public trust in political institutions [...] over several decades', with as many as 'one-fifth of Australians actively distrust[ing] the federal government and political parties'. The authors conclude that the 'crisis of trust' in Australia is largely limited to its political institutions and reflects concerns about the conduct of the political actors who inhabit these institutions (Holloway and Manwaring 2024). For our purposes, this is an important development for two key reasons. First, an increasingly sophisticated citizenry is likely to be less accepting of norm breaches by politicians – the explanations that a politician provides are less likely to be simply accepted, as we see in the Morrison ministries case. Second, the more sophisticated the citizenry is, the better placed they are to perform the role of guardians of conventions. However, to optimise citizens' convention-surveillance capacity, they must be armed with the necessary knowledge to identify and understand these most arcane of rules.

Another important change in the political context in which norms operate is the decline of the legacy media, that is, the masthead newspapers and TV news platforms that dominated journalism and political news reporting prior to the internet. Although there has always been a gap between the ideals of fourth-estate journalism and the actual practice of journalism in Australia, the legacy media outlets are closer to this ideal insofar as they have had stronger incentives to serve a broad cross-section of the population (rather than a niche audience) and relied on trained journalists for reporting, who were (and are) overwhelmingly socialised to the norms of public interest journalism. The situation was helped by the fact that legacy media outlets were more abundant and generally better staffed. All of this meant that there were more traditionally trained journalists who could act as reliable adjudicators and enforcers of violations of norms as compared with the array of internet-based commentary about political affairs. Analysts of these trends contend that 'further erosion of quality journalism threatens democracy' (e.g. Macnamara 2010, 20).

In government, the increasing use and influence of partisan political advisers in the bureaucracy has challenged traditional accountability and responsibility relationships between politicians, the public service and the public. The long-standing notion that public servants provide ministers with the information they need to make decisions, for which they are accountable to the public, has been scrambled by the rise of party political advisers (see e.g. Maley 2017; Shaw 2021). This development, as well as others such as outsourcing, often relies on informal relationships in areas where conventions/norms are not well developed.

While it might be thought that the solution to these changes in traditional oversight mechanisms is more administrative law, it is important to acknowledge that this approach would reduce flexibility in the management of relations between parliamentarians, the cabinet, public servants and advisers. This flexibility is one of the benefits of conventions to regulate political behaviour and process. If anything, the COVID-19 pandemic highlighted the increasing unpredictability and uncertainty that governments confront in a highly globalised world. Governments are expected to respond expeditiously, efficiently and creatively to any manner of challenges across the domains of public health, the environment and climate change, and economic and fiscal policy (Griffin and Clarkson 2013). These uncertainties place additional stress on norms to ensure that governments remain accountable and responsive across increasingly variegated policy platforms and elevated public expectations. In response to these changes in the modus operandi of politics and government, we should expect that new conventions have evolved and will continue to evolve, especially with regard to the relationship between politicians, political advisers, public servants and the public.

The Multiple Ministries Example

A recent Australian episode provides an important example of the challenges of norm violation in Australia – former prime minister Scott Morrison's usurpation of multiple federal ministries during the COVID-19 pandemic, which flouted the norms of responsible government. Morrison's actions became public after his government had lost office, leading to inquiries by the Commonwealth Solicitor General (2022a) and then a former High Court judge. This inquiry reached the conclusion that no laws had been broken, but important norms of representative and responsible government – which form the bedrock of democratic government in Australia – had been breached. The former prime minister did not perceive his actions to be in breach of these conventions, and the capacity for parliament and his cabinet to punish him for the breach in real time was not possible owing to the secrecy that shrouded his actions.

The dangers posed by Morrison's action were described by Anne Twomey as follows:

> Is it appropriate for ministers to be secretly appointed to exercise statutory powers? No, such matters should be notified to parliament and formally published so members of the public can know who is entitled to exercise particular powers. That is why we have Administrative Arrangements Orders and notifications of changes in ministerial responsibility that are recorded on the Federal Register of Legislation. It is inappropriate for such matters to be kept secret – especially if it is kept secret from the Cabinet and from the minister who was formally allocated responsibility for a portfolio by the governor-general. Such a lack of transparency is indicative of a lack of respect for the institutions of government and for the general public who have a right to know how power is allocated. (Twomey 2022)

Morrison justified his actions as lawful, well-intended and the product of extraordinary circumstances:

> Given the serious crises facing Australia, I considered it prudent to put these authorities in place should they be necessary as a safeguard. The authorities granted were respected in the fact they were not exercised, as the circumstances for which they were provided did not materialise. In short, the authorities were not misused. (Morrison 2022b, 3854)[3]

Morrison's action did attract sanctions but only retrospectively. Sanctions included adverse findings by the Solicitor General (2022a) as well as a public inquiry into the matter, conducted by Hon. Virginia Bell AC, which found that the former prime minister's actions were a breach of convention:

> Given that the Parliament was not informed of any of the appointments, it was unable to hold Mr Morrison to account in his capacity as minister administering any of these five departments. As the Solicitor-General concluded, the principles of responsible government were 'fundamentally undermined' because Mr Morrison was not 'responsible' to the Parliament, and through the Parliament to the electors, for the departments he was appointed to administer. Finally, the lack of disclosure of the appointments to the public was apt to undermine public confidence in government. Once the appointments became known, the secrecy with which they had been surrounded was corrosive of trust in government. (Bell 2022, 5–6)

Similarly, the Albanese Labor government, which won federal office in 2022, led a censure motion in the House of Representatives against Morrison on 30 November. Tony Burke, the mover of the censure motion, reminded the House:

> This place runs on rules and conventions. The mere existence of the office of prime minister and the existence of a cabinet is a convention. It's not in the Constitution. It's not required. It is a convention on which our system of government hangs. The concept that the parliament knows who has which job is essential to responsible government. You cannot

3. Note that Scott Prasser (2022) agrees with Morrison. Prasser argues that part of the challenge is that conventions are 'tricky' and 'political combatants in parliament have a habit of changing their views about when a convention should be followed and when it should not'.

> have responsible government if you don't know what people are responsible for, and for two years we didn't know. For two years, the ministers themselves did not know. For two years, departmental secretaries were unaware of who the ministers were to whom they had responsibility. (Burke 2022, 3854)

For his part, Morrison showed no contrition, even countering that the censure motion was nothing more than an act of 'political intimidation of this government using its numbers in this place to impose its retribution on a political opponent' (Morrison 2022b, 3854). The era of 'alternative facts' provides political actors with greater cover to reframe the narrative around their transgressions.

As noted above, parliamentary censure is one of the options available to sanction parliamentarians who violate conventions, but in this case, it was a fairly weak sanction given the seriousness of the breaches that had occurred. In addition, although Morrison was still in parliament at this stage, he was no longer prime minister or on the opposition frontbench, so the costs of censure were low. And throughout this reckoning, as is usually the case in discussions of conventions and norms, the citizenry lay in the background.

This example also reveals the way in which partisanship can influence elite responses to the violation of conventions. Morrison's fellow Coalition MPs refused to back the Albanese government's censure motion. This suggests that if the Morrison government had been returned to office (and continued to hold a majority of seats in the House), then it is unlikely that Morrison would have been censured by parliament at all. Interestingly, although elite opinion was divided along party lines, the available evidence suggests that many sections of the public took a more critical view. An opinion survey published in *The Guardian*, undertaken prior to the Bell Inquiry, found that a majority of the voting public (58 per cent and 45 per cent of Coalition voters) believed that Morrison's actions had 'diminished the reputation of his government' (Martin 2022).

Way Forward?

A key lesson from the Morrison case, which is arguably an extreme example of norm violation, is that the threat of parliamentary sanction is not sufficient to dissuade politicians, including first ministers, from violating norms. This is particularly the case in an era when political partisanship makes it unlikely that colleagues of the same party will denounce these actions, even when they become public knowledge. This raises the question of how to strengthen the disincentives for breaching conventions rather than relying on the extant sanctioning tools. (In the Morrison case, the sanction was a retrospective parliamentary censure that was somewhat 'muted' because it was supported by only one side of politics.)

What is also clear is that kneejerk solutions, such as the legal codification of conventions or the creation of extra-parliamentary expert bodies charged with enforcing conventions, are rarely able to fully address the problem of norm enforcement. Legal codification elides the fact that conventions are intended to be adaptable to changing societal and political circumstances. On the other hand, relying on experts to monitor conventions, detect breaches and sanction through critical commentary has the disadvantage of pivoting away from electors and the parliament as the anchors of representative democracy. While expert opinion plays a key role in informing communication and education about political matters, overly privileging these voices can put the system at risk of being captured by a minority who are not necessarily free of partisan influence, and who in any case lack the democratic credentials to perform this function.

The challenge is to not only bolster conventions but also to do so without weakening them or doing away with them altogether. That is, how to solidify and amplify conventions in spaces where formal laws are weak, while not inhibiting their natural malleability and flexible enforcement. It is for these reasons that we call for a greater emphasis on norm reinforcement by regular (i.e. non-elite) citizens. As guardians or caretakers of political norms, voters enjoy particular legitimacy, and their involvement has the potential to act as an antidote to both political mistrust and voter inefficacy.

Towards Citizen Custodianship of Norms

We argue that civic engagement can be a key mechanism to strengthen constitutional conventions. In an era of partisanship, the threat of electoral sanction is crucial in giving parliamentarians – and the parties they represent – an incentive to uphold conventions. However, this depends in large part on whether MPs believe they face a credible risk of electoral defeat when they violate conventions. If they judge that the electorate is likely to be indifferent to the violation of conventions and that non-observance will have minimal impact on their chances of re-election, then the threat of electoral sanction disappears. This is why it is vital that voters have an awareness of the most important constitutional conventions and an understanding of why they matter. They must also have sufficient knowledge of contemporary political events to be able to recognise when these conventions are being violated. In these ways, the challenge of upholding constitutional conventions in an inhospitable political environment is, at least, partly a problem of civic engagement.

We propose strengthening knowledge and awareness of conventions among the public by drawing on the politico-legal history of conventions, an expert knowledge base to harness the potential of information sharing and an elevation in the public's expectations of the ways in which citizens can influence public officials outside of elections. The goal, therefore, is to 'democratise' conventions and, in so doing, heighten the salience and legitimacy of conventions such that responsibility for their care and observance is shared by the public.

This approach casts citizens more directly in a re-visioned role in monitoring public officials' observance of conventions. The world of conventions is primarily an elite domain, with politicians observing each other and, ultimately, judging whether conventions have been breached. Under the prevailing chain of delegation, party leaders and whips play an especially important role in setting expectations and delivering sanctions. However, it is a mistake to view conventions purely as a matter for the political elite. For a start, doing so clashes with democratic norms, given conventions set down rules that are crucial to the system and are supposed to restrain parliamentarians. It also runs counter to contemporary attempts to develop mechanisms for involving citizens more directly in democratic government. In addition, as we have described, there are a variety of reasons to be sceptical about the willingness of elites to uphold these conventions, particularly in an era of partisan polarisation. Thus, there are positive and negative reasons to adopt an approach to constitutional conventions that is built on developing a stronger role for citizens as custodians.

Our idea of citizen custodianship can be understood through principal-agent theory, as a lens to conceptualise the problem of norm violation and its remedy. Following principal-agent theory, we conceive of the problem of norm violation as a form of 'shirking' by public officials that reflects a breakdown in the relationship between public officials (agent) and the people they serve (principal) (Braun and Guston 2003; Strøm 2003). The public (principal) delegates to public officials the authority to develop and interpret political norms on the understanding that these norms are consistent with democratic and constitutional principles and that they follow these norms unless exceptional circumstances apply that mean it would be reasonable to depart from them. Norm observance is intended to be incentivised by political rather than legal sanctions. However, public officials have a natural 'informational advantage' over the public arising from their superior knowledge of (largely) unwritten political norms. The ambiguity of conventions, arising from their form and meaning, makes it difficult for the public to observe and assess instances of norm violation and therefore harder for them to judge when electoral sanctions are appropriate. Nevertheless, principal-agent theory assumes that there are myriad ways to incentivise agents (public officials) to act consistently with the interests of the principal (the public). We propose to strengthen public official compliance by correcting the informational imbalance between agents (public officials) and the principal (the public) in relation to core constitutional conventions, which will also have the effect of demystifying conventions. Democratising awareness and understanding of constitutional conventions will increase the 'costs' for public officials who wantonly violate norms while strengthening the information base of the public in operating as citizen custodians.

Implementing Citizen Custodianship

Carving out a meaningful role for citizens in the care and maintenance of conventions may be easier in theory than in practice. There are obvious and significant hurdles to empowering citizens to take up the new responsibilities that our model requires. Among these hurdles is the need to diffuse knowledge about core political norms to foster an ethic of care in relation to these norms. Overcoming this requires a deep understanding of how and when people learn and what motivates them to do so. As a starting point, it should be recognised that conventions are ideational constructs that gain meaning through social processes (Postema 2022), which means that social learning, identity formation and social networks of practice will all have a crucial role to play in norm diffusion. Individuals (and mass publics) learn about norms through their interactions with others, and awareness of norms is therefore tied to the construction of identity within a social context. The exchange of ideas and the construction of shared meanings through discourse contributes to the understanding of norms and their diffusion.

In this vein, the diffusion of knowledge in relation to norms can occur dynamically through citizen interaction and debate. Even norm violations can present 'opportunities' for growth in the citizenry's understanding. As Stephenson explains:

> A failure can create a discursive moment, presenting constitutional actors, including the public, with a rare opportunity to discuss a neglected constitutional issue or to reframe a constitutional issue where debate has reached an impasse and become stagnant. During these moments, the doubts surrounding their content and enforceability can be a positive influence because they encourage participants to engage directly with the convention and the justifications for its existence. (Stephenson 2015, 448)

There are a range of ways that citizen custodianship can be cultivated. For example, it might be possible for citizens to be engaged directly through deliberative democratic structures such as citizens' juries and mini-publics. These could be used to debate norm violations and appropriate responses. These modes of participation engage a relatively small number of people, though there are, of course, ways to scale up the practice and impact of deliberative democratic tools (e.g. through media coverage). In 2008, the Rudd Labor government organised a national two-day 2020 Summit to bring together over 1000 citizens to discuss key policies for Australia's future across ten strategic areas. A high-profile event along these lines could also be a way of making a deliberative, group-based discussion about conventions seem relevant to the population at large.

Alongside the tools of deliberative democracy, another way that norms could be 'democratised' is through the creation of a fit-for-purpose platform that creates opportunities for citizen engagement and 'ownership' of norms. This innovation might include such features as:

- a database of constitutional conventions;
- self-paced educational modules that are suitable for different ages (see e.g. Joint Standing Committee on Electoral Matters 2024);
- archives and digitisation of important written artefacts containing mention of conventions;
- annotation of written artefacts that document conventions for accessibility; and
- a 'discussion and debate' forum where citizens can share their views about norms and reflect on contemporary political practice through this lens.

There are practical challenges to overcome to create this platform, which of course would be only a small contribution to the wider task of civic engagement on norms that we are proposing. Nonetheless, if and to the extent that it is achieved, we should expect important benefits to follow. These advantages include the following:

- increasing the transgression costs of norm violation for public officials because of the more immediate citizen and media opprobrium following norm violations;

- increasing citizens' understanding of, and engagement with, the political system and ability to discuss political matters and actions;
- building the expertise and knowledge base that makes possible deliberative moments when norms are in contention; and
- increasing citizen efficacy, with likely dividends for enhancing levels of political trust.

In addition to fostering greater knowledge of constitutional conventions, fostering a stronger role for citizens as guardians of these conventions requires them to be engaged in politics. At a minimum, this means the public need to be paying attention to what is going on in day-to-day politics, so they can observe whether conventions are being respected and respond accordingly at the ballot box when they are not. Education is going to have a key role to play in bringing about this more active form of citizenship. In this way, the kinds of reforms that are needed to strengthen civic engagement in Australia are also the kinds of reforms that are needed to strengthen citizens' role as guardians of constitutional norms.

Conclusion

There are reasons to believe that the integrity of conventions is being weakened on multiple fronts. An increasingly sophisticated citizenry represents part of the challenging context, but, we argue, it also represents an under-utilised resource in the effort to protect the integrity and legitimacy of conventions as a vital component of the political system. Getting citizens involved in monitoring norms is not to be isolated from the monitoring activities and responsibilities of other actors, such as the media, public service, parliamentarians and political staffers. However, by sharing the responsibility for safeguarding norms more widely within Australian society, the ongoing resilience of these norms is more likely to be assured along with the public's appreciation of their importance.

References

Ahmed, F., Albert, R., & Perry, A. 2019. 'Judging Constitutional Conventions'. *International Journal of Constitutional Law* 17 (3): 787–806.

Appleby, G. 2018 . 'Unwritten Rules'. In *The Oxford Handbook of the Australian Constitution,* edited by C. Saunders and A. Stone, 209–236. Oxford and New York: Oxford University Press.

Azari, J. R. and Smith, J. K. 2012. 'Unwritten Rules'. *Perspectives on Politics* 10 (1): 37–55.

Barberis, P. 1998. 'The New Public Management and a New Accountability'. *Public Administration* 76 (3): 451–470.

Barry, N., Miragliotta, N. & Nwokora, Z. 2023. 'The Prime Minister's Constitution: Cabinet Rulebooks in Westminster Democracies'. *Governance* 36 (2): 421–438.

Bell, A. C. 2022. 'Report of the Inquiry into the Appointment of the Former Prime Minister to Administer Multiple Departments', 24 November. https://apo.org.au/sites/default/files/resource-files/2022-11/apo-nid320900.pdf.

Boughey, J. and Weeks, G. 2013. '"Officers of the Commonwealth" in the Private Sector: Can the High Court Review Outsourced Exercises of Power?'. *The University of New South Wales Law Journal* 36 (1): 316–357.

Braun, D. and Guston, D. 2003. 'Principal-agent Theory and Research Policy: An Introduction'. *Science and Public Policy* 30 (5): 302–308.

Burke, A. 2022. 'Member for Cook, Censure'. *House of Representatives Debates*, 30 November: 3852–3854.

Chafetz, J. and Pozen, D. E. 2018. 'How Constitutional Norms Break Down'. *UCLA Law Review* 65: 1430–1459.

Commonwealth Solicitor-General. 2022. 'In the Matter of the Validity of the Appointment of Mr Morrison to Administer the Department of Industry, Science, Energy and Resources'. https://www.pmc.gov.au/sites/default/files/media-releases/sg-no-12-of-2022.pdf.

Dicey, A. V. 1915. *Introduction to the Study of the Law of the Constitution*. London: History of Economic Thought Books.

Flinders, M. 2017. *The Politics of Accountability in the Modern State*. London: Routledge.

Foley, M. 2013. *The Silence of Constitutions: Gaps, 'Abeyances' and Political Temperament in the Maintenance of Government*. Abingdon: Routledge.

Galligan, B. and Brenton, S. (eds). 2015. *Constitutional Conventions in Westminster Systems*. Cambridge: Cambridge University Press.

Griffin, C. M. and Clarkson, S. 2013. *Governing under Stress: Middle Powers and the Challenge of Globalization*. New York: Bloomsbury.

Harmer, D. 2004. *Can Responsible Government Survive in Australia?* Canberra: Department of the Senate, Parliament House.

Helmke, G. and Levitsky, S. 2004. 'Informal Institutions and Comparative Politics'. *Perspectives on Politics* 2 (4): 725–740.

Holloway, J. and Manwaring, R. 2024. 'The Challenge of Political Trust'. In *Australia at a Crossroads*, edited by M. Bonotti and N. Miragliotta, 57–79. London: Routledge.

Joint Standing Committee on Electoral Matters. 2024. Commonwealth of Australia, 'Inquiry into Civics Education, Engagement, and Participation in Australia'.

Levitsky, S. and Ziblatt, D. 2018. *How Democracies Die*. New York: Crown.

Lieberman, R. C. et al. 2019. 'The Trump Presidency and American Democracy: A Historical and Comparative Analysis'. *Perspectives on Politics* 17 (2): 470–479.

Macnamara, J. 2010. 'Remodelling Media: The Urgent Search for New Media Business Models'. *Media International Australia* 137: 20–36.

Maley, M. 2017. 'Temporary Partisans, Tagged Officers or Impartial Professionals: Moving between Ministerial Offices and Departments'. *Public Administration* 95: 407–420.

Martin, S. 2022. 'Guardian Essential Poll: About Half Say Morrison should Resign over Secret Ministries'. *The Guardian*, 6 September. https://www.theguardian.com/australia-news/2022/sep/06/guardian-essential-poll-majority-thinks-scott-morrison-should-resign-over-secret-ministries-decision.

Morrison, S. 2022a. 'Statement Regarding Solicitor General's Advice – The Hon Scott Morrison MP', 23 August. https://apo.org.au/sites/default/files/resource-files/2022-11/apo-nid320900.pdf.

Morrison, S. 2022b. 'House of Representatives Debates', 30 November: 3854.

Mulgan, R. 2012. 'Assessing Ministerial Responsibility in Australia'. In *Ministerial Careers and Accountability in the Australian Commonwealth Government*, edited by Keith Dowding and Chris Lewis, 117–193. Canberra: ANU e-press.

Postema, G. J. 2022. 'Constitutional Norms—Erosion, Sabotage, and Response'. *Ratio Juris* 35 (2): 99–122.

Prasser, S. 2022. 'The Scott Morrison Ministerial Appointment Saga – A Case of Political Theatrics'. *Policy Insights*. https://policyinsights.substack.com/p/the-scott-morrison-ministerial-appointment.

Rosenbluth, F., & Shapiro, I. (2018) *Responsible Parties: Saving Democracy from Itself.* Yale University Press.

Shaw, R. 2021. 'Ministerial Advisers, Contestability, and Politicization in the Core Executive in Westminster Systems'. In *The Palgrave Handbook of the Public Servant*, edited by H. Sullivan, H. Dickinson and H. Henderson, 515–530. Switzerland: Palgrave Macmillan.

Solicitor General, Commonwealth. 2022. 'In the Matter of the Validity of the Appointment of Mr Morrison to Administer the Department of Industry, Science, Energy And Resources' (SG 12, Legal Opinion), 1–29.

Stephenson, S. 2015. 'When Constitutional Conventions Fail'. *Dublin University Law Journal* 38 (2): 447–464.

Stone, B. 1995. 'Administrative Accountability in the "Westminster" Democracies: Towards a New Conceptual Framework'. *Governance* 8 (4): 505–526.

Strøm, K. 2003. 'Parliamentary Democracy and Delegation'. In *Delegation and Accountability in Parliamentary Democracies*, edited by K. Strøm, W. C. Müller and T. Bergman, 55–106. Oxford: Oxford University Press.

Twomey, A. 2022. 'Scott Morrison was Sworn in to Several Portfolios other than Prime Minister during the Pandemic. How Can this be Done?' *The Conversation*, 15 August. https://theconversation.com/explainer-scott-morrison-was-sworn-in-to-several-portfolios-other-than-prime-minister-during-the-pandemic-how-can-this-be-done-188718.

Wesley, M. 2023. 'Australian Higher Education Has Grown but Elite Universities Still Favour the Privileged'. *Guardian Australia*, 19 June. https://www.theguardian.com/australia-news/2023/jun/19/australian-higher-education-has-grown-but-elite-universities-still-favour-the-privileged.

Chapter 3

COMPULSORY VOTING IN AN ERA OF DEMOCRATIC DISENGAGEMENT

Jill Sheppard

Introduction

Australian politicians introduced compulsory voting to address what was unanimously agreed to be a crisis of falling voter turnout. That decision, waved through the federal parliament, shaped the country's party system and the nature of civic engagement for the next 100 years. In 2024, Australia faces a similar downturn in public attitudes towards politics and politicians, but politicians – led by the two major parties – have shown little interest in acting to stem the tide. We should not be surprised that parties are reluctant to act in ways that undermine their electoral interests; electoral reforms can have unexpected consequences, and the risk of, for instance, enfranchising new voters who support other parties is substantial. This chapter proposes policy solutions – mixed-member proportional representation in the House of Representatives, lower fines for abstention at federal elections and more channels for party membership – that will allow disengaged Australians to better engage with their political system without threatening either major party's strategic interests and without dismantling compulsory voting.

Compulsory voting was introduced in 1924 to arrest a rapid decline in Australians voting at federal elections. A century later, Australians' voting behaviour and responses to political surveys suggest similar signs of democratic disengagement, but the silver bullet of compulsion has already been used. Moreover, disengagement in 2024 takes more subtle forms: voters keep voting (to avoid sanction under compulsory voting laws), the major parties keep winning, and from a distance Australian politics looks to continue pretty much as usual. But a long-term and monotonic decline in the major parties' vote share, collapse of political party membership and record-low favourability towards democratic institutions all point to serious malaise.

This chapter examines the context in which compulsory voting was introduced, how it worked to reverse falling voter engagement and helped to solidify the two-party system that has dominated Australian politics, and why the stability of the last 100 years has provided the conditions for current dissatisfaction with the system. Governments and policymakers have a wide range of options to restore engagement with Australian democracy without having to remove the safety net of compulsory voting. The chapter concludes by considering policies that can make engagement easier without incurring electoral disadvantage to either side of politics: introducing (mixed-member) proportional representation to the House of Representatives, lowering the costs of voting (and of abstaining) and expanding the ways in which interested voters can engage with political parties.

Democratic Disengagement in 1924

In post-federation Australia, citizens turned up to vote in the new federal elections with little hesitation. The 1901 election saw 57 per cent of eligible voters cast a ballot, and turnout at subsequent elections rose quickly (Figure 3.1). Turnout peaked at 78 per cent in 1917 before falling to 72 per cent in 1909 and then to 59 per cent in 1922. The cause is unclear: probably not the replacement of first-past-the-post voting with alternative voting in 1919 (Green 2011); more likely the 'dullest [election campaign] yet in federal history' (Souter 1988, 192). Either way, the severe decrease clearly telegraphed some form of discontent among voters.

The idea of compulsory voting already had some purchase. The idea had popped up intermittently in pre-federation Australia as the colonial governments bedded down their separate electoral and political systems: provocative newspaper editorials here and there that achieved little political purchase (Brett 2019, 93–96). Where politicians did embrace the idea, it was less for democratic or partisan reasons (at least partially because no stable parties emerged until the 1890s) than for prideful reluctance to implore voters to the polls. Brett writes of Alfred Deakin, who promoted compulsory voting in 1888:

> It was one thing for a proud man to persuade people to vote for him because of his politics or his upright and independent character; it was another to have to coax them, as if they were doing one a favour or might expect something in return; and quite another to offer them inducements. (Brett 2019, 96)

Deakin found little support for this proposal to delegate the work of voter mobilisation to statute. The Victorian colonial government withdrew the compulsory voting clause from the 'Electoral Act 1865 Amendment Bill', claiming that the educative work of framing voting as a duty (rather than a right) was the real goal all along (Brett 2019, 95).

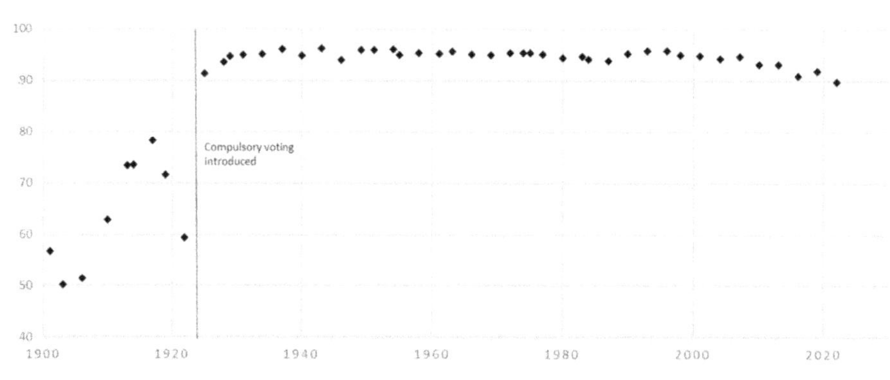

Figure 3.1 Voter turnout (percentage of enroled population) at Australian federal elections from 1901 to 2022.

After 1901, attempts to introduce compulsory voting became more explicitly strategic. This coincided with the emergence of a loose two-party system at the federal level (Sawer 2001). In 1905, a right-wing Victorian government proposed compulsion to get conservative-leaning abstainers to the polls (Brett 2021, 17). Brett (2019, 108) attributes the federal Labor government's decision to introduce compulsory enrolment but not compulsory voting in 1911 to a (possibly misguided) belief that it would 'bring to the polls those voters of the Liberal Party whose indifference at the present time is really the only reason that the Labor Party is in power' ('Party Government in Excelsis', *The Mercury*, 14 October 1911). In 1914, Queensland's Liberal government introduced compulsory voting in an attempt to counter the union movement's existing voter mobilisation strategies (Brett 2019, 117). Unfortunately for the Liberals, the subsequent election saw a swing of 5 percentage points against them. Labor parties across the country took their Queensland success as evidence that compulsion would assist them (Brett 2019, 102–3).

To that end, Labor (successfully) introduced legislation to the House of Representatives in 1915 to mandate voting at that year's proposed omnibus referendum on constitutional heads of power. The referendum was abandoned after the country's ongoing campaign in the First World War and with it the government's 'partisan experiment' (Joseph Cook, cited in Brett 2019, 120). The Victorian Labor Party (in opposition) tried and failed to introduce compulsory voting in 1917. Backbench member Ted Cotter then introduced a private member's bill annually until 1922. Federally, the Liberal government was unmoved by backbencher Sydney Sampson's argument that the burden of physically conveying thousands of voters to the polls should justify compulsion (Monnox 2019).

Although, in hindsight, compulsory voting seems an obvious solution to this relatively new problem, contemporary political actors had any number of options available to them. They could have done nothing, potentially allowing a continued decline in voter turnout (as the major parties have done with their membership bases). They could have invigorated their campaigning and policy platforms, as parties attempt to do in voluntary voting systems. Similarly, they could have continued to fundraise and spend money on transport to bring voters to polling booths. They could have legislated a 'soft' version of compulsion, wherein voting is mandatory but non-compliance is not punished in practice (e.g. Belgium) or enforced via minuscule penalties (e.g. Brazil).

Experiments and debates at the state level put compulsory voting at the top of the agenda for electoral reform in 1924. Still, the extent to which other solutions were discarded (or never even considered) is remarkable. A Nationalist Party backbencher introduced a private member's bill (which would become the Commonwealth Electoral Act 1924) to the Senate on 17 June 1924. Legislative debate on the bill was famously short, with both major parties (Nationalist and Labor) backing the bill through the Senate and the House. Only two speakers opposed the bill, and deliberation concluded in less than an hour. The bill became law on 31 July 1924 and thereafter eligible voters had to turn up or pay a £2 fine (roughly equivalent to A$290 in 2024).[1]

---

1. Adjusted for inflation using the Reserve Bank of Australia's inflation calculator (https://www.rba.gov.au/calculator/).

Given the strategic failure of Queensland conservatives in 1915, it is difficult to make sense of the federal Nationalists' decision to go 'all in' on compulsory voting in 1924. Nationalist prime minister Stanley Bruce was guided by his party in supporting the bill (Brett 2019, 135); perhaps his intra-party support was not strong enough to allow him to take a stand either way. It may also be that Nationalists believed full turnout would have different outcomes federally, and they could mandate voting without losing vote share to Labor. Certainly, the parties in 1924 did not have the kinds of electoral information or campaigning capacity available to modern-day parties, but the best available evidence seems to suggest that compulsion would benefit Labor.

An alternative reading of the 1924 debate – such that it was – is that compulsory voting was waved through the parliament because it aligned with fundamental Australian values (both then and now). This is not to say that compulsion is not in the spirit of majoritarian democracy nor that it strategically advantaged the Labor Party: both of those seem undeniable. But the instinct to compel voters rather than to entreat them to the ballot box reflects Australian society's abiding concern with material interests over concepts like natural rights (Bryce 1921; Collins 1985; Hill 2010). Rather than look inwardly at why discontent was growing among voters, legislators took the most expedient policy solution with little regard for infringing on voters' erstwhile rights (Strangio 2021).

By 1924, the major party system (with Labor on the left and a Nationalist-Country coalition on the right) had settled in place, providing voters with partisan cues with which to form their own opinions. Bryce observed:

> The average citizen cares less about public affairs than does the average Swiss or [...] American of the same class, and is less theoretically interested in democratic principles than are those two peoples. Civic responsibilities sit lightly upon him: nor does party feeling, except among Socialists, do much to stir his interest. (Bryce 1921, 269)

It is notable how similarly that sentiment describes modern-day Australians: they report comparatively high rates of partisanship, but it is not deeply held and is accompanied by little day-to-day civic engagement. Politics under these conditions can be confined to election time, as voters delegate their concerns or desires to a candidate representing a party whose ideological platform is widely known and understood. That candidate, if elected, could be expected to behave predictably throughout the parliamentary term due to an unusually strong emphasis on party discipline: Australia 'is the country in which first a closely knit party organization, compelling all members of the Legislature who belong to it to act as a compact body, became absolute master of a representative Assembly' (Bryce 1921, 189).

Australian institutions were also influenced by the principles of Chartism: payment for members of parliament, short parliamentary cycles, the secret ballot and an expansive franchise and right to nominate (Sawer 2001). Elections were orderly events and, since 1913, held on Saturdays. The combination of these institutional settings meant that, as the Chartists hoped for the United Kingdom, 'the labouring masses [...] gained control of the legal government and displayed their quality as rulers' (Bryce 1921, 189).

Contemporary accounts indicate little sense of the view of 'politicians as out of touch elites' that pervades public opinion 100 years later. Bryce (1921, 198) observed 'there is a feeling of latent antagonism or suspicion, an apparent belief among the workers that the interests of the richer and those of the poorer are and must be mutually opposed', but that the political class was mostly working men with more in common with the poor than the rich. This is partially due to the existence of salaried parliamentarians, but also to the fact that there was 'no class with leisure and means sufficient to enable it to devote itself to public life' (Bryce 1921, 207).

The parliamentarians of 1924 who chose compulsion over any other solution to decreasing engagement acted in a very specific context. Voters were disengaged from daily politics, conscious of managerial classes but not the (fledgling) political class and becoming habituated to mass political parties. These were not the cartelised parties of the late twentieth century that increasingly worked in concert to leverage resources from the state, but they were what might be termed semi-entrenched institutions, perhaps taking greater liberties with power than they had previously. While experiments with government intervention in social and economic life were mostly driven by Labor (particularly compulsory wage arbitration and compulsory unionism), the Australian public was 'generally favourable' (Bryce 1921, 208). Once one kind of compulsion in civic life was normalised, its extension to electoral participation seemed less radical.

Regardless of the actual intent of the parties in 1924, compulsory voting was immediately successful in reversing falling turnout and has sustained among the world's highest rates of electoral participation in terms of both voter enrolment and turnout. While the early penalties for abstention were much higher in relative terms – £2 in 1924 is the equivalent of almost $290 in 2024 – there is some evidence that the mere existence of compulsory voting laws helped drive turnout. Brett (2019, 114) argues that the introduction of compulsory enrolment in 1911 immediately increased turnout by more than 10 per cent points: 'making it compulsory to register seems to have impressed on voters' minds the importance of fulfilling their civic duty'. Implicit is the idea that Australians feel a latent duty to vote, which was activated by statute and has since become a widely accepted social norm (see e.g. Feitosa, Blais and Dassonneville 2020).

A less generous interpretation of early-century turnout data is that the fine really was very large and that voting – which was moved to Saturday at the same 1913 election that compulsory enrolment was introduced – is worth the hassle under such circumstances. This theory sits more easily with mainstream voting theories: turnout results from the benefits of voting (contributing to the success of a preferred candidate; the feeling of efficacy or community spirit gained from participating in an election) outweighing the costs of voting (for instance, the cost of time taken to get to the polls, learn about candidates, or line up at the booth or the price of a bus fare to a polling place). If polling places are scarce, lines long and candidates unappealing, the costs are high and the benefits low.

Compulsory voting works by increasing the cost of not voting. The Australian version did this to a radical degree; few countries of the small number with compulsory voting in the twenty-first century enforce it with any kind of fine or sanction, let alone one on the scale of £2 in 1924. The costs of abstention therefore need to be weighed against the benefits of voting (or abstaining): Voters may drive a little longer or spend a little more time researching the different candidates on the ballot if the alternative is a substantial fine. In other words, the benefits of voting don't need to be as high to justify turning out to vote. Even if a voter despises the candidates in front of them, gains nothing from the policy platforms on offer and must catch an unreliable bus to the polling place, voting under strongly enforced compulsory laws is still worth their time.

Twenty Years of Party Consolidation

The 1924 laws changed Australia's political culture forever; this much seems self-evident. In the 20 years following 1924, Australian elections saw changes consistent with the effects of compulsory voting: consistently high rates of voter turnout and a comparatively voter-friendly system of electoral administration. The introduction of Saturday voting and the widespread availability of postal voting both predated compulsory voting but contributed to the administrative culture that makes voting as easy as possible in Australia (Hill 2010). While difficult to show counterfactually, between the strength of the united Labor Party and governments' responses to the Great Depression and Second World War, which strongly centralised the Australian state, compulsory voting may also have had an impact on the consolidation of Australia's party system.

The 1920s and 1930s saw regular fragmentation and reformation of Australia's conservative parties: Labor dominated the centre-left side of the electoral spectrum while new and old parties of the right fought for dominance. Jaensch (1994, 97) characterises the period as demonstrating inertia at the level of the party system between blocs of the left and right, but constant change within that system. It was not until 1944 that Robert Menzies used his authority within conservative politics to consolidate the constellation of small parties into the Liberal Party, setting forth the two-party system that has governed Australia since. Party stability offers pros and cons for voters: on the one hand, they have consistency and simplicity of choice come election time (and the greater ability to tune out between elections); on the other, they are stuck with fewer options and can become less satisfied with how they are governed (see e.g. Blondel 1978). Additionally, voters seem more satisfied with democracy when parties are consolidated and well-resourced (Webb, Scarrow and Poguntke 2022). Additionally, resource-rich parties also attract better-quality candidates (Arriola et al. 2022).

Why might compulsion contribute to party consolidation? Voters were already compelled to vote (and doing so at rates of 90 per cent and higher), and most would have had some attachment to a political party, even if it only manifested on election day. The phenomenon of feeling closer to one party over another – what is usually called party identification – is vital to helping voters navigate complex political and policy systems. By taking cues from the party that most regularly represents their personal interests (whether those interests are material, social, ideological or just providing a sense of social identity), voters can minimise the time spent thinking about politics and ensure that they make a 'good' decision at the ballot box more often than not (Lau and Redlawsk 1997). To that end, it makes sense for parties to signal clear, stable messages to voters who would otherwise have not bothered to vote; in a voluntary system, such voters could abstain instead.

The early years of the two-party system were marked by clear and easily understood cleavages between the parties. The schisms inside Labor (over conscription and then economic management) had settled by 1941, and Menzies had been able to consolidate disparate groups on the right motivated by anti-socialism (Kemp 2021). Clear party cleavages both reflect and reproduce similar cleavages in society: voters know to which camp they belong, and belonging to the camp becomes part of their identity.

Social attachment to a party is the first step to membership, and this period had the highest rates of party membership on record in Australia. In 1939, Labor comprised as many as 370,000 members (Ward 1991), while Liberal membership was estimated at 220,000 in the early 1950s (Jaensch 2006). Not only are party members a useful resource when it comes time to campaign, but they are also a vital link to community opinion and the public mood. Perhaps most importantly, they are the main source of potential election candidates and future leaders. Through the 1940s and 1950s, Australian parties were closer to the people than they had ever been and would be in the future.

Party-Citizen Linkage under Compulsory Voting

A core criticism of compulsory voting is that it relieves parties of the task of encouraging people to vote. It fundamentally changes the relationship between parties and citizens. In voluntary voting systems, members contribute to their party's success by encouraging non-partisans to vote when they otherwise might stay home (Scarrow 2014). Compulsory systems delegate that task to the state and dampen the need for a 'standing army' of party members (see e.g. Hughes 1966). The remaining functions of party members include nominating themselves as candidates, selecting candidates from among their ranks, assisting with campaign activities and helping to administer the party organisation.

A less flattering role for political party members is legitimising parties' claims that they are representative organisations fit to govern a country (Van Biezen, Mair and Poguntke 2012). In the early days of Australia's two-party system, large membership bases made strategic sense. How could a party claim to represent half the national electorate if they could not even attract willing members? Especially for a fledgling party like the early Liberal Party, members were vital evidence that the party had a social base, not just an ideological platform.

Accordingly, as the two parties became entrenched through the 1950s and 1960s (with the Liberals in government and Labor confined to opposition), the need for members as instruments of legitimacy waned. Menzies ran a centralised party organisation with himself as the central figure: 'the Liberal Party under Menzies was designed by Menzies to be a support for Menzies' (Jaensch 1994, 136). Labor had mass membership by default via the trade union movement and yet its membership list still declined from 370,000 in 1939 to 56,000 in 1973. Liberal Party membership held up slightly better but still halved between the 1950s and 1980s (Jaensch 2006, 28).

At the same time as the party's membership bases declined, their electoral bases also disintegrated. These are surely related. Mass parties have strong identities and are motivated by well-understood ideologies. Marsh (2006, 123) argues that the period of Liberal government from 1949 to 1972 'expanded Labor's welfare state but within the framework of Keynesian-style managed capitalism' and 'significantly extended the role of the Commonwealth government in education [...] and the role of the tariff as the primary instrument of industry development'. While the subsequent Labor government under Gough Whitlam furthered the state's role in social and economic policy, the parties largely agreed on the value of government intervention and light-touch Keynesianism. Since the 1980s, bipartisan consensus has shifted back to the centre-right, with Labor driving neoliberal economic reforms (Humphrys 2018).

This approach to electoral politics – wherein competing parties share the same broad approach to governance – encourages voters to look for small differences between them. This phenomenon is commonly called valence politics. Valence issues are those where the majority of voters agree on a preferable approach or outcome; where they disagree is on which party or candidate is better placed to deliver (Green 2007). Electoral contests then weigh heavily on which party is more competent, or which leader is more commanding.

Consensus over the direction of a country is perhaps a fortunate thing: there is none of the bitter polarisation that characterises modern American politics, for instance. But it does not necessarily inspire civic engagement in political life. When the parties stand for nothing but 'doing the same as our opponents, but better', it is difficult to rally a base. Compounded by compulsory voting, parties have both little capacity and little need to recruit members.

As a counterpoint, the modern highpoint of political engagement in Australia was driven by the archetypal valence politician, Kevin Rudd. Rudd campaigned to end John Howard's 10-year Liberal government by minimising the policy differences between himself and the conservative prime minister, on all but climate change and workplace relations (Johnson 2011). Rudd was Howard-lite, but younger and more intellectual. The electoral strategy paid off handsomely: Labor won 83 of the 150 House of Representatives seats, including Howard's electorate of Bennelong. Rudd's 2007 success (discounting his evident inability to command his parliamentary party) clearly endorses the valence strategy of modern Australian parties.

However, while 'Kevin 07' briefly invigorated Australian voters, it did not lead to any sustained improvement in rates of party membership or civic engagement more broadly. Deeply entwined in this strategy is the cartelisation of the major parties: as they become closer ideologically, they have likewise cooperated more frequently and agreed to draw on state resources to entrench their two-party status (Ward 2006). Party cartelisation is not the focus here, but it is clearly important: public funding further reduces parties' reliance on volunteer campaigners, and the high barriers to entry for minor party and independent challengers mean that dissatisfied voters have had few viable alternatives.

Voter Dissatisfaction since 2007

Since the fleeting highs of 2007, most measures of Australians' democratic satisfaction have declined. The Australian Election Study (Cameron and McAllister 2022) has found the following:

- the percentage of respondents who believe politicians know what ordinary people think has fallen from 23 per cent (2007) to 14 per cent (2022);
- the percentage saying that government is run for 'a few big interests' has increased from 38 per cent to 54 per cent;
- general satisfaction with democracy has fallen from 86 per cent in 2007 (and largely stable before that) to 70 per cent (and as low as 59 per cent in 2019); and
- the belief that people in government can be trusted has declined from 48 per cent in 1996 to 30 per cent of respondents in 2022.

This shift in public mood has not yet manifested as a decline in turnout; we might expect that in a voluntary system, the disarray in Australian party politics between 2007 and 2013 would surely have led voters to stay at home. Voter turnout as a proportion of the enroled population has fallen slightly, from 93 per cent in 2010 to 90 per cent in 2022. However, at the same time, the electoral roll has grown substantially: at the 2022 federal election, 97 per cent of eligible voters were estimated to be enroled, up from 90 per cent 12 years earlier (Australian Electoral Commission 2024).[2] If we measure turnout as the number of votes cast divided by the estimated number of potential voters (i.e. voting-aged Australian citizens), the rate has increased from 85 per cent in 2010 to 87 per cent in 2022. In other words, compulsory voting and the electoral administration apparatus that supports it are working as intended, even 100 years since its introduction and while our satisfaction with politics is in general decline.

Perhaps the clearest manifestation of this dissatisfaction is the fall in primary votes for the major parties. The combined Labor and Liberal-National vote share has fallen from more than 95 per cent in 1949 to 68 per cent in 2022 (Raue 2023). The option to 'park' your vote with a minor party or independent candidate without wasting it entirely is a major advantage of Australia's system of preferential voting. If federal elections were decided by plurality ('first-past-the-post') voting, shifting your vote from a viable major party candidate to an unviable challenger would mean that your vote would effectively be uncounted. Coupling this with a fine for abstention would likely breed further discontent.

This is not to say that the movement of primary votes away from the major parties has been particularly effective, as of 2024. Australia's combination of electoral and parliamentary systems is weighed heavily in the major parties' favour: election to the House of Representatives is via single-member electorates and a simple majority in the House

2. The enrolment rate among eligible Australians has been climbing since 2010, boosted by 2012 legislation enabling the Australian Electoral Commission to identify and commence enrolment of voting-aged citizens (Australian Electoral Commission 2012).

is required to govern. In only one election since 1940 has a major party failed to win a majority of seats in the House of Representatives (when Labor governed in minority from 2010 to 2013). The 2022 federal election returned the largest crossbench in history (16, 10 more than the previous high) of the House of Representatives, including 10 independent members, but the Labor government still has two seats more than required to govern in its own right (Figure 3.2). While this likely changes the government's calculus to a small extent – it cannot withstand more than two defections from its benches – it still leaves the (lower house) crossbench sidelined on most major policy decisions.

While preferential voting means that primary votes cast for even the most niche candidates contribute to the final 'two-party preferred' totals that decide House of Representative elections, the system still favours established parties. Almost one-third (32 per cent) of all voters in 2022 gave their first preference to candidates outside the Labor-Coalition duopoly, but only 10 per cent of House seats were won by non-duopoly candidates. The situation is slightly better in the Senate, where 36 per cent of all first preference votes went to non-duopoly candidates or groups, resulting in 25 per cent of new Senators coming from minor parties or independent groups.

This has effects beyond just disproportionality between votes and seats. More than 5 per cent of the national electorate – 776,169 voters – gave their first preference vote to an independent House candidate in 2022. Less than half of those voters (341,842) saw their preferred candidate elected. 'Backing a loser' has a negative effect on 'political efficacy', or the belief that voting makes a difference (Anderson et al. 2005). While it is impossible to parse cause and effect from a snapshot survey, data from the 2022 Australian Election Study (Figure 3.3) suggest that independent voters were already less satisfied with the democratic system and less likely to believe that government is responsive to the people (Cameron and McAllister 2022).

Note: Question wording is 'C6. In general, do you feel that the people in government are too often interested in looking after themselves, or do you feel that they can be trusted to do the right thing nearly all the time?'

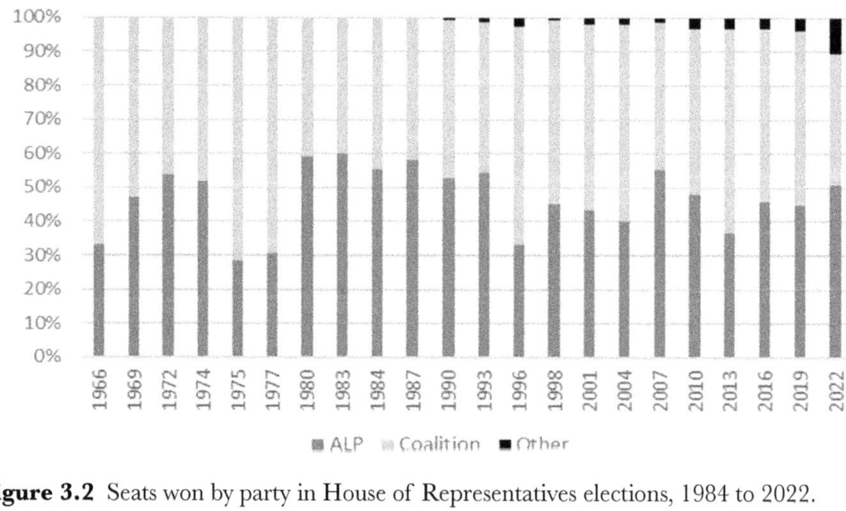

Figure 3.2 Seats won by party in House of Representatives elections, 1984 to 2022.

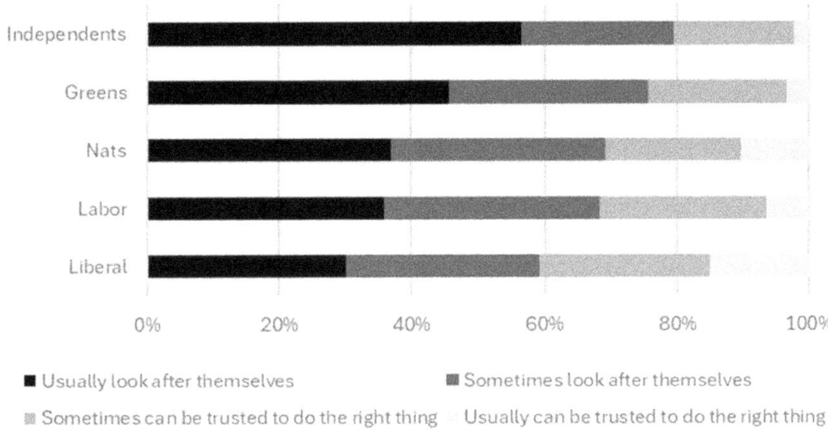

Figure 3.3 Political trust by House of Representatives vote at the 2022 election, Australian Election Study 2022.

The percentage of Australians who do not feel any kind of partisan identity is also increasing. While partisanship receives plenty of bad press (particularly with regard to affective and negative manifestations in polarised contexts like the United States), positive disposition towards parties of government is a key indicator of democratic health. In 1990, only 4 per cent of respondents to the Australian Election Study said they did not feel closer to one major party over another. In 2022, that percentage had increased to 24 (Cameron and McAllister 2022). Concurrently, Labor and Liberal partisans (combined) fell from 83 per cent of respondents to 58 per cent. Given that Australian Election Study respondents are likely more politically engaged than the wider electorate, it is reasonable to assume that substantially more than one-quarter of Australian voters feel zero attachment to a party. Political scientists have previously assumed that compulsory voting has a positive, secondary effect of prompting voters to think about parties and their policies at least once every three years (Mackerras and McAllister 1999). Without compulsion, we should expect much lower rates of partisan identification than we do now (Singh and Thornton 2013).

Under compulsory voting, voters can register their protest via a (deliberately) spoilt ballot (regardless of the intent of the original law). Informal voting – where ballots have not been filled in such a way that they convey a clear voting intent, per the Australian Electoral Commission's guidelines – has two main sources: deliberate spoilage of the ballot, so as to avoid voting for any of the nominated candidates (Hill and Rutledge-Prior 2016); and inadvertent spoilage, where the intent was to cast a valid vote but the execution was unclear (Young and Hill 2007). Informal voting is particularly high in compulsory voting systems (Kouba and Lysek 2019). The aggregate rate of informal votes cast in Australia has remained reasonably stable since 1984 (Figure 3.4), when group ticket voting was introduced in the Senate. However, there is a growing gap between informality rates in the Senate and the House, despite the Senate having the more complicated electoral system.

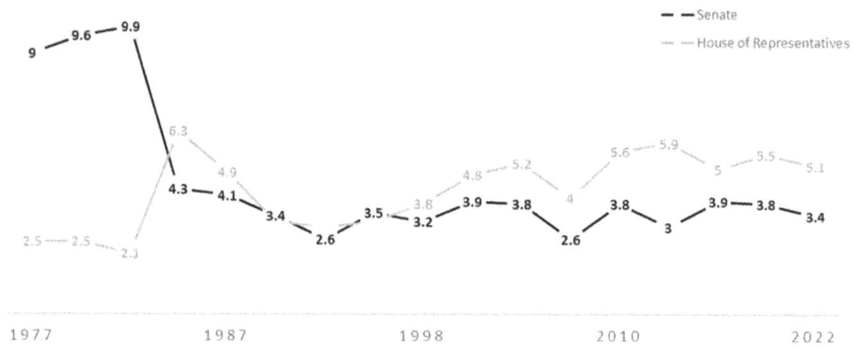

Figure 3.4 Informal voting at Australian elections 1977 to 2022, Australian Electoral Commission (2024).

If voters choose to spoil their ballot to register dissatisfaction with the electoral choices on offer, it is reasonable to expect that they will spoil House ballots at higher rates than Senate ones: the House is where government is formed and where the electoral choice is more constrained (in single-member electorates). We are more likely to see unintentional informality in the Senate, with its more complex ballot paper and much larger array of candidates (see e.g. the metre-long ballot paper in the NSW Senate election of 2013). If newly eligible citizens from non-English-speaking backgrounds were the key drivers of this growing gap (McAllister and Makkai 1993), we would expect to see it reversed, with greater informality in the Senate. Figures from 2007 further indicate that these changes are driven by intentional attempts to avoid voting: the election that saw the highest rates of voter satisfaction in recent decades also saw the lowest rates of informal voting. Other 'change of government' elections (2013 and 2022) also had below-average rates of informality.

The Voluntary Voting Counterfactual

This all leads to the question: What would Australian politics look like now without compulsory voting? We might expect the party consolidation of the first four decades to occur regardless, as similar democracies with voluntary voting but with some form of majoritarian electoral system (Duverger 1954). The United Kingdom, the United States and to a lesser extent Canada (due to linguistic and cultural cleavages) have all bedded down a stable two-party system with one centre-left and one centre-right party, without compelled voting.

It seems certain that voter turnout would have fallen significantly over the last century.[3] How the parties might have responded to lower turnout is less clear. The parties

3. One estimate suggests turnout would be as low as 50 per cent without compulsion (Dassonneville et al. 2023), but 85 per cent participation in 2017's voluntary Marriage Law Postal Survey indicates that participation norms are both real and strong.

(particularly Labor) have initiated incremental reforms over recent decades: a flurry of experiments with local primaries to select candidates, members' involvement in party leadership selection and non-member supporters' networks peaked between 2010 and 2015 (Gauja 2016), although Labor introduced lasting gender quotas in 1994 and has been successful in lifting women's legislative representation (Laing and Madden 2024). Cultural and ethnic diversity in the parliament has improved without specific intervention (Soutphommasane 2022). Similar parties in the UK and New Zealand have embarked on similar projects; however, there have been no associated gains in voter turnout (Gauja 2016).

Might the parties be more ideologically responsive under voluntary voting? The success of independent candidates in 2022 has been attributed to the Liberal Party losing support from 'moderates' (Nethery 2022), for example. The need to mobilise voters in those electorates that the Liberals lost to the independents – mostly inner suburban areas with very high household incomes and educational attainment – would plausibly have affected how the party campaigned and who they nominated. But conversely, it might have changed nothing. Parties have entrenched internal mechanisms for selecting candidates, and party members tend to be more conservative (or progressive) than the median party voter (May 1973). While the parties under voluntary voting would need to mobilise voters (as they did before 1924), it does not necessarily follow that they would take ideologically distinct positions from under compulsory voting. Existing research suggests that compulsion shifts policy very marginally to the left, so we might expect the parties to have converged slightly to the right of where they are currently (Fowler 2013; Bechtel, Hangartner and Schmid 2016).

In all, it is reasonable to say that Australian politics would look different today had compulsory voting not been introduced, but not very different. However, compelling people to vote when they are systemically displeased with the electoral options on offer is not harmless. There is, therefore, a growing percentage of Australians who do not trust the system or its actors to deliver the kind of democratic governance that they want, but who continue to vote anyway. In a voluntary system – such as Australia between federation and 1924 – we would expect these voters to abstain, revealing their dissatisfaction with the electoral choices by staying home on election day. But how do voters exit when they are compelled to stay?

Selling Policy Solutions to the Parties

Australians' attitude towards their democratic system is not dire in 2024. On this front, the country is in better shape than almost any comparable democracy. However, 100 years of stable democratic governance has failed to assure voters that this current system of elections, parties and policy is up to scratch. In 1924, the major contemporary parties responded quickly (probably too quickly, in terms of the legislative debate). In 2024, the parties have shown little interest in arresting the clear and worrying signs in the public mood; ad hoc parliamentary committees and some money for bureaucratic taskforces do not come close to compulsory voting in terms of a meaningful policy response.

In 1924, the parties ostensibly sidelined their own electoral priorities when they backed compulsory voting. It seems naïve to assume they would do the same 100 years later. On the other hand, it should not be incumbent on citizens to work to change a system that they do not feel is working for them. The optimal solution in 2024 is to persuade the parties to implement policy responses that allow citizens greater opportunities to engage and disengage from politics as they choose, without advantaging one side of politics over the other. These solutions should also align with the country's political values, as compulsory voting did in 1924.

Dissatisfied voters usually have one of three options: send a message with their vote, stay home on election day, or try to change the system from within. In Hirschman's (1972) typology, we can conceive of these choices as voice, exit or loyalty. Australia's current system of compulsory participation in elections with preferential voting (in the lower house) impinges heavily on these options. While dissatisfied or distrustful voters have the options of voting for non-major party candidates or spoiling a ballot, neither action represents a genuine exit from the electoral system. The following section considers policy options allowing voters to exercise voice, exit and loyalty while still being palatable to the established players.

Exercising Voice through Mixed-Member Proportional Representation

Although the Australian system is designed to entrench the two major parties, minor parties and independent candidates have been a long-standing feature of federal elections (and even more so at the state level). The 2022 election was notable for how many independent candidates were successful, but Australian voters are accustomed to ballot papers populated with minor party, micro party and independent candidates. Indeed, the number of unviable candidates nominating in Australia has caused consternation; voters in the electorate of Bradfield in 2022 had to rank 22 candidates to ensure their vote was counted, while the Senate ballot paper in NSW comprised 24 groups of candidates (75 candidates in total). Voters looking to send a message to the major parties are flush with options.

Obviously, the vast majority of those candidates have no real chance of winning, and preferential voting in both houses means that most votes get transferred to the major parties by the end of counting anyway. The major parties have no reason to change this, and we should not expect them to. This, more than compulsory voting, explains why the parties have been able to ignore the messages voters have been sending at recent elections: it might feel good to take your primary vote away from the unresponsive, unrepresentative parties, but your ballot will end up with one of them all the same. Independents have only very rarely managed to win.

One positive outcome for dissatisfied voters is that either major party requires support from crossbench members to form a minority government, as in 2010. From this position of power, minor party members and independents can negotiate policies in their own interest; in 2010, independents Tony Windsor and Rob Oakeshott agreed to support the Labor government in exchange for reforms to parliamentary procedure, government transparency and, probably most useful, infrastructure upgrades in rural and regional areas (including their own electorates). As it was, many of the demands included in that governing agreement – such as lowering the threshold for declaring political donations – were never enacted, and the minority government was defeated in the 2013 election. It is not within the major parties' interests to lower the barrier to entry for challenger parties and independents; even independents whose support was required to govern could not extract any real reforms. Moreover, as the crossbench grows in size, the parties will likely be even more reluctant to offer reforms that lower the barrier to entry for even more independents and minor party representatives.

The optimal way for the major parties to increase voters' voice in federal elections is to introduce a more proportional electoral system in the lower house. In moving from plurality voting to mixed-member proportional (MMP), New Zealand voters became more trusting of politicians and more efficacious about electoral politics (Banducci, Donovan and Karp 1999). Moreover, this effect was strongest among minor party and independent voters: precisely those with the lowest trust and efficacy in modern Australia.

At most points during the last century, it would have been unthinkable that the major parties would replace the current majoritarian system, so favourable to their interests, with a proportional one that diffuses their power. But the current trend in voting is long-standing and monotonic: without reform, more voters will turn to outsider candidates, and the parties will be required to negotiate with increasingly unwieldy blocs of cross-bench legislators. There is no assurance that voters' attitudes will improve under these conditions; the 2010 to 2013 experience suggests they might even fall.

While Tasmania and the Australian Capital Territory use Hare-Clarke electoral systems to produce consistently proportional outcomes, MMP is a more conservative option for Australia. Under MMP, voters cast two ballots: one for a local member, much like in the House of Representatives now, who represents a geographic-based electorate, and one for a party member, where parties designate a ranked list of candidates who are elected to the parliament based on the parties' national vote share. The result is that parliament comprises members who represent their local constituencies and members who represent their party (and their ideological and policy platform). Minor parties are much more likely to be elected via the party vote, as the necessary quota of votes is much smaller (i.e. the number of votes cast/the number of seats available + 1), similar to Australia's Senate.

The experience with MMP in New Zealand has been mixed, just like any political system. Most governments since its introduction in 1996 have required coalition arrangements; only one has governed in its own right. Minor parties have negotiated for senior executive roles (e.g. Winston Peters' three periods as foreign minister, under both conservative and progressive prime ministers), which would be a shock for many Australian voters. Importantly, neither major party has been systematically disadvantaged under MMP and elections have not produced unexpected or lopsided results. Introducing MMP to Australia's House of Representatives, combining existing electoral divisions and national party-list seats while retaining the Senate in its current form would improve democratic attitudes and preserve the major parties' positions.

Allowing Voter Exit in the Compulsory System

Voters wanting to exit the current system in Australia can stay at home and be fined or turn up and cast an informal vote. Both options incur a cost: $20 from your pocket or the time to attend a polling booth. Retaining the current settings around compulsory voting while disengagement increases seems unsustainable, as more voters want to exit the system without bearing the cost. At the same time, compulsory voting remains immensely popular: support among Australian Election Study respondents has been stable since 1990, bar the heights of 2007 (Figure 3.5). Further, of the 14 countries with enforceable compulsory voting laws, Australians stand alone in embracing rather than downplaying the nomenclature of *compulsory* voting (Birch 2009, 3).

Note: 'Supports compulsory voting' shows the percentage who responded 'compulsory better' (1967–1979) and 'favour compulsory voting' or 'strongly favour compulsory voting' (1987–2022). For would have voted if voluntary estimates combine 'definitely would have voted' and 'probably would have voted'.

Although Australian governments have tended to waive the legislated fine for non-voting in the face of reasonable explanations (illness, caring responsibilities, etc.), the existence of financial sanctions is unarguably punitive. While $20 is not considerable for many Australians, it is clearly high enough to drive even very disengaged voters to the polls: in 2022, only 10 per cent of enroled voters did not cast a vote. As that number grows, however, the cost of the fine will disproportionately affect low-income and low-wealth voters, entrenching resentment and disengagement among the very voters meant to be enfranchised by compulsory voting (Singh 2018).

There are two reasonable policy solutions to the problem of compulsory voting laws preventing unhappy voters from exiting the system. The first is to lower the fine to a less punitive amount ($5, for instance) such that there is a symbolic sanction, but no citizen is unduly penalised for abstaining. Although lowering the fine will likely mean more enrolled voters choose to abstain (Singh 2011), the abstention rate will likely increase without intervention anyway. Lowering the fine will make the cost less onerous without removing the institutional apparatus around compulsory voting.

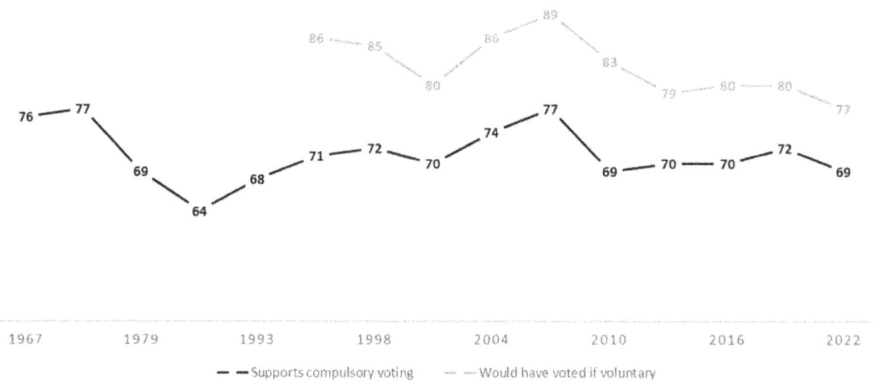

Figure 3.5 Attitudes towards compulsory voting, Australian Election Study 1987 to 2022, Australian National Political Attitudes Survey 1967 to 1979.

Second, convenience voting options can be made more convenient. For many voters, voting by post or in person before election day (as they already can) is less costly than attending a booth on election day. Removing friction from both of these options – banning parties from distributing postal vote applications, for instance, and accepting late postal votes from within Australia – would make it easier still for voters to effectively exit the system while still complying with compulsory voting requirements. Additional voting channels, such as universal telephone or internet voting, would lower the costs even further but would also introduce much greater resource requirements and potential for error, such that they should not be considered at this stage.

Compulsory voting is widely assumed to favour progressive parties (Birch 2009), but more recent evidence from early twentieth-century elections in Australia is more ambivalent (Held 2023). Certainly, recent decades have shown that Liberal politicians are more likely to want compulsory voting repealed, ostensibly for philosophical reasons, but surely the presumed strategic advantages contribute at least a little to their rationale (Strangio 2021). Given its popularity and its place in our national identity, there is almost no chance that the major parties would agree to dismantle compulsory voting entirely. Likewise, it is in the minor parties' and independents' interests to keep the current system. Making exit easier under compulsory conditions would help to ease the current pressure point, in which already unhappy voters are punished for opting out.

Fixing the System from Inside

Australia's major parties have shown little interest in increasing their membership bases in recent decades. As more of the work of campaigning and fundraising becomes professionalised, a large base of volunteers becomes less vital (Miragliotta 2015). Additionally, members can be a burden: they inevitably want more say in how the party operates, which leads to conflict between the parliamentary party and the grassroots party. The most famous recent example is UK Labor's selection of Jeremy Corbyn as leader against his colleagues' wishes, but closer to home members of the Australian Democrats chose Natasha Stott Despoja as leader of a parliamentary party that preferred her predecessor. It is reasonable that parliamentarians and party officials might be wary of their base (even though they were once part of the base themselves).

Currently, there is little benefit in staying loyal to the major parties. If you join the party, you get little say in internal decisions, save the occasional vote in a preselection contest (which might be summarily overruled by the party executive). Branch meetings are dull (McDonnell and Stanford 2024) and parliamentarians show little interest in members between elections. Most new members leave the party within two years (Miragliotta 2015). More broadly, the number of Australians who stay loyal to their party via lifelong voting is in decline: in 1967, 72 per cent of voters always voted for the same party; in 2022 that had fallen to 37 per cent. There is currently little payoff for loyalty within the system.

Improving their membership offerings will not engage citizens who only want to think about politics cursorily, and so internal party reform is not a panacea. It may only barely grow the formal membership base of either party. But the current perception of parties as indifferent to their members at best and hostile at worst is likely contributing to low political trust. Providing new channels for engagement outside of formal party branch structures – like supporter groups, primaries for candidate selection and encouraging debate and expression within the party – may not revive the post-war culture of party membership in Australia, but it is a very small risk worth taking. Extending participation in parliamentary leadership ballots, as Labor has already done, comes with known risks and is not necessarily any more effective in terms of improving members' feelings of efficacy.

Conclusion

Compulsory voting has performed admirably well at maintaining high levels of voter turnout while remaining popular among the vast majority of voters. It has also had many ancillary benefits not discussed here, such as widespread but relatively shallow party identification, high rates of political knowledge across the whole population and probably contributed to the country's moderate and stable political culture. But it might mask deep-seated dissatisfaction and even further it by compelling citizens to engage with a system of elections, parties and candidates they distrust and dislike. Surveys such as the Australian Election Study will not necessarily pick up on the early warning signs, as the most disengaged tend to ignore requests to respond. Voters are steadily moving away from the major parties, but single-member electoral districts, alternative voting and compulsion work to maintain their hold on executive power. Deliberate abstention via informal voting remains rare but climbs during the lifespan of a government. With the compulsory voting silver bullet already used, politicians in 2024 will require more innovative solutions to address low trust and democratic malaise.

References

Anderson, Christopher J., Blais, André, Bowler, Shaun, Donovan, Todd and Listhaug, Ola. 2005. *Losers' Consent: Elections and Democratic Legitimacy.* Oxford: Oxford University Press. https://doi.org/10.1093/0199276382.001.0001.

Arriola, Leonardo R., Choi, Donghyun Danny, Davis, Justine M., Phillips, Melanie L. and Rakner, Lise. 2022. 'Paying to Party: Candidate Resources and Party Switching in New Democracies'. *Party Politics* 28 (3): 507–520. https://doi.org/10.1177/1354068821989563.

Australian Electoral Commission. 2024. 'Enrolment Statistics'. Australian Electoral Commission. https://www.aec.gov.au/Enrolling_to_vote/Enrolment_stats/ (accessed 24 April 2024).

Banducci, Susan A., Donovan, Todd and Karp, Jeffrey A. 1999. 'Proportional Representation and Attitudes about Politics: Results from New Zealand'. *Electoral Studies* 18 (4): 533–555. https://doi.org/10.1016/S0261-3794(99)00019–0.

Bechtel, Michael M., Hangartner, Dominik and Schmid, Lukas. 2016. 'Does Compulsory Voting Increase Support for Leftist Policy?' *American Journal of Political Science* 60 (3): 752–767. https://doi.org/10.1111/ajps.12224.

Birch, Sarah. 2009. *Full Participation: A Comparative Study of Compulsory Voting.* Tokyo and New York: United Nations University Press.

Blondel, Jean. 1978. *Political Parties: A Genuine Case for Discontent?* London: Wildwood House.

Brett, Judith. 2019. *From Secret Ballot to Democracy Sausage: How Australia Got Compulsory Voting.* Melbourne: Text Publishing.

Brett, Judith. 2021. 'How Australia Got Compulsory Voting'. In *A Century of Compulsory Voting in Australia: Genesis, Impact and Future*, edited by Matteo Bonotti and Paul Strangio, 15–32. Singapore: Springer. https://doi.org/10.1007/978-981-33-4025-1_2.

Bryce, James. 1921. *Modern Democracies, vol. 2.* New York: Macmillan. http://oll.libertyfund.org/?option=com_staticxt&staticfile=show.php%3Ftitle=2090&chapter=159262&layout=html&Itemid=27.

Cameron, Sarah M. and McAllister, Ian. 2022. *Trends in Australian Political Opinion: Results from the Australian Election Study, 1987–2022.* https://australianelectionstudy.org/publications/.

Collins, Hugh. 1985. 'Political Ideology in Australia: The Distinctiveness of a Benthamite Society'. *Daedalus* 114 (1): 147–169. https://doi.org/10.2307/20024958.

Dassonneville, Ruth, Barbosa, Thiago, Blais, André, McAllister, Ian and Turgeon, Mathieu. 2023. *Citizens Under Compulsory Voting: A Three-Country Study.* Elements in Campaigns and Elections. Cambridge: Cambridge University Press. https://doi.org/10.1017/9781009071116.

Duverger, Maurice. 1954. *Political Parties: Their Organization and Activity in the Modern State.* London: Methuen; New York: J. Wiley.

Feitosa, Fernando, Blais, André and Dassonneville, Ruth. 2020. 'Does Compulsory Voting Foster Civic Duty to Vote?' *Election Law Journal: Rules, Politics, and Policy* 19 (1): 19–44. https://doi.org/10.1089/elj.2018.0539.

Fowler, Anthony. 2013. 'Electoral and Policy Consequences of Voter Turnout: Evidence from Compulsory Voting in Australia'. *Quarterly Journal of Political Science* 8 (2): 159–182. https://doi.org/10.1561/100.00012055.

Gauja, Anika. 2016. *Political Parties and Elections: Legislating for Representative Democracy.* New York: Routledge.

Green, Antony. 2011. 'No Link between the Alternative Vote and Compulsory Voting in Australia'. *ABC News* (blog), 17 March 2011. https://www.abc.net.au/news/2011-03-18/no-link-between-the-alternative-vote-and-compulsory-voting-in-au/9389704.

Green, Jane. 2007. 'When Voters and Parties Agree: Valence Issues and Party Competition'. *Political Studies* 55 (3): 629–655. https://doi.org/10.1111/j.1467–9248.2007.00671.x.

Held, Alexander. 2023. 'Compulsory Voting, Turnout, and Support for Left-Wing Parties: The Case of Australia'. *Electoral Studies* 81 (February): 102569. https://doi.org/10.1016/j.electstud.2022.102569.

Hill, Lisa. 2010. 'Public Acceptance of Compulsory Voting: Explaining the Australian Case'. *Representation* 46 (4): 425–438. https://doi.org/10.1080/00344893.2010.518089.

Hill, Lisa and Rutledge-Prior, Serrin. 2016. 'Young People and Intentional Informal Voting in Australia'. *Australian Journal of Political Science* 51 (3): 400–417. https://www.tandfonline.com/doi/abs/10.1080/10361146.2016.1200534.

Hirschman, Albert O. 1972. *Exit, Voice, and Loyalty.* Harvard University Press.

Hughes, Colin A. 1966. 'Compulsory Voting'. *Politics* 1 (2): 81–95. https://doi.org/10.1080/00323266608401077.

Humphrys, Elizabeth. 2018. *How Labour Built Neoliberalism.* Netherlands: Brill.

Jaensch, Dean. 1994. *Power Politics: Australia's Party System*, 3rd edn. St. Leonards: Allen & Unwin.

Jaensch, Dean. 2006. 'Party Structures and Processes'. In *Political Parties in Transition?*, edited by Ian Marsh, 24–45. Sydney: Federation Press.

Johnson, Carol. 2011. 'Gillard, Rudd and Labor Tradition'. *Australian Journal of Politics & History* 57 (4): 562–579. https://doi.org/10.1111/j.1467–8497.2011.01614.x.

Kemp, David. 2021. *A Liberal State: How Australians Chose Liberalism Over Socialism, 1926–1966.* Melbourne: Miegunyah Press.

Kouba, Karel and Lysek, Jakub. 2019. 'What Affects Invalid Voting? A Review and Meta-Analysis'. *Government and Opposition* 54 (4): 745–775. https://doi.org/10.1017/gov.2018.33.

Laing, Kate and Madden, Cathy. 2024. 'Gender Composition of Australian Parliaments by Party: A Quick Guide'. Canberra: Australian Parliamentary Library. https://www.aph

.gov.au/About_Parliament/Parliamentary_departments/Parliamentary_Library/pubs/rp/rp2324/Quick_Guides/CompositionPartyGender2024.

Lau, Richard R. and Redlawsk, David P. 1997. 'Voting Correctly'. *American Political Science Review* 91 (3): 585–598. https://doi.org/10.2307/2952076.

Mackerras, M. and McAllister, Ian. 1999. 'Compulsory Voting, Party Stability and Electoral Advantage in Australia'. *Electoral Studies* 18, no. 2: 217–233. https://doi.org/10.1016/S0261-3794(98)00047-X.

Marsh, Ian. 2006. 'Policy Convergence between the Major Parties and the Representation Gap in Australian Politics'. In *Political Parties in Transition?*, edited by Ian Marsh, 116–142. Sydney: Federation Press.

May, John D. 1973. 'Opinion Structure of Political Parties: The Special Law of Curvilinear Disparity'. *Political Studies* 21 (2): 135–151. https://doi.org/10.1111/j.1467–9248.1973.tb01423.x.

McAllister, Ian and Makkai, Toni. 1993. 'Institutions, Society or Protest? Explaining Invalid Votes in Australian Elections'. *Electoral Studies* 12 (1): 23–40. https://doi.org/10.1016/0261-3794(93)90004–4.

McDonnell, Duncan and Stanford, Bartholomew. 2024. 'The Party on Remote Ground: Disengaging and Disappearing?' *Parliamentary Affairs* 77 (1): 46–61. https://doi.org/10.1093/pa/gsac026.

The Mercury. 1911. 'Party Government in Excelsis', 14 October 1911. http://nla.gov.au/nla.news-article10117308.

Miragliotta, Narelle. 2015. 'Parties and the Mass Membership'. In *Contemporary Australian Political Party Organisations*, edited by Narelle Miragliotta, Anika Gauja and Rodney Smith, 62–75. Clayton: Monash University Publishing.

Monnox, Chris. 2019. '"Men, Money, and Motors": The Motor Car as an Emerging Technology in Australian Federal Election Campaigns, 1903–31'. *The Journal of Transport History* 40 (2): 232–250. https://doi.org/10.1177/0022526619831396.

Nethery, Amy. 2022. 'Why Teal Independents Are Seeking Liberal Voters and Spooking Liberal MPs'. *The Conversation*, 3 May 2022. http://theconversation.com/why-teal-independents-are-seeking-liberal-voters-and-spooking-liberal-mps-182133.

Raue, Ben. 2023. 'The House of Representatives Results'. In *Watershed*, edited by Marian Sawer, Anika Gauja and Jill Sheppard, 335–359. Canberra: ANU Press. https://doi.org/10.22459/W.2023.

Sawer, Marian. 2001. 'Inventing the Nation Through the Ballot Box'. Canberra: Parliament of Australia. https://www.aph.gov.au/About_Parliament/Senate/Powers_practice_n_procedures/pops/pop37/sawer.

Scarrow, S. 2014. *Beyond Party Members: Changing Approaches to Partisan Mobilization*. Oxford: Oxford University Press.

Singh, Shane. 2011. 'How Compelling Is Compulsory Voting? A Multilevel Analysis of Turnout'. *Political Behavior* 33 (1): 95–111. https://doi.org/10.1007/s11109-010-9107-z.

Singh, Shane and Thornton, Judd. 2013. 'Compulsory Voting and the Dynamics of Partisan Identification'. *European Journal of Political Research* 52 (2): 188–211. https://doi.org/10.1111/j.1475–6765.2012.02071.x.

Singh, Shane P. 2018. 'Compulsory Voting and Dissatisfaction with Democracy'. *British Journal of Political Science* 48 (3): 843–854. https://doi.org/10.1017/S0007123416000041.

Souter, Gavin. 1988. *Acts of Parliament: A Narrative History of the Senate and House of Representatives Commonwealth of Australia*. Carlton South: Melbourne University Press.

Soutphommasane, Tim. 2022. 'We're about to Have Australia's Most Diverse Parliament yet – but There's Still a Long Way to Go'. *The Conversation*, 24 May 2022. http://theconversation.com/were-about-to-have-australias-most-diverse-parliament-yet-but-theres-still-a-long-way-to-go-183620.

Strangio, Paul. 2021. '"A Lonely and Quixotic Battle": A Short History of Agitation Against Compulsory Voting in Australia'. In *A Century of Compulsory Voting in Australia: Genesis, Impact and Future*, edited by Matteo Bonotti and Paul Strangio, 33–57. Singapore: Springer. https://doi.org/10.1007/978-981-33-4025-1_3.

Van Biezen, Ingrid, Mair, Peter and Poguntke, Thomas. 2012. 'Going, Going, . . . Gone? The Decline of Party Membership in Contemporary Europe'. *European Journal of Political Research* 51 (1): 24–56. https://doi.org/10.1111/j.1475-6765.2011.01995.x.

Ward, Ian. 1991. 'The Changing Organisational Nature of Australia's Political Parties'. *The Journal of Commonwealth & Comparative Politics* 29 (2): 153–174. https://doi.org/10.1080/14662049108447608.

Ward, Ian. 2006. 'Cartel Parties and Election Campaigns in Australia'. In *Political Parties in Transition?*, edited by Ian Marsh, 70–93. Sydney: Federation Press.

Webb, Paul, Scarrow, Susan and Poguntke, Thomas. 2022. 'Party Organization and Satisfaction with Democracy: Inside the Blackbox of Linkage'. *Journal of Elections, Public Opinion and Parties* 32 (1): 151–172. https://doi.org/10.1080/17457289.2019.1698047.

Young, Sally and Hill, Lisa. 2007. 'Protest or Error? Informal Voting and Compulsory Voting'. *Australian Journal of Political Science* 42 (3): 515–521. https://www.tandfonline.com/doi/abs/10.1080/10361140701513646.

Chapter 4

EARLY VOTING AND THE DEMOCRATIC IDEAL

Lachlan Umbers

Recent years have witnessed a sharp increase in early voting in Australian elections.[1] In the 2004 Federal election, just over 10 per cent of voters cast their ballot early (whether by mail or pre-poll) (Muller 2022). In 2019, however, over 40 per cent of voters did so. In 2022, over half of all voters cast their ballots prior to election day (Coma and Smith 2023, 413). This rise appears to have been largely driven by changes to the *Commonwealth Electoral Act* (1918) passed in 2010. Schedule 2 of the Act outlines a list of circumstances in which citizens are eligible to vote early (e.g. being a patient in hospital). However, the 2010 reforms enabled pre-poll ballots to be counted as 'ordinary ballots', removing the requirement for citizens to submit a declaration that they were formally eligible to vote early.

Despite the fact that Schedule 2 does not list convenience as a reason why citizens may vote early, survey data collected in 2010 and 2013 by the Australian Electoral Commission (AEC, hereafter) found that over 30 per cent of early voters cited convenience as their principal reason for casting their ballots prior to election day (Rojas and Muller 2014). It is likely that the proportion is much higher, today.[2] Even in 2013, over 75 per cent of respondents on the AEC survey admitted that had early voting been unavailable, they would have been able to vote on election day (Rojas and Muller 2014, 6). Moreover, rates of early voting in 2010 and 2013 were much lower than in more recent elections – under 20 per cent in 2010 and just over 26 per cent in 2013, as opposed to over 50 per cent in 2022.

Notwithstanding legal technicalities, then, Australians now arguably enjoy virtually universal access to early voting, de facto. This represents a major shift in the way Australians participate in the electoral process. Despite this, the normative

1. For invaluable comments and suggestions, I should like to thank attendees at the 2024 UWA 'Civic Participation in Australian Democracy' workshop and a 2024 UWA Philosophy Society Seminar. My thanks also to Ten-Herng Lai for written comments.
2. Empirical research is unfortunately rather limited – though see ERRN (2018) and Sheppard and Beauregard (2018).

considerations raised by early voting have been little discussed.[3] In particular, though much has been written about the right to vote, generally, little has been said about the basis of the right to vote *early*. Or, more particularly, whether that right ought to be extended to all citizens or whether we instead ought to favour arrangements in which opportunities for early voting are restricted to certain citizens only. In this chapter, then, I begin by reconstructing what seems to me to be the strongest case for universal early voting, which appeals to the value of political equality. In the following section, however, I argue that the considerations to which this argument appeals, on closer examination, entail only that opportunities for early voting ought to be extended to citizens for whom election-day participation would be unreasonably costly. They do *not* show that *all* citizens must be afforded such rights. I then go on to argue that we have powerful reasons to *only* extend the right to vote early to such citizens. Citizens for whom voting early would be a matter of mere convenience ought to be instead required to vote on election day.

The Egalitarian Case for Universal Early Voting

The rise in early voting has not been a subject of significant controversy in Australia. In the United States, however, matters are very different. In response to Republican attempts to limit ballot access for partisan advantage, a range of influential bodies now advocate explicitly for universal early voting. The Brennan Centre for Justice, for instance, has argued that states should afford all citizens a two-week early voting window prior to major elections (BCJ 2018). The arguments offered in defence of such arrangements often appeal to the value of *equality*. Since theorists often take egalitarian considerations to be central to the case for democracy itself, we would do well to begin by considering the egalitarian case for universal early voting.

It will be helpful to begin by introducing a model of the calculus of voting.[4] Let $G: \{1, 2, \ldots n\}$ be the set of all eligible voters. Then, $\forall i \in G$, the utility of voting will be given by the formula $U_i(V) = P_i(D) \times [R_i(A) - R_i(B)] - C_i + D_i$, where $U_i(V)$ is the utility, for i, of voting, $P_i(D)$ is the probability of i being decisive over the outcome, $R_i(A)$ is the net benefit, to i, of their preferred candidate winning, $R_i(B)$ is the net benefit, to i, of their non-preferred candidate winning, $[R_i(A) - R_i(B)]$ is (therefore) the *marginal* benefit, to i, of their preferred candidate winning, C_i is the cost, to i, of voting and D_i is any 'non-instrumental' benefits of voting (e.g. feeling that one has expressed support for a favoured political cause).[5]

In English, this formula simply states that the utility of voting in an election, for any given individual, i, will be given by the marginal benefit of their preferred candidate emerging victorious, weighted by the probability of their being decisive over the

3. Indeed, with the exception of Thompson (2004, 2005, 2008), early voting appears to have been largely neglected by political theorists.
4. Here I largely follow Riker and Ordeshook (1968).
5. We assume two-party competition for simplicity.

outcome (i.e. the probability of an exact tie among all other voters that *i* gets to break in favour of their preferred candidate), minus the costs of participating (time, transport costs, cognitive effort, etc.), plus any returns from voting unrelated to the extent to which *i* probabilifies their favoured outcomes (e.g. the value of expressing one's political attitudes – c.f. Brennan and Lomasky 1993).

Importantly, in any realistic election, $P_i(D)$ will inevitably be extremely close to zero. Thus, the marginal benefit, to *i*, of their preferred candidate emerging victorious will be of very little significance (because aggressively discounted) in determining whether *i* will participate or not. We should therefore expect that whether some individual will participate in some election will largely be determined by the relative magnitudes of C_i and D_i – i.e. by the *costs* of voting and its *non-instrumental benefits*.

Even where elections are well-administered, the costs of participating on election day vary significantly between citizens. A wealthy retiree who lives next door to a polling place and has few competing calls on their time can cast their ballot on election day at very little cost. For an impecunious casual employee forced to decline a work shift in order to vote, matters may be very different. The fact of this variation lends support to two separate (though compatible) egalitarian arguments for universal early voting.

First, the *appeal to equality of opportunity*. Democrats plainly ought to favour a principle of equality of opportunity to vote. Arrangements in which some face formal impediments to accessing the franchise that others do not (e.g. race-based disenfranchisement) seem plainly unjust. Yet so, too, do states of affairs in which exercising the franchise is *excessively costly* for certain citizens. For instance, Australian elections are invariably held on Saturdays. Certain members of the Jewish faith, however, do not work or travel on Saturdays for religious reasons. A requirement to vote on election day, then, would impose a serious burden upon such persons (a choice between declining to participate or violating the tenets of one's religion) that others in the community do not face. Thus, a system in which early voting was unavailable to any citizen would fall afoul of the ideal of equality of opportunity. Even if no citizen faced any formal barrier to exercising the franchise, certain citizens would nevertheless find participating on election day *costly* in a way others would not.[6]

If we wish to ensure equality of opportunity to vote *in substance*, then, voting must not be excessively costly. By permitting all citizens to vote prior to election day, should they wish to, citizens would be able to vote at a time which *minimises* the opportunity costs of doing so. Shift workers who typically work Saturdays, for instance, could elect to vote on days when they are not 'rostered on' and thereby avoid foregoing income. Thus, universal early voting helps ensure (though, of course, does not guarantee) that citizens for whom election-day participation would be particularly burdensome do not face excessive costs in exercising the franchise, thereby promoting substantive equality of opportunity to vote.

---

6. This argument has particular force where voting is compulsory and where such voters effectively face a choice between the high costs of participation on election day or incurring a fine (exemptions notwithstanding).

The second argument is the *appeal to responsiveness*. Persons of lower socioeconomic status often confront a higher cost of voting than persons of higher socioeconomic status, for a wide variety of reasons. Poorer citizens, for instance, are more likely to be employed casually and may therefore be required to sacrifice some proportion of their income in order to attend the polls in a way that other citizens typically will not be. Moreover, empirical studies suggest both that citizens of lower socioeconomic status are more likely to be disinterested in politics than citizens of higher socioeconomic status (Prior 2019, ch. 12) and that citizens disinterested in the political process are significantly less likely to vote (see e.g. Blais and Daoust 2020), presumably because there is a connection between political interest and the utility one derives from participating in elections (i.e. the magnitude of the D_i term). Thus, it is significantly more likely that for citizens of lower socioeconomic status, $C_i > D_i$ – that is, that the costs of voting will outweigh the benefits – than for more privileged citizens. As such, we should expect citizens of lower socioeconomic status to be significantly less likely to vote – a finding borne out by many empirical studies (see e.g. Leighley and Nagler 2014).

The problem, of course, is that insofar as elected officials may be certain ex ante that the worse-off will under-participate in elections, relative to more privileged citizens, they will have weaker incentives to protect and promote such persons' interests. And, indeed, there is a large body of empirical research that lends powerful support to this conjecture. Elected officials do, indeed, appear to be significantly less responsive to the interests of the worse-off where they under-participate in elections. Lower rates of participation on the part of the worse-off appear to be associated with higher Gini coefficients (see e.g. Avery 2015, 964–71) and reduced state welfare spending (see e.g. Severson 2018, 285), for instance. Insofar as opportunities for early voting help to minimise the costs of voting for the worse-off, then, we ought to expect universal early voting to help minimise under-participation on the part of the worse-off and to help mitigate its harmful, inegalitarian effects.

Against the Egalitarian Case

Unfortunately, neither of these arguments survives close examination. We can quickly dismiss the appeal to responsiveness. In the case of Australia, concerns around socioeconomic bias in turnout largely do not arise due to the fact of compulsory voting.[7] Second, in voluntary voting contexts, though convenience voting measures such as universal early voting undoubtedly lower the costs of participation, empirical studies overwhelmingly find that such measures disproportionately mobilise *politically engaged* citizens, who are (as noted above) also more likely to belong to more socioeconomically advantaged groups (see esp. Berinsky 2005; Gronke et al. 2008, 442–47). Universal early voting, then, may *worsen* the (relative) under-participation of the worse-off in elections. The appeal to responsiveness, then, fails to survive contact with empirical reality.

7. Though compulsory voting is controversial. For criticisms, see Brennan (2014) and Lever (2010). For defences, see (among many others) Hill (2014) and Umbers (2020a, 2021b).

The appeal to equality of opportunity requires more careful treatment. Notice, first, that the ideal of substantive equality of opportunity to vote is ambiguous between two potential interpretations. On the *comparative* interpretation, we might insist that $\forall i, j \in G$, $C_i \cong C_j$. Or, less formally: the costs of voting must be approximately equal for all citizens. On the *non-comparative* interpretation, we might instead hold that there is some threshold cost of voting M_i, beyond which the costs of participation are *unreasonably* great. We might insist, then, that $\forall i \in G$, $C_i < M_i$. Or, less formally: for all citizens, the costs of participation in elections must not exceed some absolute threshold. Both interpretations are obviously egalitarian – though in different ways. The former insists that voting must be approximately equally costly for all citizens, while the latter insists that all citizens must have an equal right to participate without unreasonable cost.[8]

It is important to see, however, that the appeal to equal opportunity presupposes the comparative interpretation. The most important question the proponent of this argument needs to confront is: why does equality of opportunity require extending the right to vote early to *all* citizens, not merely to those for whom $C_i \geq M_i$ (i.e. all those for whom election-day participation is unreasonably costly)? The only possible answer, it seems, must be that this would still allow for inequalities in the cost of voting between citizens for whom $C_i < M_i$ (i.e. those citizens for whom election day participation would not be unreasonably costly). This, they must insist, is both unjust and would be mitigated by universal early voting.

However, while there is a powerful argument for the non-comparative interpretation, I think that there is no similarly compelling argument for the comparative interpretation. For comparison, consider the following argument for equality of substantive opportunity to access higher education. Here, the reasons for embracing a comparative principle are straightforward. Given the ways in which we have collectively chosen to structure our societies, the degree of access each citizen can expect to have to the 'social primary goods' necessary for pursuing a conception of the good (income and wealth, the social bases of self-respect, and so on) depends very substantially upon their profession. And one's access to the professions, in turn, depends upon one's level of educational attainment.

Yet social primary goods are also the product of *social co-operation*. It would be impossible for any citizen to accumulate a non-trivial amount of income and wealth, for instance, without the basic legal architecture necessary to establish a market, ensure the efficacy of contract, provide individuals with a guaranteed minimum level of personal security and so on. Such goods are provided only by virtue of enormously complex schemes of collective action regulated and co-ordinated by the state, to which citizens are required to contribute (typically, though not exclusively, via taxation) on pain of coercion. It would seem obviously to strike at the fundamental equality of persons if citizens could be coerced into *contributing* to institutions that afforded them *unequal access* to the goods of social co-operation that it is the fundamental purpose of those institutions

8. Note that the two interpretations are not mutually exclusive – one could insist that the costs of voting must be both approximately equal *and* not unreasonably high for all citizens.

to produce. Thus, since in societies like ours access to higher education substantially conditions the degree to which citizens are in fact able to enjoy access to such goods, it follows that access to higher education ought to be at least approximately equal for all citizens.

Arguments of this form are both compelling and, since largely appropriated from the influential work of Rawls (1971), very familiar. They are often appealed to in defence of requirements that citizens be afforded equality of opportunity to access some good or other. Yet no similar argument is available in the case of voting. For, unlike higher education, one's access to the benefits of social co-operation will *not* depend upon one's opportunities to exercise the franchise. To the contrary, we can be certain ex ante that whether or not we (just as individuals) participate in some election and/or who we cast our ballots for will make *no difference* to the outcome of the election, to the policies subsequently implemented or to the parties' incentives to protect and promote the interests of the social groups to which we belong. Our access to the benefits of social co-operation – and, hence, our quality of life – is simply *unaffected* by whether we, as individuals, enjoy access to the franchise at all, let alone the *costs* we face in exercising it.

Of course, as noted above, if members of my social group(s) characteristically face greater costs of participation, en masse, then this is liable to have a very adverse impact on my access to the goods of social co-operation by weakening politicians' incentives to protect and promote my interests. But whether I *personally* face greater costs than other citizens in exercising the franchise is simply irrelevant. What matters is whether a *sufficient proportion* of my social group faces costs in exercising the franchise that others do not. Whether there is some inequality between the costs of *my* participating in elections and those confronted by any other citizen has no non-trivial bearing on the outcomes that will be produced by the democratic process.

However, there is a very powerful rationale available for the *non-comparative* interpretation, which lends powerful support to the claims of citizens for whom election-day participation would be *unreasonably costly* to be extended the right to cast their ballots prior to election day. Our enjoyment of the goods of social co-operation depends fundamentally upon a range of basic social institutions. Many of these institutions take the form of rules. Systems of economic exchange, for instance, depend fundamentally upon the ability of governments to establish and enforce rules of property. The *distribution* of such goods also depends ultimately upon such rules. Each person's share of total income and wealth depends heavily upon the extent to which the rules of economic activity mandate redistribution. Since we plainly have powerful reason to ensure both the production of certain public goods (e.g. roads, transport, health, defence) and for those goods to be distributed in certain ways, we have reason to favour a system for the *determination* of such rules that will most efficiently ensure the production of such goods and guarantee their appropriate distribution (subject to appropriate procedural constraints – see below).

Any plausible system must delegate responsibility for most decisions concerning such rules to representatives whose role it is to specialise in the making of policy. Most issues of public policy are highly complex, and most citizens have neither the time nor inclination to acquire the relevant expertise. The consequences of any system of pure direct decision-making on the part of the entire citizenry, then, would be deleterious. Political representation, however, gives rise to a (very familiar) principal-agent problem. The fundamental purpose of representative government is to organise and regulate social co-operation to advance the citizenry's interests. Yet given (a) the extraordinary power wielded by political representatives and (b) the limited ability of citizens to monitor their activities, there is an obvious risk that representatives will tend to illicitly favour their *own* interests (and the interests of members of their own social groups) at the expense of the interests of the citizenry more generally.

The only feasible (albeit imperfect) solution is to insist that representatives must be *elected*.[9] Office-seeking politicians have powerful incentives to protect and promote the interests of those citizens upon whom their re-election depends in decision-making and to call out abuses of power by the opposition. This, however, immediately gives rise to a very wide range of questions concerning the method of election we have reason to favour. One salient possibility is *unanimity*. Yet given the obvious infeasibility of obtaining unanimous agreement, the inefficiencies this would generate (and the resultant inability of government to make rules for the production and distribution of the goods of social co-operation) would render any such requirement plainly unjustified.[10] Elections, then, must be held on the basis of some form of *majority rule*.

Yet this, too, entails an obvious risk. If elected officials do not need support from *all* citizens, they may choose to simply neglect certain subsets of the citizenry and concentrate their efforts upon others. The maldistribution of the benefits of social co-operation seems a virtually inevitable result. We cannot hope to eliminate this problem. But, in order to *mitigate* it, we must insist that elections be structured such that all citizens can participate *without excessive cost*. Citizens must be able to join (with or without formal co-ordination efforts) with fellow members of the social groups to which they belong at the ballot box to demand that their interests be afforded weight in policymaking. In this way, we might hope that elected officials will have an incentive to attend to all (or, at least, the vast majority of) citizens' interests – not merely those of particular social classes. Plainly, this will only be the case if politicians *cannot* reasonably anticipate that certain ex ante identifiable subsets of the population will tend to under-participate in elections given the unreasonably great costs of their participation.

Thus, we have very powerful reason to favour a *non-comparative* interpretation of equality of opportunity to vote. All citizens must be able to vote without excessive cost. And this, in turn, lends powerful support to institutions that make opportunities for early voting available to those citizens for whom election-day participation would, indeed, be unreasonably costly. It also, clearly, entails that election-day participation must also not be excessively costly. Yet this rationale gives us little reason to insist upon the comparative interpretation. For if no citizen faces a cost of participation that is unreasonably great, such that elected officials do *not* confront a situation in which they

9. Certain figures have argued in recent times that *random selection* would be more efficient in this respect. See esp. Guerrero (2014). For a response, see Umbers (2021a).
10. On this point, see esp. Buchanan and Tullock (1962, ch. 6).

can be certain ex ante that some group of citizens is less likely to participate owing to their confronting a significantly greater cost of participation than others, then we presumably have little reason to think that disparities in the costs of voting *under* our threshold are liable to give rise to problematic incentives for elected officials to attend to the interests of social groups unevenly in co-ordinating the production and distribution of the benefits of social co-operation. And it is the *avoidance* of such effects that constitutes our fundamental reason for insistence upon a principle of substantive equality of opportunity to vote, in the first place.

Thus, important though it surely is to ensure that many citizens have access to early voting, the egalitarian case for *universal* early voting fails. What, then, should we make of the practice?

Early Voting and Openness

Criticising expanding access to early voting beyond those who face particular difficulties in participating on election day, Thompson (2004, 58) writes that

> When citizens go to the polls on the same day, publicly participating in a common experience of civic engagement, they demonstrate their willingness to contribute to the democratic process on equal terms. [...] election-day voting serves an important expressive purpose in a democracy. It enables citizens to express their commitment to a common project in which they participate on equal terms – the process of choosing the leaders who will represent them.

In a similar vein, Orr (2014, 155) writes that

> Polling in person on election day is more than an empty ritual; it may be a richer form of participation. There is an important distinction – both symbolic and real – between polling day as a communal event and the elongated process by which individuals vote over many days or weeks, ensconced in their own homes or pre-polling in electoral offices.

These passages are highly suggestive. There does, indeed, seem to be an important symbolic difference between an election that takes place over many days and an election that (largely) takes place on a single day. But what, exactly, does this difference consist in? If election-day participation is, indeed, a *richer* form of participation, Orr does not explain in any detail why this is the case – beyond the suggestion that early voting is more *private* than election-day voting (an argument which presumably applies much more clearly to the case of mail balloting than pre-polling, particularly in an era in which *many* citizens are choosing to pre-poll). Nor does Thompson state with any precision why it is the case that election-day participation implies a commitment to the common democratic project, whereas early voting does not. Why should the *timing* of participation be thought to make a difference, in this respect?

In what remains of this chapter, I aim to sketch an answer to this question. I shall argue against universal early voting by appeal to the idea that citizens have *duties of openness* derived from more fundamental duties of respect for their fellow citizens as equal, autonomous agents.[11] It will be easiest to begin with a non-political case. Consider:

> *Meeting*: Harold is a member of a corporate board and he is currently attending a meeting at which a decision will be taken by majority vote as to which of two contractors, A or B, the company should engage to perform some service. Three people are scheduled to give presentations on the topic – Seth, Colin and Jennifer. Jennifer gives the first presentation, arguing in favour of A. Harold, convinced by Jennifer's arguments and eager to beat the traffic on his commute home, writes A on a piece of paper, hands it to the chairperson and walks out without waiting to listen to Seth or Colin.

I think that there is a powerful intuition in this case that Harold – in casting his vote early – has acted wrongly, insofar as his conduct is *disrespectful* of Seth and Colin. It is worth spelling out more precisely the sense in which this is so, beginning with the notion of respect.

The concept of respect I have in mind is what Darwall refers to as recognition-respect, which consists in 'giving appropriate consideration or recognition to [some object or property thereof] in deliberating about what to do' (Darwall 1977, 38). Respect in this sense will characteristically be extended to persons as bearers of significant, valuable properties. The intentional infliction of unnecessary pain upon another person, for instance, evinces a failure of appropriate deliberative consideration for that person as a bearer of the valuable property of sentience. It thereby constitutes a failure of recognition-respect for that person as a sentient being and is wrongful, as such. I think that all persons have a wide variety of morally significant properties and that each of us has a correspondingly wide range of moral duties of recognition-respect to others in virtue of these properties. Amongst the most important, I suggest, is individual autonomy.

Autonomy is a matter of *self-governance*: 'being one's own person, directed by considerations, desires, conditions and characteristics that are not simply imposed externally on one, but are part of what can somehow be considered one's authentic self' (Christman and Anderson 2005, 3). To be autonomous, in this sense, is to possess and exercise a range of significant capacities. The most important of these, for our purposes, is the capacity to *recognise and respond to reasons*. Autonomy paradigmatically requires acting on the basis of considerations one recognises as counting in favour of some course of action. Persons with highly severe cognitive impairments do not plausibly amount to fully autonomous agents, for instance, precisely because their behaviour cannot be understood as being directed by reasons in this way.

Respect for others as autonomous agents, then, requires us to afford appropriate weight to their autonomy-constituting capacities in our own deliberations. Actions will be wrongful where they evince a failure of such consideration. Consider paternalistic interference (interference visited upon some target agent with the aim of promoting the target's interests). It is widely thought that paternalism is disrespectful of persons

11. In other work, I have argued that such duties explain the objectionable character of vote buying (Umbers 2020b).

as autonomous agents, insofar as it characteristically implies an unwarranted negative judgement as to the capacities of the agent in question to recognise the considerations that bear upon their interests and respond appropriately (Shiffrin 2000, 220). And it is for this reason (among others) that paternalism is generally taken to be wrongful, *pro tanto*.

The objection to Harold's conduct is similar in certain respects. In *Meeting*, a joint decision must be made, presumably on the basis of considerations raised in the deliberative process preceding the final vote. Ordinarily, where one becomes cognisant of a fact relevant to the making of some collective decision, the appropriate response is to give that consideration some weight in determining the outcome one will support (i.e. to treat the fact in question as a reason for action), just as one would do in a decision one has the authority to make unilaterally. That, in turn, suggests that the appropriate attitude to take towards one's deliberative partners is a kind of *openness*. One has a duty of recognition-respect to treat others as though their contributions to the deliberative exercise in question *could* raise considerations relevant to the outcome the group ought to favour and which it would be appropriate to afford weight to in working out one's own view of the matter in hand.

To do otherwise – that is, to *fail* to be open in this way – expresses the conviction that some or all of one's deliberative partners *lack* the capacity to identify such reasons. That, plainly, is objectionably disrespectful. And it is this, I suggest, which accounts for the objectionable character of Harold's conduct in *Meeting*. In withdrawing prematurely from the collective decision-making process, Harold expresses the conviction that the considerations that might have been advanced by Seth and Colin *could not* amount to considerations of a kind Harold has reason to give weight to in determining whether he ought to vote for A or B at the end of the meeting. Harold, thus, fails to discharge his duties of openness with respect to Colin and Seth.

Elections are not closely analogous to workplace meetings. Nevertheless, the same considerations which explain the wrongness of Harold's conduct in *Meeting* suggest that voting early, for reasons of mere convenience, may be objectionable. Elections, after all, are also moments of collective decision. Citizens are called upon to decide who should form the next government and therefore (indirectly) how their collective affairs ought to be regulated, going forward.

Election outcomes, moreover, ought to depend – at least in part – upon the considerations brought to light in the deliberative period prior to election day. It is the role of citizens, to the extent possible, to weigh the considerations advanced in that period and cast their ballots accordingly.[12] Elections, after all, are occasions for parties to present a policy agenda for the next term of government. There is invariably a vast range of considerations that militate for and against each party's platform. Such competing considerations are central to the public debate that precedes elections. Yet no citizen could reasonably expect to ascertain anything like the full range of facts relevant to each party's proposals, alone. Citizens must rely extensively on others' testimony, as

12. Very many citizens *do not* do this, of course. Nevertheless, I think they *ought* to do so.

communicated in political deliberation. There are, therefore, powerful *epistemic* reasons to want election outcomes to depend, at least in part, upon the balance of considerations advanced prior to election day.[13]

Moreover, it is commonplace among liberal political theorists that political institutions must be justified to all citizens as equal, autonomous agents.[14] It is not sufficient, however, that such justifications merely be available in principle. Rather, as deliberative democrats rightly emphasise (see esp. Cohen 1989), insofar as political decisions for the regulation of basic social institutions authorise the use of coercive force and therefore constrain individuals' autonomy, such decisions ought to be made in accordance with a *procedure* in which reasons militating for and against different potential ways of structuring our political institutions are exchanged. Such procedural considerations are an important constraint on the set of admissible processes for the determination of the rules according to which social co-operation is to be structured.

Respecting this constraint, in turn, requires citizens to engage in a process of good-faith deliberation. Only by doing so can we adequately express an appropriate regard for others' capacities as autonomous agents with the ability to recognise and respond to the reasons relevant to the issues before the electorate. Engaging in deliberation implies a recognition of others' capacities to recognise the considerations one is advancing *as reasons* which ought to count in favour of the course of action one is seeking to justify. And it similarly implies a recognition that the considerations *they* might advance in discussion could amount to reasons that ought to bear upon one's own view of the matter in hand. In affording such consideration to *all* agents, one would necessarily be treating all such agents as equals (at least, in the context of political decision-making).

Needless to say, *ideal* deliberative democracy is unrealisable. Given the sheer number of citizens in modern democracies, conducting a large-scale deliberative exercise during which all citizens' views were heard and responded to would obviously be infeasible (Fishkin 2009, ch. 1). Citizens could not be compelled to engage in good faith with one another. Material and social inequalities would doubtless cause some voices to be afforded more weight than others (Sanders 1997). And so on.

Nevertheless, political institutions may *approximate* that ideal. And our own contemporary electoral institutions (imperfect though they are) may be seen in this light. Elections, after all, are processes by which persons with the power to enact laws that will subject citizens to coercion and thereby limit each citizen's autonomy are appointed. We, therefore, have powerful reason to desire a period of deliberation preceding elections in which citizens have opportunities to share with one another (in formal and informal settings) the considerations they take to bear upon the choice before the electorate and to hear and respond to the same from others.

This furnishes us with what I take to be the fundamental objection to universal early voting. Just as we ought to be open to the possibility that our co-workers might

13. As such, I broadly agree with figures like Landemore (2013), who maintain that the value of democratic deliberation at least partly rests upon its *epistemic* value.

14. See for instance Waldron (1987).

raise considerations of relevance to matters of joint decision-making in the workplace, so too ought we be open to the possibility that our fellow *citizens* might raise considerations of relevance to which candidate ought to prevail in a given electorate, or which party ought to form government. Electing to cast one's ballot early (for reasons of mere convenience) expresses the opposite conviction; in effect, *no* considerations that might be raised during the remainder of the election campaign by *any* of one's fellow citizens could make any difference to how one ought to cast one's vote.

That, I suggest, constitutes a failure of respect for one's fellow citizens. By foreclosing the possibility of further deliberation, one implicitly fails to recognise others' capacities to bring forth further considerations that one ought to treat as reasons relevant to the collective decision. And since we have reason to favour a set of electoral institutions that, in themselves, respect persons as equals, we have reason to favour a system in which the vast majority of citizens are not permitted to fail to discharge their duties of openness in this way. It is in this sense, I claim, that universal early voting is problematic. To the extent that such a system effectively prevails in Australian elections, at present, we have reason to return to a more restrictive approach.

Yet perhaps this is unnecessary.[15] After all, it is hardly as though political deliberation occurs only during election campaigns. On the contrary, the parties debate one another *continually*. Their interactions are the subject of extensive media commentary. Many ordinary people discuss and debate political matters at all points of the political cycle. Citizens, then, have *ample* opportunity to communicate their political views to one another well in advance of the formal declaration of an election campaign. We need not think that voting on any particular date, then, is necessary to express appropriate respect for our fellow citizens.

However, it seems to me that this significantly under-emphasises the importance of election campaigns. Parties typically only make the bulk of their plans for the next term of government known to the electorate within weeks of polling day, presumably with the twin aims of minimising public scrutiny and being able to declare a 'mandate' for their implementation, should they prevail. It is therefore necessarily the case, then, that citizens *cannot* take adequate account of the considerations relevant to the election raised by others in deliberation prior to the campaign, for the simple reason that matters crucial to the *subject* of that deliberation – who should form the next government – are simply *unavailable* for informed deliberation until close to polling day. It is for this reason that, I think, it is reasonable to demand that citizens cast their ballots on election day unless doing so would be unreasonably costly.

Yet perhaps this proves too much. An expectant mother due to give birth on election day, in casting her vote early, forecloses the possibility of taking account of any further considerations raised in the period of deliberation prior to election day just as surely as a citizen who casts their ballot early for reasons of mere convenience. Surely, we should not conclude that early voting should not be open to *anyone*.

15. I thank Paul Kildea and Ten-Herng Lai for pushing me to address this issue.

Yet recognition-respect for persons as autonomous agents merely requires that we give *appropriate* deliberative weight to others' autonomy-constituting capacities in determining what we ought to do. But appropriate deliberative weight is *not* absolute weight. There are reasons of many kinds that bear upon what we ought to do, all things considered, including the protection and promotion of our own legitimate interests. If the difference in cost, for some agent, between voting early and voting on election day is sufficiently great, then that agent may do so consistently with discharging their duties of recognition-respect, insofar as their own legitimate interests may outweigh their reasons to remain open to considerations that might be advanced in deliberation by others prior to the conclusion of the election process. There is no incompatibility between my account and ensuring that citizens for whom participation on election day would be unreasonably costly continue to have access to early voting.

There is another respect, however, in which the account might still seem overly demanding. One might argue that my account shows not merely that (most) citizens ought to vote on election day but also that they ought to vote *as late as possible* on election day in order to ensure that they remain 'open' to others' potential deliberative contributions for as long as possible.[16] Yet this invites an obvious reply: if it is indeed the case that a requirement to vote at a particular *time* on election day would be excessively demanding, then that fact would surely undermine any claim to the effect that affording others' autonomy-constituting capacities appropriate deliberative weight requires us to do so. We presumably have legitimate interests in mostly being able to dispose of our time as we choose – and these interests will also weigh in the overall calculus as to what we ought to do all things considered. Provided all citizens have reasonable opportunities to communicate with one another prior to election day, there would seem to be no reason to insist upon a requirement to wait until the *last possible moment* to vote.

Yet it is important to acknowledge that my account does not furnish us with any specific guidance as to when, precisely, it is permissible or impermissible for citizens to vote. Suppose the Electoral Commission has opened an 'all night' early voting location. Simon has chosen to cast his ballot on the night immediately preceding election day. If he were to arrive at the polling station at 11:59 PM, it would be absurd to insist that he must wait until 12:00 AM to ensure that he casts his ballot on election day and thereby discharges his duties of openness to his fellow citizens.

Yet this need not be seen as a deficiency. It is important to distinguish between questions concerning the ethics of voting and those concerning the ways in which our democratic institutions should be arranged. I do not think it is plausible that all cases of voting prior to election day, for reasons of mere convenience, are wrongfully disrespectful. Simon's case, above, illustrates this. Yet I *also* think that there are many cases of early voting that *are* objectionable in this respect. There is a significant difference between a citizen choosing to cast their ballot a fortnight prior to election day (for reasons of mere convenience) and that same citizen choosing to cast their ballot on election day, following the deliberations that take place during the election campaign. The trouble,

16. I thank Andrew Goddard for pressing me on this point.

of course, is that there is no principled way to specify a precise 'cut-off' point beyond which someone votes *too* early, from a moral point of view. Vagueness of this kind is simply inherent in any ethical theorising that aims to take seriously the significance of ideals – such as recognition-respect – whose precise extension may be at least somewhat opaque to us.

What does this imply for the ways in which our electoral institutions ought to be structured? The answer, I think, is simply that even if it is (say) conceptually possible that at least some citizens could cast their ballots prior to election day (for reasons of mere convenience) without necessarily breaching their duties of openness, we should nevertheless require all citizens to vote on election day (setting aside those who could not do so without unreasonable cost). We should favour a set of electoral institutions that (within reasonable constraints) renders it most *probable* that citizens will discharge their duties to one another in the course of political deliberation. Election-day voting does not, of course, *guarantee* that citizens will do so. But, in preventing individuals from formally foreclosing the possibility of further engagement in the deliberative process by casting their ballots early, it does make it *more likely*.

Of course, this is likely to invite a final response, to the effect that requiring (most) citizens to vote on election day, itself, would be unjust if at least some such citizens would not (necessarily) be breaching any duty owed to any other citizen by casting their ballots beforehand. The trouble with this response, however, is that it presupposes that citizens possess some *right* to cast their ballots prior to election day. That, presumably, is implied by the assertion that *denying* citizens this opportunity is unjust. But it is simply unclear why we should accept this. We have already investigated what would seem, antecedently, to be the most promising basis for such a right – political equality – and found that such considerations only entail such rights on the part of citizens for whom election-day participation would be unreasonably costly.

The only other obvious alternative basis for such a right would appeal to the idea that citizens have *liberty-based* claims to vote prior to election day. Under my preferred set of arrangements, after all, most citizens would not be free to vote prior to election day. Yet the sense of 'unfreedom' here is at best metaphorical. After all, at least on the orthodox conception, liberty is abridged by *coercion* (see e.g. Berlin 1958). A citizen denied the right to vote prior to election day is not subject to coercion of any kind. The state simply fails to extend an opportunity to them. Citizens denied the right to vote early, then, do not suffer any diminution of liberty. And for this reason, it is hard to see quite how liberty might be thought to provide a basis for the right to vote early.

Conclusion

The consequences of the recent rise in early voting in Australian elections are likely to remain unclear for some time. In this chapter, however, I have sought to show that there are at least some reasons to be concerned by such developments, *irrespective* of their consequences. The legitimacy of the democratic process itself depends upon the extent to which the institutions that determine the rules in accordance with which social co-operation proceeds respect all citizens as equal, autonomous agents. A system that allows a large proportion of the population to cast their ballots prior to election day, I think, undermines this ideal.

References

Avery, James M. 2015. 'Does Who Votes Matter? Income Bias in Voter Turnout and Economic Inequality in the American States from 1980 to 2010'. *Political Behaviour* 37 (4): 955–976.

BCJ (Brennan Centre for Justice). 2018. 'Democracy: An Election Agenda for Candidates, Activists, and Legislators'. USA: The Brennan Centre for Justice.

Berinsky, Adam J. 2005. 'The Perverse Consequences of Electoral Reform in the United States'. *American Politics Research* 33 (4): 471–491.

Berlin, Isaiah. 1958. 'Two Concepts of Liberty'. In *Contemporary Political Philosophy: An Anthology (Second Edition)*, edited by Robert E. Goodin and Philip Pettit, 369–386. Oxford: Blackwell.

Blais, André and Daoust, Jean-François. 2020. *The Motivation to Vote: Explaining Electoral Participation*. Toronto: UBC Press.

Brennan, Geoffrey and Lomasky, Loren E. 1993. *Democracy and Decision: The Pure Theory of Electoral Preference*. Cambridge: Cambridge University Press.

Brennan, Jason. 2014. 'Medicine Worse Than The Disease? Against Compulsory Voting'. In *Compulsory Voting: For and Against*, edited by Jason Brennan and Lisa Hill, 1–110. Cambridge: Cambridge University Press.

Buchanan, James M. and Tullock, Gordon. 1962. *The Calculus of Consent*. Ann Arbor: University of Michigan Press.

Christman, John and Joel Anderson. 2005. 'Introduction'. In *Autonomy and the Challenges to Liberalism*, edited by John Christman and Joel Anderson, 1–26. Cambridge: Cambridge University Press.

Cohen, Joshua. 1989. 'Deliberation and Democratic Legitimacy'. In *Contemporary Political Philosophy: An Anthology (2nd Edition)*, edited by Robert E. Goodin and Philip Pettit, 159–170. Oxford: Blackwell.

Coma, Ferran Martinez i and Smith, Rodney. 2023. 'The Rise and Rise of Early Voting'. In *Watershed: The 2022 Australian Federal Election*, edited by Anika Gauja, Marian Sawer and Jill Sheppard, 413–432. Canberra: ANU Press.

Darwall, Stephen L. 1977. 'Two Kinds of Respect'. *Ethics* 88 (1): 36–49.

ERRN (Electoral Regulation Research Network). 2018. 'Implications of Changes to Voting in Australia'. Melbourne: ERRN.

Fishkin, James S. 2009. *When the People Speak*. Oxford: Oxford University Press.

Gronke, Paul, Galanes-Rosenblum, Eva, Miller, Peter A. and Toffey, Daniel. 2008. 'Convenience Voting'. *The Annual Review of Political Science* 11: 437–455.

Guerrero, Alexander A. 2014. 'Against Elections: The Lottocratic Alternative'. *Philosophy & Public Affairs* 42 (2): 135–178.

Hill, Lisa. 2014. 'Compulsory Voting Defended'. In *Compulsory Voting: For and Against*, edited by Jason Brennan and Lisa Hill, 111–204. Cambridge: Cambridge University Press.

Landemore, Hélène. 2013. *Democratic Reason*. Princeton: Princeton University Press.

Leighley, Jan E. and Nagler, Jonathan. 2014. *Who Votes Now? Demographics, Issues, Inequality, and Turnout in the United States*. Princeton: Princeton University Press.

Lever, Annabelle. 2010. 'Compulsory Voting: A Critical Perspective'. *British Journal of Political Science* 40 (4): 897–915.

Muller, Damon A. 2022. 'Trends in Ēarly Voting in Federal Elections'. Australian Parliamentary Library. https://www.aph.gov.au/About_Parliament/Parliamentary_Departments/Parliamentary_Library/FlagPost/2022/May/Early_voting_at_the_2022_federal_election (accessed 17 January 2023).

Orr, Graeme. 2014. 'Convenience Voting: The End of Election Day?' *Alternative Law Journal* 39 (3): 151–155.

Prior, Markus. 2019. *Hooked: How Politics Captures People's Interest*. Cambridge: Cambridge University Press.

Rawls, John. 1971. *A Theory of Justice*. Cambridge: MA: Belknap.

Riker, William H. and Ordeshook, Peter C. 1968. 'A Theory of the Calculus of Voting'. *American Political Science Review* 62: 25–42.

Rojas, Angelo J. and Muller, Damon A. 2014. 'Early Voting in Australian Federal Elections: Causes and Consequences'. Sydney: Australian Political Studies Association.

Sanders, Lynn M. 1997. 'Against Deliberation'. *Political Theory* 25 (3): 347–376.

Severson, Alexander. 2018. 'Transparency, Class Bias, and Redistribution: Evidence from the American States'. *State Politics & Policy Quarterly* 18 (3): 271–295.

Sheppard, Jill and Beauregard, Katrine. 2018. 'Early Voting in Australia: The Costs and Benefits of Convenience'. *Political Science* 70 (2): 117–134.

Shiffrin, Seana Valentine. 2000. 'Paternalism, Unconscionability Doctrine, and Accommodation'. *Philosophy & Public Affairs* 29 (3): 205–250.

Thompson, Dennis F. 2004. 'Election Time: Normative Implications of Temporal Properties of the Electoral Process in the United States'. *American Political Science Review* 98 (1): 51–64.

Thompson, Dennis F. 2005. 'Democracy in Time: Popular Sovereignty and Temporal Representation'. *Constellations* 12 (2): 245–261.

Thompson, Dennis F. 2008. 'Electoral Simultaneity: Expressing Equal Respect'. *Journal of Social Issues* 64 (3): 487–501.

Umbers, Lachlan Montgomery. 2020a. 'Compulsory Voting: A Defence'. *British Journal of Political Science* 50 (4): 1307–1324.

Umbers, Lachlan Montgomery. 2020b. 'What's Wrong with Vote Buying'. *Philosophical Studies* 177 (2): 551–571.

Umbers, Lachlan Montgomery. 2021a. 'Against Lottocracy'. *European Journal of Political Theory* 20 (2): 312–334.

Umbers, Lachlan Montgomery. 2021b. 'Assessing Objections to Compulsory Voting in Australia'. In *A Century of Compulsory Voting in Australia: Genesis, Impact and Future*, edited by Matteo Bonotti and Paul Strangio, 59–82. Palgrave-MacMillan.

Waldron, Jeremy. 1987. 'Theoretical Foundations of Liberalism'. *The Philosophical Quarterly* 37 (147): 127–150.

Chapter 5

MERELY ADVISORY OR EFFECTIVELY BINDING? THE STATUS OF PLEBISCITE RESULTS IN AUSTRALIA

Paul Kildea

Introduction

In 2017, the Australian government surveyed the Australian people on whether they supported a change to the law to allow same-sex marriage. Despite the non-binding nature of the survey, there was a widespread expectation that the government would implement the result. In the end, more than 60 per cent of survey participants voted 'Yes'. On the day that the result was announced, Prime Minister Malcolm Turnbull declared: 'The people have voted "Yes" for marriage equality, now it's our job to deliver it' (Turnbull 2017). A few weeks later, the Commonwealth Parliament amended the *Marriage Act 1961* (Cth) to make same-sex marriage lawful.[1]

The marriage survey illustrates one of the curious features of the advisory referendum, or 'plebiscite' as the device is often called in Australia.[2] The result is not binding on the parliament but may nonetheless be treated as if it is. Lawmakers remain free to respond as they wish, but there is a strong political incentive for the parliament to act in line with the result, as disregarding it could risk a severe backlash from voters. For this reason, some view the plebiscite as 'effectively binding' (Gallagher 1996, 246). Viewed in this way, the plebiscite can be seen as a device that empowers citizens and, potentially, weakens parliaments (Suksi 1996; Psycharis 2022, 233).

However, others challenge the idea that plebiscites are politically binding and question their value as a mechanism for citizen participation in the making of policy decisions. They point to examples where advisory votes have been ignored by political actors (Cheneval and El-Wakil 2018). Some view plebiscites as nothing more than

1. The author thanks Stella Wailes and Kelly Yoon for their excellent research assistance.

2. The use of the term 'plebiscite' to denote an advisory popular vote on a policy issue is not widely shared outside of Australia, where terms such as 'advisory referendum' or 'consultative referendum' are more common. This chapter, being focused on the Australian experience, primarily uses the word 'plebiscite' but occasionally refers to the term 'advisory referendum', notably when discussing the international literature. For discussion of the use of 'plebiscite' in Australia, see Kildea (2016, 292).

official opinion polls given that they provide a mechanism for people to express a view on a policy proposal but deny them the final say (noted by Setälä 1999, 87). And it is said that advisory votes, if anything, empower politicians at the expense of citizens, as political actors remain free to manipulate the results to their own advantage (Cheneval and El-Wakil 2018). On this account, the plebiscite offers an illusion of popular control but preserves the power of political elites.

This chapter investigates which of these two accounts of the plebiscite is most applicable to Australia. It does this by examining the immediate aftermath of the 44 plebiscites that have been held by federal, state and territory governments since federation in 1901.[3] In doing so, it adds to an emerging literature on plebiscites (see e.g. Orr 2000; Kildea 2016; Twomey 2015; Kildea 2022; Psycharis 2022). These devices remain understudied in Australia, particularly at the subnational level, despite the intense academic interest in federal constitutional referendums. This chapter is the first attempt to provide an empirical analysis of how political representatives have responded to plebiscite outcomes.

This chapter is organised as follows. The first section explains key features of the plebiscite in the Australian context and reviews the literature on advisory referendums as democratic devices. The following section examines how political representatives have responded to plebiscite results. It finds that governments and parliaments have typically viewed plebiscites as binding and, in almost all cases, have acted in line with their outcomes. At the same time, there have been numerous instances in which small groups of political actors have contested the authority of a plebiscite result and argued that it be disregarded or revisited. The final section proposes three possible explanations for the general deference of political representatives towards plebiscite outcomes: the identity of the initiator, the interests of politicians and a widely held, principle-based view of the plebiscite as binding. Overall, my empirical research supports the notion that plebiscites are effectively binding. However, despite this conclusion, plebiscites are best understood as democratic devices that can foster both citizen empowerment and elite control.

The Plebiscite as a Democratic Device

The Plebiscite in Australia

In Australia, the term 'plebiscite' means 'a legally non-binding poll of electors which does not cause a constitutional amendment' (Psycharis 2022, 220; Twomey 2015). In more simple terms the plebiscite can be described as an advisory popular vote on a policy issue. All plebiscites held in Australia have shared two other basic characteristics: they have been initiated by the government or parliament (rather than by citizens, as is the case with a popular initiative), and they have been optional in the sense that they have been held at the discretion of the government in the absence of any legal

3. Excluded from my analysis are plebiscites conducted in island territories, local government polls and local option polls (such as Western Australia's 1911 and 1921 votes on liquor licensing).

requirement to do so (Kildea 2021, 92). The plebiscite can be contrasted with the constitutional referendum which, in the Australian context, refers to a mandatory and binding poll initiated by the parliament on a proposal for constitutional amendment.

The difference between an advisory and a binding vote refers to the legal effect of the outcome. To describe a plebiscite as advisory is to say that its result is not binding on the parliament. The parliament retains the final say on the issue at hand (Uleri 1996; Setälä 1999, 70–75). By contrast, where a popular vote is binding, the parliament is constitutionally obliged to follow the outcome. This is the case, for instance, for federal constitutional referendums, where the parliament lacks the capacity to legislate against the outcome.

On occasion, a parliament may attach legal consequences to a plebiscite. I call this 'legislative pre-commitment' as it involves the parliament legislating, in advance, to give effect to a plebiscite result. One common form of legislative pre-commitment occurs where a parliament passes an act before polling day that enacts the proposed policy change but makes the act's commencement contingent on a majority 'Yes' vote. The presence of legislative pre-commitment, however, cannot transmute an advisory poll into a binding one. This is because, even when the vote triggers preset legal consequences, the parliament retains the capacity to reverse them.

Since federation, there have been 4 federal plebiscites and 40 state and territory plebiscites (see Table 5.1). They have been held on a wide range of topics, including conscription, prohibition, daylight saving and, most recently, same-sex marriage. In most instances, they have been instigated by the government and formally initiated by an act of Parliament, but some (including the marriage survey) have been initiated by executive action alone. In some cases, the Commonwealth has taken a poll of electors residing in a territory, as was the case in all three Australian Capital Territory plebiscites (on prohibition, self-government and the territory's electoral system) and the Northern Territory's sole plebiscite (on statehood).

The Plebiscite as a Democratic Device

The relationship between plebiscites and democracy has been described as 'ambiguous' (Folkestad, Klausen and Segaard 2021, 214). This ambiguity arises from the fact that an advisory vote offers citizens the opportunity to have a direct say over a policy issue while leaving final decision-making authority in the hands of elected representatives. The same might be said of other devices that invite public input, such as parliamentary inquiries and government consultations. But the plebiscite is distinctive in that it takes the form of an electoral process and can therefore foster strong expectations that the outcome will be acted upon (Psycharis 2022, 237). It is arguably unique as a democratic device in that it is formally advisory but may nonetheless be treated as binding. Ultimately, the democratic role of plebiscites in a particular polity will depend a great deal on how political actors respond to them.

There is a debate in the international literature on whether advisory referendums can, in an empirical sense, be genuinely advisory. The predominant view is that advisory referendums are generally treated as binding by political actors and are therefore

Table 5.1 Plebiscites in Australia, 1901–2024

Where	Year	Topic	Result	For %	Was result implemented?
CTH	1916	Military service	Defeated	48.4	Yes: no change
CTH	1917	Military service	Defeated	46.2	Yes: no change
CTH	1977	National song	Adv Aust Fair	43.2	Yes: change adopted
CTH	2017	Same-sex marriage	Approved	61.6	Yes: change adopted
NSW	1903	Legislative Assembly size	90 MPs	73.0	Yes: change adopted
NSW*	1916	Hotel closing hours	6pm	62.4	Yes: change adopted
NSW*	1928	Prohibition	Defeated	28.5	Yes: no change
NSW*	1947	Hotel closing hours	6pm	62.4	Yes: no change
NSW	1954	Hotel closing hours	10pm	50.3	Yes: change adopted
NSW	1967	New state in NE NSW	Defeated	45.8	Yes: no change
NSW	1969	Sunday hotel trading	Defeated	42.0	Yes: no change
NSW	1976	Daylight saving	Approved	68.4	Yes: no change
VIC	1904	Secular public education	Approved	58.6	Yes: no change
VIC	1904	Scripture in schools	Approved	53.0	No: change not adopted
VIC	1904	Prayer & hymn use	Approved	53.2	No: change not adopted
VIC*	1930	Liquor license abolition	Defeated	43.1	Yes: no change
VIC*	1938	Liquor license abolition	Defeated	33.8	Yes: no change
VIC	1956	Hotel closing hours	Defeated	39.7	Yes: no change
QLD	1910	Religion in schools	Approved	56.7	Yes: change adopted
QLD*	1920	Prohibition	Continuance	50.3	Yes: no change
QLD*	1923	Prohibition	Continuance	59.3	Yes: no change
QLD	1992	Daylight saving	Defeated	45.5	Yes: no change
SA	1911	Member salaries	Defeated	32.5	Yes: no change
SA	1915	Hotel closing hours	6pm	56.9	Yes: change adopted
SA	1965	State lotteries	Approved	70.8	Yes: change adopted
SA	1970	Retail trading hours	Defeated	48.2	Yes: change adopted
SA	1982	Daylight saving	Approved	71.6	Yes: no change
WA*	1925	Prohibition	Defeated	34.9	Yes: no change
WA	1933	Secession	Approved	66.2	No: change not adopted
WA	1933	Secession Convention	Defeated	42.6	Yes: no change
WA*	1950	Prohibition	Defeated	26.5	Yes: no change
WA*	1975	Daylight saving	Defeated	46.4	Yes: no change
WA*	1984	Daylight saving	Defeated	45.7	Yes: no change
WA*	1992	Daylight saving	Defeated	46.9	Yes: no change
WA	2005	Weeknight trading	Defeated	41.3	Yes: no change
WA	2005	Sunday trading	Defeated	38.6	Yes: no change
WA*	2009	Daylight saving	Defeated	45.4	Yes: no change
TAS	1916	Hotel closing hours	6pm	58.7	Yes: change adopted
TAS*	1968	Hotel casino license	Approved	53.0	Yes: change adopted
TAS	1981	New dam location	G-b-F†	85.6	No: change not adopted
ACT*	1928	Prohibition	Private sale	50.7	Yes: change adopted
ACT	1978	Self-government	Status quo	63.8	Yes: no change
ACT	1992	Electoral system	Hare-Clark	65.3	Yes: change adopted
NT	1998	Statehood	Defeated	48.1	Yes: no change

Note: * Parliament legislated, in advance of vote, to attach legal consequences to plebiscite outcome.

† Gordon below Franklin: the proposal was for the new dam to be located on the Gordon River below its junction with the Franklin River.

Note: Data from Parliamentary Library (2024) and Kildea (2022).

best understood as politically or 'effectively' binding (Gallagher 1996, 246; Setälä 1999, 87). The basic observation made is that the legal status of an advisory referendum – that is, its non-binding nature – becomes irrelevant once it encounters political reality. In simple terms, it is 'very difficult to go against popular opinion' (Budge 1996, 52). Michael Gallagher (1996, 246) writes that 'it is clear that in practice these [advisory referendums] develop their own momentum and become effectively binding' and, further, that the 'fallout would be severe' were a parliament to disregard a popular verdict on a major issue. Similarly, Vernon Bogdanor (1981, 77–78), writing about advisory referendums in the United Kingdom context, concludes:

> Although in theory Parliament cannot be bound by a referendum result, in practice, provided that the result is clear-cut and there has been an adequate turnout, then it would be almost impossible for either Parliament or government to ignore it. It is only if the result is a very close one [...] or the turnout is very low, that Parliament really retains its discretion. (Bogdanor 1981, 77–78)

Existing empirical studies lend support to this account of advisory referendums. Surveys of national referendums in Europe have found that parliaments tend to follow citizen advice, with a 2006 study finding no instances of legislatures ignoring advisory outcomes (Setälä 2006; Gallagher and Uleri 1996). A review of local council referendums in Norway found that politicians had occasionally departed from citizen advice but that, overall, the outcomes were respected. The authors concluded that it was difficult to view advisory referendums as 'a tool for information seeking – as one of many inputs to a decision made by others' and that the legal status of advisory votes 'appears to be somewhat at odds with the real-world political stature of these referendums' (Folkestad, Klausen and Segaard 2021, 225).

The notion that plebiscites, despite their advisory nature, are practically binding has implications for the role they play in democracies. It conceives of plebiscites as a device of citizen empowerment. It confers an influential role on citizens, enabling them to not only have a say on a question of public policy but also to have a say that is treated as decisive. One must be careful not to overstate this, as the power to initiate a plebiscite remains in the hands of the government or parliament, and the role of citizens is constrained to approving or rejecting the proposal(s) that have been put before them. But, once a plebiscite has been put in train, the people arguably take on the role of policymakers and not just policy advisors (Jäske 2017, 51).

This view of the plebiscite carries implications for parliaments, too. If the people are empowered, it may follow that the legislature is weakened. Matthew Psycharis (2022, 233) writes that 'the plebiscite may, in practice, *constrain* the policymaking latitude or legislative competence otherwise afforded to government and Parliament under law'. Along similar lines, Marrku Suksi (1996, 61) has written that advisory referendums, once they take on a binding character, can 'emerge as a second sovereign, competing in this matter for authority with the formally final decision-maker, parliament'. On this view, the parliament, by treating an advisory vote as binding, is ceding some of its authority to the people. There are also implications for individual members of parliament. It might be said that, on the issue at hand, members of parliament are deferring to public opinion and are therefore assuming a delegate role with respect to their constituents rather than acting as a trustee (Pitkin 1967). Alternatively, it could be argued that political representatives who choose to follow a plebiscite outcome are adopting a majoritarian stance on the ballot issue by deferring to the preferences of a majority of voters (Setälä 2006, 713).

An alternative account of the plebiscite views it as genuinely advisory and offers different conclusions about its contribution as a democratic device. The idea that advisory referendums are practically binding is challenged as 'problematic if not downright wrong' (Cheneval and el-Wakil 2018, 301). Various examples are cited to support this. It is noted that the Greek government ultimately accepted harsh bailout conditions to address a debt crisis despite voters overwhelmingly rejecting this course of action in a 2015 referendum. Local councils in Finland and (as noted above) Norway have sometimes departed from citizen advice (Jäske 2017). Research on popular initiatives in New Zealand and California has also shown that politicians are willing to act contrary to advisory outcomes (Qvortrup, Morris and Koboro 2018, 255; Gerber et al. 2001). In other words, this account takes the legal status of advisory referendums seriously and does not accept that the difference between a binding and a non-binding poll will always dissolve in practice.

Understood in this way, the plebiscite has a very different democratic role from the one outlined above. The plebiscite is an instrument for popular input but not popular rule. It leaves the final, determinative say with politicians and therefore does not empower citizens in the same way as a vote that is treated as binding (Cheneval and el-Wakil 2018, 301–2). More than that, it arguably reinforces the power of political representatives. Not only does the parliament get to initiate a plebiscite – and thus determine the topic and timing of a vote – but it also decides whether and how to respond to the outcome. Lawmakers can ignore the result, act contrary to it or interpret it in a way that suits their agenda or creates uncertainty (Hollander 2019, 50). It might be objected that the opportunity for citizens to articulate their preferences in a public vote is itself a valuable form of engagement in the decision-making process. On the other hand, it is said that, compared to a legally binding vote, the type of popular control offered by an advisory poll 'is significantly diluted by its contingency' (Lacey 2017, 118).

This conception of the plebiscite poses no challenge to the authority of parliaments. Their legal and political competence remains intact. The individual role assumed by political representatives is also different. Parliamentarians are seen to take on more of a trustee role in relation to their constituents, retaining a discretion to bring an independent cast of mind to the issue on the ballot paper as they consider – but do not necessarily follow – the popular verdict. Looked at from a different perspective, representatives could be said to adopt more of a deliberative, as opposed to majoritarian, stance on the status of plebiscites (Setälä 2006, 713). Advisory polls are seen as fostering public participation and voice without denying politicians the scope to exercise their capacities and judgment when it comes to making the final decision.

To sum up, there are two broad empirical accounts of the plebiscite. One views it as politically binding and the other sees it as genuinely advisory. Each account provides a different perspective on the democratic role of the plebiscite. The next section reports on which account is most applicable to the Australian experience.

How Australian Politicians Have Responded to Plebiscites

This section reports on the results of my analysis of the 44 plebiscites held by federal, state and territory governments. I reviewed the immediate aftermath of each plebiscite to assess whether the relevant parliament or government implemented the outcome. In most instances, the delivery of a plebiscite outcome required the passage of legislation and therefore depended on the parliament taking appropriate action. In a small number of cases, such as the 1977 poll on the national song, it was possible for the executive to implement the proposed change by itself. In those instances where the people voted to retain the status quo, I considered inaction by the government or parliament to signal respect for the result.

High Compliance with Plebiscite Results

My review of Australian plebiscites shows that governments or parliaments have almost always followed the majority (or plurality) view recorded at the ballot box. Out of the 44 cases, there have been only 3 instances, discussed further below, in which a plebiscite result has not been followed. In none of those instances was the failure to implement the result due to obstruction by political actors; instead, the key factors were confusion regarding public preferences and intervention by a higher level of government. In all other cases, the government or parliament took steps consistent with citizen advice and usually did so without delay.

We can divide the sample into those instances where voters supported change as opposed to the status quo. Voters supported the status quo in 27 cases (i.e. 61.4 per cent of the time) and, in each instance, the parliament respected this by taking no further action in relation to the proposal on the ballot paper. Voters opted for change in response to 17 proposals. The parliament implemented the requested change in 13 of those 17 instances. The four that were not acted on were part of the three cases mentioned above.

Most plebiscites have delivered a clear outcome on a high turnout. But even when that has not been the case, the parliament has acted in line with the result. Proposals that have won only small victories have been implemented. For instance, the New South Wales Parliament legislated to introduce 10:00 p.m. closing for licenced premises after this option won just 50.3 per cent of the vote in a 1954 plebiscite. Similarly, plebiscites that recorded low turnouts, a more common occurrence prior to the introduction of compulsory voting, were respected by lawmakers.[4] To cite two examples, majority votes in favour of reducing the size of the New South Wales Legislative Assembly and intro-

4. Queensland's 1920 vote on prohibition was the first plebiscite to employ compulsory voting, and votng has been mandatory at all state/territory plebiscites since 1925. By contrast, for

ducing religious instruction in Queensland schools were implemented despite turnout rates of 47.2 per cent and 49.7 per cent, respectively.

On several occasions, the majority or plurality vote has gone against the preferred policy position of the government or its leader. However, this has generally not had an impact on implementation. For instance, when South Australians rejected a government proposal to increase the salaries of members of parliament in 1911, the Premier responded by saying that he 'willingly accepted the will of the people' ('Tremendous Negative Vote', *The Advertiser*, 28 April 1911, 6). And in 1992, when electors in the ACT voted to adopt Hare-Clark as their electoral system, the chief minister said she was disappointed with the result but would take steps to implement the result regardless (Lamberton 1992). Other examples of plebiscite results going against the government or its leader include the Queensland ballot on religion in state schools (1910), the votes for 6:00 p.m. closing in South Australia (1915) and New South Wales (1916), the two federal conscription polls (1916, 1917), the secession vote in Western Australia (1933), the vote in Tasmania for the building of a dam (1981) and the twin votes on weeknight and Sunday trading in Western Australia (2005). It is notable that in only one instance, the 1916 vote against conscription, did the losing leader take the issue back to the people in the hope of obtaining a different result. In the case of secession and the dam, the popular verdict was ultimately not implemented but for other reasons.

The parliament attached legal consequences to the plebiscite result through a form of legislative pre-commitment, in relation to 15 of the 44 plebiscites (see asterisked entries in Table 5.1; for more on this topic, see Kildea 2022, 40). This signalled that the legislature viewed the poll as binding, and as such we might have an especially high expectation that the result would be respected. Indeed, the outcomes of all 15 polls were implemented. Having said that, the result in most cases was a vote for the status quo. The people voted for change on only 3 of those 15 occasions – NSW 1916, ACT 1928, TAS 1968 – and in each case, the relevant authority honoured the pre-commitment. However, in the case of the 1928 vote in the Federal Capital Territory (now the ACT) to end certain restrictions on the sale of alcohol, the federal government delayed implementation for over a year despite the enabling law providing that the referendum would have 'full force and effect'. The remaining 29 plebiscites did not feature legislative pre-commitment. The government and/or parliament implemented votes for change on 10 of those occasions – including, most recently, through the introduction of same-sex marriage in 2017. This suggests that whatever influence legislative pre-commitment has had in encouraging compliance with advisory outcomes, politicians have also proven responsive to non-legal forces.

My review reveals that intergovernmental dynamics have sometimes had an impact on the implementation of a plebiscite result. This finding underscores the importance of paying attention to federalist factors when studying the conduct of plebiscites in a federal system. The potential for intergovernmental dynamics to come into play arises

---

various reasons, voting at all four federal plebiscites has been voluntary. See further Kildea (2022, 50–51); Kildea (2021, 93, 99).

from the fact that the implementation of an advisory result will sometimes require the consent or action of a higher level of government. In the lead-up to some of the 40 state and territory referendums, it was accepted that the execution of the result would require action by the Commonwealth or, in one case, the parliament at Westminster. Those cases were: ACT 1928 (prohibition), WA 1933 (secession), NSW 1967 (establishment of a new state in northeast New South Wales), ACT 1978 (self-government), ACT 1992 (electoral system) and NT 1998 (statehood). In one other case (TAS 1981), the significance of intergovernmental factors arose only after the vote. Overall, the intergovernmental dimension adds a layer of complexity due to the potential for questions to be asked about the legal competence of subnational political authorities to implement the popular will.

There have been two instances in which such intergovernmental factors have proven decisive in the sense of preventing the implementation of a plebiscite result. The earliest case occurred in the 1930s when the British Parliament blocked a proposal for Western Australia to secede from the Commonwealth despite two-thirds of voters having supported secession at a 1933 plebiscite. The state government, despite its opposition to secession, sent a delegation to London to make the secessionist case. But, following a lengthy process, during which time public enthusiasm for secession cooled, the British Parliament rejected the state's petition to be recognised as an independent self-governing colony (Besant 1990, 252; Watt 1958, 81).

The second instance related to Tasmania's 1981 vote to build a hydroelectricity dam at a certain location on the Gordon River. After a period of political turmoil following the vote, a newly installed Liberal government committed to the dam's construction, and preliminary work had begun by the end of 1982. Commonwealth intervention soon brought this to a halt. In 1983, the newly elected Hawke government passed legislation to block the dam. There was doubt as to whether the federal parliament had the power to intervene in a state's affairs in this way, but the law was eventually upheld by the High Court as a valid use of the Commonwealth's external affairs power. This intervention ensured that the public vote relating to the dam would not be implemented. In both of these cases, the popular will as expressed at the ballot box was stymied by the actions of a higher level of government. In both cases, too, it is arguable that the intervening government may have felt more emboldened to act contrary to public opinion given that it was less directly accountable to the electors who voted in the plebiscite.

Another factor that has stood in the way of plebiscite implementation is ambiguity around public preferences. As noted above, some scholars have said that compliance with advisory votes is to be expected where the result is 'clear-cut', so the idea that ambiguity could prove to be a barrier to implementation is to be expected.

Ambiguity accounts for the third instance in which political authorities have not implemented a plebiscite result. In 1904, Victoria held a referendum on the teaching of scripture in schools. The government submitted three questions to voters, asking if they supported, respectively, the continuation of secular education, the teaching of scripture lessons in schools and the use of certain prayers and hymns. In a confusing outcome, majorities voted Yes to all three ('The Religious Instruction Referendum', *Daily Telegraph*, 14 June 1904, 4). Poor question design resulted in the electorate giving mixed signals. This led to debate in parliament on how the result should be interpreted.

Some argued that the responses to questions 2 and 3 were only to be considered in the event of question 1 being rejected. That interpretation resolved the issue in favour of retaining secular education. Others put forward an alternative argument that the parliament should disregard the ballots cast by voters who made inconsistent choices. On one member's calculation, that would have delivered a win for question 2 ('Scripture in Schools', *The Age*, 24 August 1905, 5). In the end, the government took no action in response to the referendum, effectively endorsing the majority response to question 1 while disregarding the answers to questions 2 and 3. The confusing result prompted the government to ignore what, at least on one interpretation, was a majority call for change.

There have been other instances in which ambiguity about public preferences has arisen after a plebiscite, including in relation to Tasmania's 1981 dam vote, which recorded an unusually high informal vote. These examples demonstrate that the people sometimes 'speak' in ways that require interpretation, and this opens a space for contestation about what the public wants and what action should be taken.

Overall, then, my analysis shows that Australian governments and parliaments have generally taken a deferential stance towards plebiscite results. They have implemented the popular verdict in all but three cases, and those few instances of non-compliance were not due to manipulation or obstruction. The majority or plurality vote has been respected even where the government or its leader has held a different policy preference. It is fair to say the idea that plebiscites are generally treated as politically binding holds in the Australian context.

Resistance to Plebiscite Implementation

My survey of Australian plebiscites also reveals that it is not uncommon for the implementation of plebiscite results to be contested by individual members or small groups of parliamentarians. This finding provides a counterweight to the overall conclusion of high compliance with advisory results. The reasons that lawmakers have given for resisting the implementation of a plebiscite outcome include concerns about the legitimacy of the vote, loyalty to the views of local constituents, personal conscience and misgivings about the proposed means of implementing the result.

An illustrative state example is South Australia's 1970 poll. Electors narrowly rejected a proposal for Friday night trading in Adelaide, with a 'Yes' vote of 48.2 per cent. But preferences varied considerably between inner city areas (which recorded a 'No' vote) and outer metropolitan areas (which already had Friday night trading and delivered an overwhelming 'Yes' vote). When the state parliament debated implementing legislation, some representatives of outer metropolitan Adelaide voted against it, or expressed misgivings about it, citing a range of legitimacy concerns relating to the ballot question and the unusually high informality rate (11 per cent) and, especially, the importance of giving voice to the wishes of local electorates. As one member put it, he was 'duty-bound' to take note of the views of his constituents and to try to amend the implementing legislation to take account of their preferences (South Australian Legislative Council 1970, 2459).

The aftermath of the same-sex marriage survey provides another example of individual lawmakers resisting the implementation of a plebiscite result. A Bill to introduce same-sex marriage was introduced into the federal parliament after a clear national majority of 61.6 per cent voted 'Yes'. Some members disregarded the national result and instead voted in line with the preferences of their local constituency or their personal conscience. There were 12 recorded votes against the third reading of the Bill in the Senate and 4 such votes in the House, although 11 lower house MPs were known to have abstained by leaving the chamber before the vote occurred, presumably as a way of reconciling their personal views with those of the overall majority. In some cases, as with Nationals MP David Littleproud, who voted against the Bill, a commitment to respect local views happened to align with personal opinion. It is noteworthy that several other members did not feel constrained by the preferences of their local constituency. Ten members of the lower house, most of them Labor representatives sympathetic to same-sex marriage, voted for the Bill despite representing electorates that returned a majority 'No' vote. One Labor senator acknowledged the tension at play, noting the 'huge disconnect' between residents of some Western Sydney electorates and their local members on the issue of same-sex marriage (McGowan 2017).

There are numerous other examples of parliamentarians mounting resistance to the implementation of plebiscite outcomes. These instances show that political actors have not always viewed advisory votes as politically binding. At the same time, it must be acknowledged that in no case has this type of resistance occurred in sufficient numbers to put the implementation of a majority or plurality verdict at risk. It may be, as with the two examples cited above, that individual actors have felt emboldened to argue against public opinion due to the knowledge that their resistance would not ultimately obstruct the execution of the popular will.

Possible Reasons for High Compliance with Plebiscite Results

The reasons why politicians comply with plebiscites will vary across cases, as each individual poll takes place in its own individual context. Having said that, my survey of the 44 Australian plebiscites and their aftermaths suggests 3 general explanations for high compliance. The first is that all plebiscites were initiated by the government or parliament. The second is that compliance has often been in the interests of political representatives. The third provides that implementation is consistent with a principled view that public opinion, as expressed at a plebiscite, supersedes the judgment of parliament.

Initiation by Government or Parliament

The fact that all plebiscites have been initiated by the government or parliament in the absence of a constitutional requirement to do so probably helps to explain the high compliance rate. This arrangement means that representatives control the decision to hold a plebiscite and to determine its topic, timing and question wording. We would therefore generally expect that when the initiating authority triggers an advisory vote on an issue, it has some confidence about the likely result and a degree of comfort about the prospect of implementing it. By contrast, we would expect a lower level of compliance with popular initiatives (see above). Such polls are more likely to concern policy proposals with which legislators disagree and/or present implementation difficulties (Gerber et al. 2001; cf. Ferraiolo 2007).

Interests

The idea that the interests of politicians might help to explain the high compliance rate is not surprising. As noted earlier, the strategic concerns of representatives are cited as the reason why, in practice, advisory votes often end up being treated as binding. As Ian Budge succinctly puts it, it is 'very difficult to go against popular opinion' (Budge 1996, 52).

The fear of suffering severe public fallout (Gallagher 1996, 246) has almost certainly contributed to the deferential stance taken by parliaments towards plebiscite results. Although it is difficult to locate express statements from politicians to the effect that they are implementing the majority verdict to avoid the risk of a public backlash, common sense indicates that such electoral self-preservation is a prominent consideration. The idea that this is the case comes out more clearly in commentary on individual plebiscites. For instance, following the ACT's vote to adopt a Hare-Clark electoral system, which both the territory and federal governments opposed, a reporter remarked that 'it would be a brave Federal government which ignored such an overwhelming result' (Lamberton 1992). In short, politicians have likely treated plebiscites as binding in some cases because to do otherwise would be politically difficult.

The implementation of Australian plebiscite outcomes has often aligned with another facet of political interest. In many instances, governments have held plebiscites to resolve internal party or coalition divisions on an issue (e.g. same-sex marriage) or to depoliticise a contentious social issue by removing it from the parliamentary agenda (e.g. daylight saving and 6:00 p.m. closing) (Phillips 1980; Twomey 2016; Kildea 2022). In such cases, it is the act of holding the plebiscite that benefits the governing authority, with the result being of secondary importance. We would expect the rate of compliance with such votes to be high. In other words, the government and parliament have likely been moved to implement some plebiscite results because doing so is aligned with their motivation for holding the vote in the first place. In such cases, it is politically expedient for political actors to comply with the popular will.

Principle

My review of Australian plebiscites also suggests that the high rate of compliance can be attributed to a general perception among politicians that advisory votes should, as a matter of principle, be treated as if they were binding. There is a commonly expressed view that, once a decision is made to hold a plebiscite, it is the duty of representatives to implement it. The view that emanates is that public opinion, as expressed at the ballot box, possesses a special force and that elected politicians are bound to follow.

The idea that politicians are obliged to respect advisory votes was expressed after the continent's first post-federation plebiscite and has endured over time. After New

South Wales electors voted overwhelmingly in 1903 to reduce the size of the state's Legislative Assembly, Premier John See recalled parliament early to give effect to the result. See said that his government was 'obeying the mandate of the people' and called on members to 'trust the people' and implement the result (New South Wales Legislative Assembly 1904, 6). More than a century later, Prime Minister Malcolm Turnbull made a very similar pronouncement in the aftermath of the same-sex marriage vote. He drew attention to the imperative of 'respect[ing] the voice of the people' and declared that it was parliament's 'job to deliver it' (Turnbull 2017).

It is not uncommon to find statements to the effect that elected politicians must abide by citizen advice whether they agree with it or not. Queensland Premier William Kidston gave voice to this idea after the public voted for religious teaching in schools, saying that representatives were 'under an obligation to abide by the decision of the people of Queensland [...] [n]o matter what his personal opinions are' (Queensland Legislative Assembly 1910, 475). Another clear encapsulation of this idea was given by a New South Wales minister after the state voted against Sunday hotel trading: '[w]hatever the reasons for the result of the vote, this Government will abide by it' (New South Wales Legislative Council 1970, 4400).

These statements present a view of the popular voice as sitting above the parliament. On occasion, ministers have articulated this very idea. Turnbull, having learnt of the majority 'Yes' vote for same-sex marriage, invoked the idea that politicians receive instructions from their constituents: 'They are our masters, we who were elected to Parliament' (Turnbull 2017). This notion of the people as sitting above politicians was also given voice after New South Wales's 1947 poll on hotel closing hours. Premier Jim McGirr, remarking on the majority verdict in favour of retaining 6:00 p.m. closing, said: '[t]he people are the highest authority in this country and they have spoken' ('Premier Says Club Hours Fixed', *Sydney Morning Herald*, 15 July 1947, 3). Conveyed in these statements is a sense that, once a plebiscite is called, members of parliament cede their power on whatever issue is on the ballot paper. Decision-making authority is, on this view, transferred from representatives to voters.

These declarations regarding popular power align with a strain of constitutional theory that sees 'the people' as the fundamental source of legitimacy for the exercise of public power and views the popular voice as sitting above that of the parliament (Psycharis 2022, 237). There is perhaps reason to not take them entirely at face value – after all, such statements have invariably been made by politicians who have decided to implement a popular verdict and, perhaps, have calculated that it is in their interests to do so. All the same, they suggest a widely held view among representatives that a decision to hold a plebiscite constitutes more than a request for information and can signal a delegation of decision-making authority on the issue at hand.

Conclusion

This chapter has examined whether Australian governments and parliaments have treated plebiscites as genuinely advisory or practically binding. My analysis of 44 federal, state and territory plebiscites has shown that political actors have typically adopted a deferential stance towards advisory votes. The majority or plurality vote has been implemented in almost all cases. There have been only three instances of non-compliance, which were related to intergovernmental resistance and preference ambiguity.

It is clear, then, that Australian politicians typically treat plebiscites as binding despite their formally advisory nature. It is therefore fair to describe plebiscites as devices of citizen empowerment in the Australian context. These advisory ballots have enabled citizens to have a decisive say over policy proposals, including in cases where the popular vote has run counter to the preferences of the government or leader. The holding of plebiscites has, in effect, constrained the policy latitude of parliaments. And numerous politicians accept this as a matter of principle, viewing the plebiscite as a vehicle for delegating decision-making authority to the people on a policy question.

At the same time, plebiscites can also serve as instruments of elite control. They provide less scope for popular influence than bottom-up votes like popular initiatives. Governments and parliaments control the decision to hold a plebiscite and get to decide its topic, timing and question wording. In many cases, the interests of political actors are served simply by holding a plebiscite. And, while plebiscite results have almost always been followed in Australia, my analysis shows the potential for intergovernmental factors to counter the popular voice and for the majority or plurality view to be contested by parliamentarians at the implementation stage. This illustrates that plebiscite results are not self-executing and must pass through the filters of federal and representative government.

The plebiscite, as practised in Australia, therefore has the capacity to serve both as an instrument of citizen empowerment and elite control. The extent to which it advances one or the other of these outcomes will likely be dependent on the circumstances surrounding individual polls, including the motivations of the initiating authority, the clarity of the result and the potential for intervention from another level of government.

References

Besant, Christopher W. 1990. 'Two Nations, Two Destinies: A Reflection on the Significance of the Western Australian Secession Movement to Australia, Canada and the British Empire'. *Western Australian Law Review* 20: 209–310.

Bogdanor, Vernon. 1981. *The People and the Party System: The Referendum and Electoral Reform in British Politics.* Cambridge: Cambridge University Press.

Budge, Ian. 1996. *The New Challenge of Direct Democracy.* Cambridge: Polity Press.

Cheneval, Francis and El-Wakil, Alice. 2018. 'The Institutional Design of Referendums: Bottom-Up and Binding'. *Swiss Political Science Review* 24 (3): 294–304.

Ferraiolo, Kathleen. 2007. 'Preserving the Initiative: State Legislative Response to Direct Democracy'. *Polity* 39 (4): 425–448.

Folkestad, Bjarte, Klausen, Jan Erling and Segaard, Jo. 2021. 'When Do Consultative Referendums Improve Democracy? Evidence From Local Referendums in Norway'. *International Political Science Review* 42 (2): 213–228.

Gallagher, Michael. 1996. 'Conclusion'. In *The Referendum Experience in Europe*, edited by Michael Gallagher and Pier Vincenzo Uleri, 226–252. Basingstoke: Macmillan Press.

Gallagher, Michael and Uleri, Pier Vinchenzo. (eds.). 1996. *The Referendum Experience in Europe.* Basingstoke: Macmillan Press.

Gerber, Elisabeth R., Lupia, Arthur, McCubbins, Matthew D. and Kiewiet, D. Roderick. 2001. *Stealing the Initiative: How State Government Responds to Direct Democracy*. Upper Saddle River: Prentice-Hall.

Hollander, Saskia. 2019. *The Politics of Referendum Use in European Democracies*. London: Palgrave Macmillan.

Jäske, Maija. 2017. '"Soft" Forms of Direct Democracy: Explaining the Occurrence of Referendum Motions and Advisory Referendums in Finnish Local Government'. *Swiss Political Science Review* 23 (1): 50–76.

Kildea, Paul. 2016. 'The Constitutional and Regulatory Dimensions of Plebiscites in Australia'. *Public Law Review* 27: 290–310.

Kildea, Paul. 2021. 'Australia's Same-Sex Marriage Survey: Evaluating a Unique Popular Vote Process'. *Monash University Law Review* 46 (2): 85–118.

Kildea, Paul. 2022. 'The Law and History of State and Territory Referendums'. *Sydney Law Review* 44 (1): 31–76.

Lacey, Joseph. 2017. *Centripetal Democracy: Democratic Legitimacy and Political Identity in Belgium, Switzerland, and the European Union*. Oxford: Oxford University Press.

Lamberton, Hugh. 1992. 'Resounding "Yes" for Hare-Clark'. *Canberra Times*, 16 February: 1.

McGowan, Michael. 2017. 'Dastyari: High Number of No Votes in Labor Seats Shows "Huge Disconnect"'. *The Guardian*, 15 November. https://www.theguardian.com/australia-news/2017/nov/15/dastyari-high-number-of-no-votes-in-labor-seats-shows-huge-disconnect.

New South Wales Legislative Assembly. 1904. *Debates*, 19 January. https://api.parliament.nsw.gov.au/api/hansard/search/daily/searchablepdf/HANSARD-290296563-2951.

New South Wales Legislative Council. 1970. *Debates*, 18 March. https://api.parliament.nsw.gov.au/api/hansard/search/daily/searchablepdf/HANSARD-290296563-1655.

Orr, Graeme. 2000. 'The Conduct of Referenda and Plebiscites in Australia: A Legal Perspective'. *Public Law Review* 11: 117–132.

Parliamentary Library. 2024. 'Referendums and Plebiscites'. *Parliamentary Handbook*. Department of Parliamentary Services, Parliament of Australia. https://handbook.aph.gov.au/Referendums.

Phillips, Walter. 1980. '"Six O'Clock Swill": The Introduction of Early Closing of Hotel Bars in Australia'. *Australian Historical Studies* 19 (75): 250–266.

Pitkin, Hanna. 1967. *The Concept of Representation*. Berkeley: University of California Press.

Psycharis, Matthew. 2022. 'Locating Plebiscites in the *Australian Constitution*'. *Melbourne University Law Review* 46 (1): 218–280.

Queensland Legislative Assembly. 1910. *Debates*, 17 August. https://documents.parliament.qld.gov.au/events/han/1910/1910_08_17_A.PDF.

Qvortrup, Matt, Morris, Caroline and Kobori, Masahiro. 2018. 'Australasia'. In *Referendums Around the World*, edited by Matt Qvortrup, 237–262. London: Palgrave Macmillan.

Setälä, Maija. 1999. *Referendums and Democratic Government: Normative Theory and the Analysis of Institutions*. Basingstoke: Macmillan.

Setälä, Maija. 2006. 'On the Problems of Responsibility and Accountability in Referendums'. *European Journal of Political Research* 45: 699–721.

South Australian Legislative Council. 1970. *Debates*, 10 November. https://hansardsearch.parliament.sa.gov.au/daily/uh/1970-11-10/pdf/download.

Suksi, Markku. 1996. 'Finland: The Referendum as a Dormant Feature'. In *The Referendum Experience in Europe*, edited by Michael Gallagher and Pier Vincenzo Uleri, 52–65. Basingstoke: Macmillan Press.

Turnbull, Malcolm. 2017. *Transcript*, Press Conference with Prime Minister Malcolm Turnbull and Senator Mathias Cormann, Parliament House, Canberra, 15 November.

Twomey, Anne. 2015. 'Plebiscites and Referenda'. *Australian Law Journal* 89: 832–835.

Twomey, Anne. 2016. 'Let's Not Demonise the Plebiscite in the Heat of the Debate Over Our Marriage Laws'. *The Australian*, 7 October: 28.

Uleri, Pier Vincenzo. 1996. 'Introduction'. In *The Referendum Experience in Europe*, edited by M. Gallagher and P. Uleri, 1–19. Basingstoke: Macmillan Press.

Watt, Edward. 1958. 'Secession in Western Australia'. *University Studies in Western Australian History* III (2): 43–86.

Chapter 6

REFLECTIONS ON THE VOICE REFERENDUM

Ryan Cox

Introduction

On 14 October 2023, the Australian people voted against a referendum proposal 'To alter the Constitution to recognise the First Peoples of Australia by establishing an Aboriginal and Torres Strait Islander Voice'.[1] Of those who cast a valid vote, 39.9 per cent voted 'Yes', and 60.1 per cent voted 'No'. Politicians and journalists were quick to draw conclusions about what the outcome of the vote meant. Former prime minister Tony Abbott (2023) wasted no time in announcing that 'if the people's vote is to be respected, it should mean abandoning, or at least scaling back, recent concessions to separatism'. Coalition Senator Jacinta Nampijinpa Price (2024) claimed the vote was 'an affirmation of every Australian's equal right to be heard, of every Australian's equal right to have a say'. Indigenous leaders stayed silent for a week after the referendum before releasing an anonymous open letter claiming the outcome was a 'repudiation of our peoples and the rejection of our efforts to pursue reconciliation in good faith'.[2]

It is, however, extremely difficult to draw conclusions about the meaning or significance of the vote from the result of the vote itself. As the authors of the ANU 'Detailed Analysis of the 2023 Voice to Parliament Referendum' write: 'there is a real risk of reading too much into a single vote on a very specific and narrow question about a Constitutionally enshrined Voice for Aboriginal and Torres Strait Islander Australians' (Biddle et al. 2023, 61). Indeed, neither Abbott's conclusion nor that drawn by the signatories of the open letter is justified by the survey data. This should not be surprising, for, as the authors of the analysis write: 'without asking questions directly about people's views towards Aboriginal and Torres Strait Islander issues, it is not really possible to infer what those views are, let alone whether those views have changed during or because of the campaign' (Biddle et al. 2023, 61).

---

1. For details on the proposal, see National Indigenous Australians Agency (2021) and Davis and Williams (2021). The Uluru Statement can be found here: https://ulurustatement.org/the-statement/view-the-statement/ (Accessed 31 January 2024).
2. The letter was published by 'A group of First Nations leaders, community members and organisations who supported Yes'. It can be found here: https://ulurustatement.org/statement-for-our-people-and-country/ (Accessed 2 February 2024).

In what follows, I will reflect on what the vote and the data tell us about the attitudes of Australians towards Indigenous issues and how this, in turn, bears on how we should think about arguments for proposals for reform in the future. I will then reflect on some of the arguments for the Voice in light of the outcome of the referendum. I will focus, in particular, on arguments for the Voice which cast the proposal as a way of addressing the legitimacy deficit faced by the Australian state with respect to its exercise of political power and authority over Indigenous Australians, where 'legitimacy' is understood as 'moral legitimacy' (I will not address questions of legal legitimacy). What does the outcome of the referendum tell us about the prospects for legitimating the exercise of power and authority of the Australian state over Indigenous Australians?[3]

Before beginning in earnest, I should briefly note that this chapter is written from the perspective of a Non-Indigenous Australian. It is written from the perspective of someone who believes that all Australians have a responsibility to be fully informed, from multiple perspectives, about the history of settlement and the contemporary injustice faced by Indigenous Australians and to have this inform their perspective on political issues that have consequences for Indigenous Australians. As the content of this chapter makes clear, it is my view that the question of the legitimacy of the exercise of political power by the Australian state over Indigenous Australians turns significantly on whether that exercise can made acceptable to the point of view of those over whom it is exercised. This is a matter for Indigenous Australians themselves to decide, and the chapter takes no stand on this matter at all. Whether the question of legitimacy turns significantly on whether that exercise can made acceptable to the point of view of those over whom it is exercised is a philosophical matter and one that this chapter does take a stand on.

Division and Unequal Rights

What does the outcome of the vote tell us about the inevitably varied attitudes of the Australian population towards the Voice proposal itself and towards some of the political values and principles that were offered for and against it? Consider the headline conclusion of the ANU survey:

> The data suggests that Australians voted no because they didn't want division and remain sceptical of rights for some Australians that are not held by others. The data suggests that Australians think that Aboriginal and Torres Strait Islander Australians continue to suffer levels of disadvantage that is both caused by past government policies and that justified extra government assistance. They did not see the Voice model put to them as the right approach to remedy that disadvantage. (Biddle et al. 2023, iii, 81)

3. Duncan Ivison has argued for the importance of this question in thinking about the relationship between settler states and Indigenous peoples. See Ivison (2002), Ivison (2017) and Ivison (2020). Paul Patton has raised a similar question in more Rawlsian terms. See Patton (2009).

Talk of 'division' here might seem to support Abbott's claim that 'if the people's vote is to be respected, it should mean abandoning, or at least scaling back, recent concessions to separatism'. Indeed, as the authors write elsewhere: 'Amongst those who voted no, the factor that was most likely to be given as very important was concern about dividing the country. This was given by 66.1 percent of no voters' (Biddle et al. 2023, 77). If division was the main concern, what were the grounds for the concern? I take it that grounds for the concern were that unequal rights, that is, 'rights for some Australians that are not held by others', would lead to or constitute social division. The survey also revealed that people thought that it was 'unfair' for some to be granted rights that others do not have. But what were the rights at issue when it came to the Voice proposal? Talk of people remaining 'sceptical of rights for some Australians that are not held by others' is ambiguous. I take it the scepticism here is over unequal legal rights and, in particular, over unequal political rights. The proposal, in a sense, was to grant Indigenous Australians, collectively, a political right that other groups do not have, that is, a right to advise parliament on matters relating to Indigenous Australians. And this may correctly have been perceived as granting Indigenous Australians, collectively, a right to greater influence over certain political decisions than they otherwise would have had. If the heart of the concern was over unequal political rights related to influence over political decisions, then this might seem to partly vindicate Price's claim that the outcome of the vote was 'an affirmation of every Australian's equal right to be heard, or every Australian's equal right to have a say'.

Concerns about division and unequal rights had been salient in public discourse since the Voice was first proposed. Malcolm Turnbull, the prime minister at the time the Referendum Council delivered its final report, rejected the proposal on the grounds that the proposed advisory body 'would inevitably become seen as a third chamber of parliament' and that, as such, it was not capable of winning acceptance in a referendum. He claimed it would 'undermine the universal principles of unity, equality and "one person one vote"'.[4] Prior to this, the Institute of Public Affairs had put out a 'research note' entitled 'Four Reasons to Reject the Referendum Council Recommendations'. One of the reasons the IPA offered was that 'Indigenous Australians already have a voice in parliament' since they already have the vote. Another reason given was that 'A voice to parliament for one race is divisive and undemocratic – we are all equal'. The essential point, as the note put it, was this: 'Every Australian should be treated equally under the constitution. No special privileges should be afforded to any group of individuals based on race, gender, sexuality, or religion. No group should be singled out for special treatment. We are all equal under the Australian constitution'. It is clear that the concern was not merely about formal recognition, however, but was about political inequality and division: 'Granting a special constitutional privilege to one segment of

---

4. Australian Government, 'Response to Referendum Council's Report on Constitutional Recognition'. *Media Release*, 26 October 2016. https://www.malcolmturnbull.com.au/media/response-to-referendum-councils-report-on-constitutional-recognition (Accessed 5 February 2024).

our community is also undemocratic. The creation of a body to exclusively represent one group elevates members of that group above others in our community'.

Proposals for special legal or political rights for Indigenous Australians have rarely gone over well with the majority of Non-Indigenous Australians.[5] What was special about the Voice proposal, however, was that it did not concern land rights, or even, in the first instance, rights to self-determination and self-government. (Although, as we will see, arguments for the proposal often appealed to the latter.) It was, at most, a proposal for a right to greater political influence for Indigenous Australians, collectively, than they currently have. And it was justified, for the most part, on the grounds that it would lead to better decisions and outcomes and address Indigenous disadvantage.

It may have been somewhat surprising that granting Indigenous Australians *this* right should have been perceived to be unfair. Why should it have been perceived to be unfair? I suspect that resistance to land rights or rights to self-determination and self-government stems from a certain degree of scepticism about the moral claims that are meant to underwrite these claims. But, unless this political right was being argued for on the basis of independent moral rights to self-determination and self-government, this kind of scepticism would be out of place.

Is there anything beyond a general concern about unequal treatment that could explain the depth of this concern about the proposal? I suspect that part of what explains the depth of the concern, in this case, is the perception that it conflicts with deeply held and jealously guarded assumptions about the distribution of influence over political decisions and the justification of political power in democracies. In the first instance, the assumption is that in a democratic society, nobody has a prior and independent claim to greater influence over political decision making than anyone else. This is one kind of equality that goes into our thinking about democracy. As a consequence of this assumption, we hold that, as far as possible, or at least as an ideal, everyone is to have roughly the same (opportunity for) informal influence over political decisions. So I think that this concern over the proposal was not just 'more of the same' scepticism about Indigenous rights. The supposedly unequal rights cut close to home and to some cherished democratic assumptions.

The 'Yes' campaign did not do enough to address this kind of concern. While there were many illegitimate concerns that were easily dismissed, no attempt was made to address any underlying reasonable concern. It is crucial that we get clear on these concerns in order to understand how to argue for reform in the future. Addressing the concern here would have involved two things: offering arguments *against* misunderstandings, but also having a sense of the concern in providing a positive case *for* the proposal and ensuring that one's argument for the proposal would not exacerbate any reasonable (even if ultimately illegitimate) concerns. One of the more philosophical points I will be making in this chapter is the following: that the perceived fairness or unfairness of a proposal is not just a matter of features of the proposal itself but involves

5. See Ivison (2002, 113–114) for a brief discussion of responses to calls for Indigenous Rights, especially the quotations on the top of p. 114.

the argumentative context it is set in. Some arguments for the proposal may only have served to exacerbate concerns about fairness and unequal rights.

Influential contributors to the 'Yes' campaign often seem to have thought there was no serious 'No' case to answer. In her *Quarterly Essay* 'Voice of Reason', Davis, for instance, writes: 'Conservatives are busy carving out a convenient narrative for themselves that there is a reasoned and respectable case for "No"; there isn't' (Davis 2023, 4). No doubt much of the 'No' campaign was cynical, and there was a significant amount of dog-whistling and misinformation. But that does not mean that there was not a case to be answered as to why the proposal should not be seen as unfair from the point of view of political equality. Yes, formal equality is beside the point. But the point may nonetheless have needed making: what is the case for the proposal such that it does not amount to an unfair granting of greater collective political influence (than they already have) to some and not others?

This is not to say that there were no attempts to address the 'myth' that the proposal would be divisive or that it was unfair or involved unequal rights. Among the many articles that emerged debunking myths about the proposal, some claimed that 'a First Nations Voice will not give First Nations peoples special rights' (O'Bryan and Gerber 2023). This, of course, is partly right. It is true that Indigenous Australians were not being granted individual rights that Non-Indigenous Australians were not. The article also addressed the myth that the proposal 'offends against the notion of equality that underpins the Constitution and our democracy'. It claimed, in response, that 'Our Constitution does not protect equality' and that 'The structure of our Parliament is also not equal' (O'Bryan and Gerber 2023). But both of these claims are beside the point. The first is largely irrelevant. The second is questionable in fact and likely to be unconvincing in practice. Sure, the state of Tasmania has the same number of senators as the state of Victoria. From the point of view of someone who cares about political equality, that will seem like a bad thing. It is not enough to merely point out that the structure of parliament is already not equal. That will not convince someone who thinks that such inequality is regrettable. One needs to make an independent argument to the effect that *this* inequality is justifiable (just as those who argued for the structure of the Senate did).

Suppose, then, that rather than taking the 'No' voter to have some mistaken view about the proposal, we take them to think that it was unfair, or a departure from political equality, for a formal body to be enshrined to ensure that some had greater influence over certain decisions, decisions primarily concerning themselves.[6] Their concern is not, at least in the first instance, one about racial divisiveness, nor about dividing the country. The division they are concerned about, in the first instance, is a division in political power: the unfairness relates to (perceived) political inequality. My view is that it is *this* concern which (if we are to extend a charitable interpretation to them) prevented many 'No' voters from being able to see the proposal as the right proposal for addressing

6. These distinctions in kinds of influence made in this paragraph are taken from Kolodny (2014). For an application in this context, see Cox (2023, 9).

the issue. It is this concern which led them to see the proposal as an unjustifiable *means* to an otherwise worthy end.

Arguments for the Voice in Retrospect

I now want to consider some of the arguments that were made for the proposed Voice in light of the referendum outcome and political attitudes that we have just been examining. Arguments for and against the proposed Voice drew on a wide range of moral and political values and combined them in different ways. Many put social justice at their heart. Many appealed to democratic ideals. Others appealed to Indigenous rights and Indigenous sovereignty. Others still appealed to considerations of political legitimacy. I will consider these in turn.

Many arguments for the proposed Voice were straightforward arguments that drew on claims about *social justice*. Arguments for 'better' decisions and outcomes are best seen as being of this kind. What we need are better political decisions to achieve more just outcomes. The proposed Voice was a means to better decisions and achieving these outcomes. This, plausibly, was the central argument of the 'Yes' campaign. Their main pitch was that Australians should vote 'Yes' because a constitutionally enshrined advisory body has the best prospects among the available alternatives for achieving better outcomes for Indigenous Australians. Their argument for this primarily consisted, on the one hand, of demonstrating the need to achieve better outcomes for Indigenous Australians and, on the other hand, of demonstrating that the proposal had the best prospects among the available alternatives for achieving better outcomes. The argument for the latter involved showing how the failure to achieve better outcomes was largely a consequence of a failure on the part of the government to listen and showing that alternative mechanisms for listening, such as a legislated voice, would likely not be as effective as a constitutionally enshrined voice. In my view, most of the arguments for these claims are impeccable and were well made by the most articulate Yes campaigners.

One shortcoming of the direct style of argument, however, is that it merely offered a reason or consideration in favour of the proposal without addressing potential conflicts with other political values. The reason may have been a weighty one, but to settle the question in favour of the proposal, the campaign would have had to address any reasonable and legitimate arguments against the proposal. Unfortunately, the Yes campaign was too confident in thinking that *all* of the counterarguments or considerations fell on the illegitimate side of the divide. But the direct argument *does* raise a concern that it does not alone address. It motivates giving one group greater influence over certain decisions than they otherwise would have had. And it does so on the ground that doing so would bring about better outcomes for that group. It argues for the means merely on the basis of a just end. The argument doesn't answer concerns about whether the end justifies the means. This argument also doesn't address another kind of unfairness objection, which points out that others face disadvantage and are not thereby granted greater influence over decisions as a means of addressing that disadvantage. Is it merely that Indigenous Australians face greater injustice than these other disadvantaged groups? It is here, of course, that considerations outside of the direct argument itself might have been appealed to – for instance, one might simply appeal to facts about the history of settlement. But it seems to me that, for the most part, this kind of worry was not addressed by proponents of the direct argument.

Another kind of direct argument appealed to democratic values. Indeed, one relatively straightforward argument for the Voice is that it would merely serve to rectify a certain *democratic deficit* faced by Indigenous Australians. The thought here is that the ideal of political equality is one in which all members of society, individually and collectively, have roughly equal contributory influence over decision-making. Mere formal equality isn't enough to ensure that this value is realised, because it is a familiar point that various kinds of social advantages and disadvantages contribute to differences in political influence. As Noel Pearson put it in his *Quarterly Essay* 'A Rightful Place', Indigenous Australians are an *extreme minority* and as such have less informal influence over political decision making, both individually and collectively, than many Non-Indigenous Australians (Pearson 2014, 37–38). The proposed Voice could be seen as a mechanism for addressing this democratic deficit then.

Again, there is much to be said for this style of argument. For one, it goes some distance towards answering the unfairness objection because the argument simply claims to ensure that Indigenous Australians are collectively brought up to parity with Non-Indigenous Australians concerning political influence. They are not being granted a political privilege that others do not have. They are being granted a political privilege that they lack and others already enjoy. Note, however, that this argument would be an argument for giving Indigenous Australians more influence than they currently have over *all* political decisions, and not specifically decisions that affect them. Moreover, there is a concern that the proposed Voice would do more than just bring Indigenous Australians to parity with Non-Indigenous Australians with respect to influence over decisions that affect them; it would give them *greater relative influence* over such decisions than Non-Indigenous Australians have. And rightly so, because it is arguably *this* amount of influence that would be necessary to address the kinds of social injustice appealed to by arguments from social injustice. Admitting this, however, puts the burden back on defenders of the proposal to explain why *this* is not an unfair political advantage. How is the tension we identified at the end of the previous section to be resolved?

Was there a good argument that could have been given for a proposal for greater relative contributory influence over certain matters that addressed concerns around unfairness? Here we must look to deeper philosophical justifications than the two we have examined so far. The justification at this stage may appeal to unceded sovereignty or to a right to self-determination. Perhaps Indigenous Australians have a *prior and independent* claim to exercise a certain degree of control over their own political and economic destiny. I think that there is a good case to be made, in many cases, for the right to Indigenous self-determination. That is, I think that a people with a collective and shared identity, or a sense of nationhood, may have a claim to decide collectively matters that concern their own community (Miller 2000, 27). I take it that it was a right of this kind that Davis was appealing to in speaking of the right of Indigenous peoples 'to participate in decisionmaking in matters that impact on their lives' (Davis 2017, 65).

This, of course, echoes Article 18 of the UN Declaration of the Rights of Indigenous Peoples (UNDRIP): 'Indigenous peoples have the right to participate decisionmaking in matters which would affect their rights'.[7]

As progressive 'No' campaigners effectively pointed out, however, *if* Indigenous Australians do have such a right to self-determination, it is not clear how the proposed Voice would satisfy it.[8] One does not exactly have collective control over decisions that affect one by having an advisory body that at best grants greater relative contributory influence. Suppose, however, one argued that the Voice was to be seen as a compromise of sorts, a partial concession. The proposed Voice could then be seen as at least partly satisfying claims to self-determination (it is better than nothing) or even as a means to further such claims down the path. Would this then answer the fairness worry? Is it what the arguments from social justice or democracy need in order to justify greater relative contributory influence for Indigenous Australians over matters affecting them?

In my view, this form of argument was always likely to be politically ineffective (even though it may be cogent). As we have seen, many 'No' voters accept the claims about social injustice. But I suspect that far fewer would sign on to claims about Indigenous rights to self-determination and unceded sovereignty if these claims entailed greater influence over political decisions.[9] I suspect that they simply do not think that anybody has a *prior and independent* claim to a certain degree of political influence (other than a claim to *equal* political influence). Or, at least if they do, they do not think that such rights should be recognised in a democratic society governed by the ideal of political equality. If they were even remotely disposed to reject the proposal as unfair on the grounds that it gave some greater relative influence over certain matters, they would be even more strongly disposed to reject it on the grounds that some have a *prior and independent* claim to greater influence. For them, that would seem to go against the spirit of democracy and political equality.

Political Legitimacy and the Voice

One political value or concept that did not get much traction in the public debate over the proposed Voice was political legitimacy. This is unfortunate, as I think that this is the concept that the debate needed most and is the most relevant to theorising proposals like the Voice. My own contribution to the academic debate put questions of political

7. See also Article 3: 'Indigenous peoples have a right to self-determination. By virtue of that right the freely determine their political status and freely pursue their economic, social and cultural development.'
8. Progressive 'No' campaigners were also concerned that by supporting the Voice, they would be seen as conceding the legitimacy of the Australian state, something that, at least on the face of it, is in conflict with Indigenous sovereignties and claims to self-determination.
9. Patton refers to the 'stark evidence of the plurality of religious, moral and philosophical views on the basis of which different citizens address the question of the rights of Indigenous people' and writes that 'Agreement on the moral basis of lack of basis for distinctively Aboriginal rights seems unlikely' (Patton 2009, 62). These points apply in this context.

legitimacy at its heart.[10] And others have seen legitimacy as central to thinking about Indigenous issues in Australia (and elsewhere).[11]

One initial advantage arguments from legitimacy have over arguments from self-determination and unceded sovereignty is dialectical. They put the burden on the opponent to argue that the Australian state has a legitimate claim to exercise political power over Indigenous Australians. Showing that there is such a burden need not involve establishing that Indigenous Australians have a right to self-determination or a claim to sovereignty, although this would certainly bolster the case.[12] One might appeal to facts about the history of settlement in order to call the legitimacy of the Australian state into question;[13] but one might also argue that a combination of the factors we have discussed so far serves to call the Australian state's claim into question. Let me first set out what is at stake in asking about political legitimacy before showing how considerations of political legitimacy can be used to support a proposal like the Voice.

On the approach to political legitimacy I adopt, an approach due in broad outline to Bernard Williams, whether the exercise of political power by some authority is legitimate or not is a matter of whether it meets the basic legitimation demand.[14] This demand arises whenever some purported authority exercises political power and claims to have the right or authority to do so (Williams 2005, 4). What does meeting the basic legitimation demand involve? According to Williams, meeting the demand 'implies a sense in which the state has to offer a justification of its power *to each subject*' (Williams 2005, 4), the basic legitimation demand requires 'a legitimation be given to every subject' (Williams 2005, 6). Such a justification or a legitimation must be one that 'makes sense' as a justification or legitimation of that power to those subject to it.[15] Whether there exists such a justification or legitimation of political power will then be something determined by the shared moral and political outlooks of those over whom that power is exercised.

While it is necessary for legitimacy that a legitimation of power exist that makes sense as a legitimation of power, it is not sufficient. In addition to such a legitimation existing, it must be the case that it is not accepted merely as a consequence of exercises

10. See Cox (2023).
11. Patton (2009); Ivison (2002); Ivison (2017); Ivison (2020). See Patton (2009, 60–62) for an excellent overview of the issue of legitimacy with respect to Indigenous Australians.
12. This burden-shifting point is nicely made by Ivison. Cf. 'Despite the focus on [...] justification and legitimacy in recent political theory, it's still not clear that liberal egalitarians really do put power at the heart of their analysis. If they did, it would shift the onus of justification from resting mainly with Indigenous polities to the settler state' (Ivison 2020, 87). See also Ivison (2020, 104).
13. See Patton (2009, 61) for a brief discussion of this issue. Patton is drawing on Mulgan (1998).
14. Williams (2005, 4). See also Ivison (2008, 7, 209–211) on the demand for legitimisation.
15. There is a lot to be said about the idea of 'making sense' as a legitimation of power here. Williams appeals to the notion here (Williams 2005, 10–11). He says that making sense is a category of human understanding (Williams 2005, 11). He also speaks of 'the human capacity to live under an intelligible order of authority' Williams (2005, 10).

of that power itself.[16] This is what Williams calls the 'critical theory test'. Since it is possible for political power to be exercised in such a way that those it is exercised over are coerced into accepting some legitimating story of that power, and such cases appear to be cases where the basic legitimation demand is not met, we will want a way of excluding such cases. How we exclude such cases is a difficult matter, because it is not sufficient that acceptance of the legitimating principle be causally explicable in terms of exercises of the power it is meant to legitimate. No doubt liberal legitimations are by and large part of contemporary moral and political outlooks as a consequence of the exercise of political power in liberal states.

With this understanding of legitimacy in mind, I want now to briefly restate my own 'argument from legitimacy' for the proposed Voice, showing how it improves on the arguments considered in the previous section. I will then reflect on what I see as some shortcomings of this argument.

The first question to ask is what kind of legitimation of political power makes sense according to the moral and political outlooks of those living in modern liberal democratic societies. I think that it is reasonable to suppose that modern states like Australia are legitimated partly in terms of the source of authority – the principle of popular sovereignty – and partly in terms of the ends the government seeks to attain – it seeks to attain, among other things, an adequate level of social justice. That is, the exercise of political power by a modern state like Australia is legitimated for us because we take the authority of the state to be ultimately given by the people through democratic means, and because we see the state as seeking to attain an adequate level of social justice. Suppose, for now, that such a legitimating principle is widely accepted by those living under the power of the Australian state, where this is taken to include Indigenous Australians.

In order to make out the argument from legitimacy, we then need the concept of a legitimacy deficit. The thought here is that a legitimacy deficit involving the ends of government arises when the governing conventions of a society are inadequate for achieving those ends.[17] Governments are always failing to achieve the ends of social justice. But not all governments are such that their governing conventions are inadequate for achieving those ends. A legitimacy deficit arises when it is clear that if the government were to continue in line with the prevailing governing conventions, there would be little hope of redressing some injustice. With the concept of a legitimacy deficit in place, we can set out an argument for a proposal like the Voice. Such a proposal can be seen as a proposal to change the governing conventions of a society to address such a deficit. And it is plausible that the Voice would address such a deficit due to the nature of the injustice at play. The injustice faced by Indigenous Australians is partly structural. It is partly a consequence of their not having enough of a say over matters that concern them. So,

16. Williams spells out his account of non-coercively formed beliefs in more detail in Ch. 6 of Williams (2002).

17. I take this expression and idea from David Beetham. See Beetham (1991, 18). Hobbs and Jones speak of a 'legitimacy gap' but do not pursue the issue of legitimacy at length. See Hobbs and Jones (2022, 7). See also Beetham (1991, 207–208).

it is reasonable to think that a proposal like the Voice would address such a legitimacy deficit. More needs to be said to support each of these claims.[18] However, my aim here is only to set out the argument from legitimacy in broad outline.

There is an obvious sense in which the argument from legitimacy does little more than set the argument from social justice in a new context. This is true, but the new context matters. It calls into question the Australian state's claim to have a legitimate claim to exercise political power over Indigenous Australians. It shows that the matter is not simply one of the state failing to live up to its promise of achieving social justice for all. It shows that since there is so little hope of redress within the prevailing governing conventions, for the Australian state to continue to exercise its political power over Indigenous Australians is, in a sense, for it to partly *dominate* Indigenous Australians. For, to the extent that political power is exercised over some in the absence of full legitimacy, those over whom it is exercised are dominated.

The argument from legitimacy has the advantage that it motivates a departure from a strict understanding of political equality as a means to addressing a legitimacy deficit with respect to the ends of government and not on the grounds that a particular group in society has a prior and independent claim to greater influence (if only with respect to matters that primarily affect them). This is not to say that Indigenous Australians do not have such a claim. It is only to suggest that there is an argument available for a proposal like the Voice that does not appeal to such a claim. My thought was that such an argument would do less to offend against a widely accepted understanding of popular sovereignty and political equality.

The argument for legitimacy has two shortcomings, however. The first is that it may be too sanguine about a departure from political equality not offending against such an understanding just because it is not argued for on the grounds that some have a prior and independent claim to greater influence. In light of the outcome of the referendum vote and the survey data, it is plausible to think that any departure from political equality would still have been seen as a violation of a widespread understanding of the principle of popular sovereignty. The second is that the argument did not address the question at all of whether the Australian state could ever become fully legitimate. It merely assumed that there was a shared understanding of legitimacy according to which the Australian state faced a legitimacy deficit. It did not address the question of whether there is or could be a shared understanding of political power in Australia, an understanding endorsed by Indigenous and Non-Indigenous Australians alike, according to which the Australian state could (with feasible changes) become fully legitimate. Both of these concerns will need addressing in an adequate treatment of the question of political legitimacy.

Legitimacy Reconsidered

Granting that the exercise of political power by the Australian state is less than fully legitimate, can it be made legitimate? This question can be divided into two parts: one

18. See Cox (2023, 4–7) for such support.

concerning what kind of legitimating principles can form part of a shared moral and political outlook in a settler state like Australia and another concerning the feasibility of the Australian state coming to conform to such legitimating principles. These questions are made all the more pressing for a 'realist' approach to legitimacy of the kind I have adopted.

Let me begin by addressing an initial challenge. It might be thought that the critical theory test, appealed to by Williams, rules out the possibility of the Australian state ever being legitimated because, even if Indigenous Australians did accept some liberal democratic principle of legitimation, it would only be as a result of the power exercised over them by a settler state. Here is how Ivison puts the challenge:

> The challenge for any conception of legitimacy [...] is how to ensure that the acceptance of a justification for the exercise of power is not itself produced by the coercive power that is being justified. Does the colonial past and present of liberal settler states make political legitimacy impossible in this sense? Are the institutions and practices of contemporary settler states so saturated by the legacy of colonialism that any claim to legitimacy – either now or in the future – is hopeless? (Ivison 2017, 126–27)

As a merely causal claim, it is, of course, going to be true that the moral and political outlooks of Indigenous Australians today have been influenced by settlement. But this is not enough to justify the claim that their outlooks, therefore, are just the product of coercive power and cannot be appealed to in order to legitimate the Australian state. Mere causation is not the relevant test. The relevant test is whether Indigenous Australians can reflectively endorse the legitimating principles implicit in their moral and political outlooks in full knowledge of the facts about how they have come to have them.[19] There is no reason to think that this is impossible.

However, this initial challenge only leads to another. The starting assumption of the argument from political legitimacy was that we could speak of a shared moral and political outlook according to which broadly liberal democratic legitimating principles were endorsed. It is not obvious that this is the right starting assumption when considering legitimacy in the context of settler states and Indigenous peoples. A better starting assumption is that of the *distinct* but possibly overlapping moral and political outlooks of peoples living within the settler state. There are many ways of drawing distinctions between such outlooks. But suppose for the moment that we can speak of a shared moral and political outlook of Indigenous Australians taken collectively. Now, we know that such an outlook will not be the outlook of a particular First Nation. Rather, it will be a shared moral and political outlook of Indigenous Australians as a consequence of their having a shared history of colonisation in Australia. Such a shared outlook will be informed by more local outlooks. But it is distinct from the outlook of Non-Indigenous Australians, where this is taken to include those who do and do not have immigrant identities. What I am calling a 'moral and political outlook' here Ivison calls

19. This would involve recognising the diversity of normative perspectives among Indigenous Australians themselves.

a 'normative order', where a normative order is 'a cluster of values, beliefs and legitimation "narratives" (religious, cultural, moral, political and legal) that people appeal to in order to justify (and contest) the practices and institutions they are both subject to and help create' (Ivison 2017, 123). The challenge, from this perspective, is, as Ivison puts it, to answer the following question: 'On what basis can a liberal political order be considered legitimate given this plurality [of normative orders]'? (Ivison 2020, 124). Or, as I would put it: how can Indigenous and Non-Indigenous Australians come to share a moral and political outlook which includes a legitimation of the exercise of political power of the Australian state that makes sense as a legitimation of such an exercise?

This question is particularly difficult to answer from a realist approach to political legitimacy. Indeed, on such an approach, the question becomes a political question, not a philosophical one. Although it is tempting to find a philosophical answer to the question, this temptation needs to be resisted. Philosophy tells us that the legitimating principles must be freely accepted and that they must make sense of political power as political power. But that is about all that philosophy allows itself to say here. Philosophy cannot *answer* questions about political legitimacy as such. This may have been the case when the philosopher's moral and political outlook could just be assumed to be that of the broader society he or she lived in. For then the philosopher could play a role in explicating the sense in which some legitimation of political power made sense as a legitimation of political power within that moral and political outlook. This is not the situation of the philosopher today. Indeed, the question of legitimacy has become more than just a first-order question about the legitimating features of political power but has become a critical or reflective question, one concerning whether legitimations make sense only as a consequence of the exercise of that power itself.

Paul Patton has considered the question of political legitimacy in this context from a Rawlsian perspective, and he has made a suggestion about how the approach might be adapted to this context. Patton argues that Rawls's political conception of legitimacy 'provides us with resources to answer the question of the conditions under which government can be legitimate in postcolonial societies such as Australia' (Patton 2009, 60). As Patton notes, Rawls suggests that liberal legitimation can be modelled in terms of something like the original position in which '[w]e suppose the parties to know the facts of reasonable pluralism and of oppression along with other general information' (Rawls 2005, 137; Patton 2009, 66). Patton then asks: 'Should the general knowledge about human society available to the parties include the fact that many societies have been established by colonisation, some of them relatively recently, and that culturally different peoples still coexist side by side on the same territory?' (Patton 2009, 66). As Patton notes, this kind of information is meant to be available at the 'constitutional stage' of deliberation in Rawls's model in any case (Patton 2009, 66). Patton suggests that as an upshot of this, it may be possible to find 'constitutional essentials that *all* citizens may reasonably be expected to endorse' which grant distinctive rights to Indigenous citizens (Patton 2009, 66–67).

It is not obvious to me that exactly the principles one would like to see fall out of a Rawlsian theory can be derived from some combination of the original position and the constitutional convention stage of deliberation, however. Who is to say whether it would be reasonable or unreasonable for some to reject constitutional essentials that grant some greater influence over particular decisions, even if those decisions only affect those who are to have greater influence over them? I suspect that the outcome that would be reached by contracting parties given this kind of information would just become undefined. And, even if it is defined, what if a significant number of citizens *do* reject such constitutional essentials? That is, what if, as a matter of fact, many of those living in settler societies would reject constitutional essentials involving departures from strict political equality? Is the Rawlsian argument meant to show that they are simply wrong and must accept the power exercised over them on these terms (shall we just say that they are unreasonable)? It seems as bad to say this to Non-Indigenous Australians who reject departures from political equality as it would be to say to Indigenous Australians that even though they happen to reject the constitutional essentials of the liberal settler state, those essentials are such that all citizens may be reasonably expected to endorse them. The main shortcoming of the Rawlsian approach is that although it can provide the contracting parties with additional information about the history of settlement, it nonetheless works with an abstract model of the parties to the contract. It does not incorporate *their* perspectives.

If we are going to reject a Rawlsian resolution and continue to work with a critical or reflective understanding of political legitimacy, then the project of legitimating the Australian state is a political one. It is a political one that we should consider in light of the referendum result and the survey data. Suppose that the result and the data reveal a commitment to popular sovereignty as a legitimating principle, as well as a particular understanding of political equality on that principle. I think that the question to ask about this is whether this is a principle that should continue to make sense as a legitimation of power in settler states like Australia. We have already seen how it might reasonably fail to make sense as a legitimation for Indigenous Australians themselves who are acutely aware of their history and of the ways in which the governing conventions of the Australian state are inadequate to redress the kinds of structural injustice they face. But should it really make sense as a legitimation of power for Non-Indigenous Australians? There are good reasons to guard against the suggestion that nobody has a prior and independent claim to greater influence over political decisions. But does it make sense, in a settler state, to hold onto a legitimating principle that cannot allow a historically and contemporaneously dominated people to have greater influence over decisions that currently affect them than they currently do? We do not need a Rawlsian original position to see that this does not make sense in light of our historical circumstances. We need only to be able to imagine ourselves in the shoes of Indigenous Australians and to ask whether it would make sense to accept anything less in light of the facts of history and their current circumstances.

So, to sum up, I think that if there is going to be a way forward for Australia with respect to addressing the legitimation deficit, it is going to involve negotiating or renegotiating our shared understanding of the legitimation of the exercise of political power in a society like ours, with a history like ours. For Non-Indigenous Australians to insist on a principle of legitimation that requires strict political equality, and for the Australian state to continue to exercise political power over some who reject such a principle of legitimation, is for the Australian state to be less than fully legitimate. For Indigenous Australians to refuse to endorse principles of legitimation that the Australian state could feasibly be brought into line with, may well be their prerogative, and if they choose to exercise it, the Australian state should (all else being equal perhaps) refrain from exercising its political authority over those who refuse to endorse such principles. But the hope remains, however, that there may be a legitimation that can be accepted from all points of view.

References

Abbott, Tony. 2023. 'Voice Defeat a Decisive Blow to Identity Politics'. *The Australian*, 20 October.

Beetham, David. 1991. *The Legitimation of Power.* Basingstoke: Palgrave MacMillian.

Biddle, Nicholas, Gray, Matthew, McAllister, Ian and Qvortrup, Matt. 2023. 'Detailed Analysis of the 2023 Voice to Parliament Referendum and Related Social and Political Attitudes ANU Centre for Social Research and Methods'.

Cox, Ryan. 2023. 'Political Legitimacy and the Indigenous Voice to Parliament'. *Journal of Applied Philosophy* 41 (3): 423–441. https://doi.org/10.1111/japp.12692.

Davis, Megan. 2017. 'Self-Determination and the Right to Be Heard'. In *A Rightful Place: A Road Map to Recognition*, edited by Noel Pearson and Shireen Morris. Collingwood: Black Inc.

Davis, Megan. 2023. 'Voice of Reason: On Recognition and Renewal'. *Quarterly Essay*, no. 90: 1–70.

Davis, Megan and Williams, George. 2021. *Everything You Need to Know about the Uluru Statement from the Heart.* Sydney: NewSouth Publishing.

Hobbs, Harry and Jones, Benjamin T. 2022. 'Egalitarian Nationhoods: A Political Theory in Defence of the Voice to Parliament in the Uluru Statement from the Heart'. *Australian Journal of Political Science* 57 (2): 129–44.

Ivison, Duncan. 2002. *Postcolonial Liberalism.* Cambridge: Cambridge University Press.

Ivison, Duncan. 2008. *Rights.* New York: Routledge.

Ivison, Duncan. 2017. 'Pluralising Political Legitimacy'. *Postcolonial Studies* 20 (1): 118–130.

Ivison, Duncan. 2020. *Can Liberal States Accommodate Indigenous Peoples?* Cambridge: Polity.

Kolodny, Niko. 2014. 'Rule over None I: What Justifies Democracy?' *Philosophy and Public Affairs* 42: 195–229.

Miller, David. 2000. 'In Defence of Nationality'. In *Citizenship and National Identity*, edited by David Miller, 24–40. Cambridge: Polity Press.

Mulgan, Richard. 1998. 'Citizenship and Legitimacy in Post-Colonial Australia'. In *Citizenship and Indigenous Australians: Changing Conceptions and Possibilities*, edited by Nicolas Peterson and Will Sanders, 179–195. Reshaping Australian Institutions: Cambridge University Press.

National Indigenous Australians Agency. 2021. *Indigenous Voice Co-Design Process Final Report to the Australian Government.* Canberra: Commonwealth of Australia.

O'Bryan, Katie and Gerber, Paula. 2023. 'Voice to Parliament: Debunking 10 Myths and Misconceptions'. *Monash Lens.* https://lens.monash.edu/@politics-society/2023/02/27/1385518/voice-to-parliament-debunking-10-myths-and-misconceptions.

Patton, Paul. 2009. 'Rawls and the Legitimacy of Australian Government'. *Australian Indigenous Law Review* 13 (2): 59–69.

Pearson, Noel. 2014. *A Rightful Place: Race, Recognition and a More Complete Commonwealth.* Quarterly Essay 55. Collingwood: Black Inc. Books.

Price, Jacinta Nampiginpa. 2023. 'Media Statement: 24 October 2023'. https://www.jacintaprice.com/24_october_2023 (accessed 5 February 2024).

Rawls, John. 2005. *Political Liberalism*, Expanded edition (2nd edn). New York: Columbia University Press.

Williams, Bernard. 2002. *Truth and Truthfulness: An Essay in Genealogy*. Princeton: Princeton University Press.

Williams, Bernard. 2005. 'Realism and Moralism in Political Theory'. In *In the Beginning Was the Deed: Realism and Moralism in Political Argument*, edited by Geoffrey Hawthorn, 2–15. Princeton: Princeton University Press.

Chapter 7

UNDERSTANDING THE COMPETING SOVEREIGNTY CLAIMS OF THE VOICE REFERENDUM

Ron Levy and Justin McCaul

Introduction

In a 'constitutional legitimacy crisis' (Appleby, Levy and Whalan 2023), two or more parties view the values underlying a constitution markedly differently, such that there is no single, practically authoritative view of how a constitutional disagreement between them should be resolved. The parties disagree not only about a constitution's essential normative foundations but also about who is authorised to resolve the disagreement. There are many kinds of constitutional legitimacy crises. But our interest in this chapter is in competing claims to constitutional sovereignty of Indigenous groups and the settler state – in particular, the Australian Commonwealth and its federal subunits.

Sovereignty claims are claims to legitimate ownership and authority over the land, law and political life within a given territory or in relation to a set of people (Cobb 2005, 118). Sovereignty conflicts raise a particularly caustic form of constitutional legitimacy crisis, due partly to divergent ideas about the foundations and implications of sovereignty. As Davis and Williams write, the 'term "sovereignty" is a widely used but contested term that can mean different things to different people' (2023, 165). Indeed, competing visions of sovereignty were mainstays of the rhetoric leading up to the 2023 referendum on the Aboriginal and Torres Strait Islander Voice. All sides made claims based on distinct perspectives of sovereignty. In this chapter, we focus on this competition of ideas in the Voice debate.

Claims of the state's *exclusive* sovereignty commonly arose. However, a close look reveals these claims' normatively problematic foundations. Some varieties of exclusive claims understood exclusivity as self-evident. Others relied for support on the authoritative statements of state institutions, notably courts. Neither type of argument could escape the problem of self-reference – or 'normative bootstrapping' (Levy 2025). Claims to the state's exclusive sovereignty relied on state perspectives, or on state institutions themselves, to justify the state's normative primacy.

The consequence of such bootstrapping rhetoric first may have been to contribute to the Voice reform's rejection by generating fears about creating (Albrechtsen 2023b) or amplifying Indigenous sovereignty. This rhetoric misunderstands the status of

Indigenous sovereignty, which – as a normative and political matter, rather than positive law – is already widely understood by Indigenous people and their supporters as existing. The bootstrapping perspective overlooks this normative and political reality.

A second consequence may be that, as bootstrapping assumptions seek to wish away sovereign divisions rather than address them via measures such as the Voice, they cause the constitutional legitimacy crisis to persist. As we will see, concretely this may seed Indigenous people's further frustration over their normative exclusion and deepen doubts about the legitimacy of the state's governance over their affairs. An enduring legitimacy crisis may be a source of legal inefficacy, poor policymaking, social harm and – ironically – worsening divisions.

We proceed as follows. We begin by outlining the general contours of constitutional legitimacy crises. We then analyse Voice campaign rhetoric, focusing in turn on normative claims of exclusive state sovereignty and of Indigenous sovereignty. We will see the bootstrapping pattern arise especially in the former. Indeed, after this discussion, bootstrapping may appear to have a certain inevitability in constitutional legitimacy crises implicating sovereignty. However, we will consider (necessarily briefly) potential crisis solutions that draw on the canon of deliberative democracy research and more particularly on 'deliberative constitutionalism' (Levy et al. 2018). We will argue that managing a constitutional legitimacy crisis effectively requires open and inclusive deliberation about constitutional foundations, including about questions of sovereignty.

Constitutional Legitimacy Crises and Intractability

Recall that a constitutional legitimacy crisis arises when the parties involved cannot agree which essential normative foundation of the constitution should resolve a constitutional dispute between them, nor who should be authorised to give a binding answer to the question. There are many kinds of constitutional legitimacy crises. For instance, budget crises arise in both established and incipient democracies in the context of separations of power. In Australia, the Dismissal was a budget dispute in which the underlying question concerned the relative powers of the chambers of parliament – a profoundly important question with contested answers. Elsewhere, budget crises have been both endemic and intractable, or even notorious. The United States has experienced cycles of federal government shutdowns since the 1970s, such as when Democrats have held the presidency and Republicans at least one chamber of Congress (Young 2014). The English Civil War was a formative contest between the king and Parliament over the 'power of the purse'.

These instances illustrate how foundational and divisive constitutional legitimacy crises may be. Yet, our specific interest in this chapter is in how Indigenous and other groups' claims of sovereignty raise a commonplace but unusually intractable species of constitutional legitimacy crisis. During the Voice debate, ideas of sovereignty often surfaced in the rhetoric of Voice opponents (both right and left) and proponents. As Hobbs (2020, 624) notes, '[i]n its Final Report, the Expert Panel noted that "at almost every consultation Aboriginal and Torres Strait Islander participants raised issues of sovereignty."' We will see that sovereignty talk also recurred in media and academic commentary. At root, whatever its many nuances, the sovereignty dispute in Australia is a contest between competing and often incompatible sovereignty claims. Claims on one side imagine ultimate and exclusive sovereignty residing in the state. Yet, for their part, Indigenous people and their supporters tend to recognise unceded Indigenous sovereignty, or sovereignties, challenging the state's exclusive claim (National Constitutional Convention 2017; Bedford 2023).

Variations of this type of dispute are globally ubiquitous and often far from harmless. The inclination to obey the law may require, in the first place, a sense of authorship over the law (Habermas 1998, 121). The disagreement over constitutional legitimacy in Australia has indeed led to a sense of exclusion among many Indigenous people who perceive their sovereignty ambitions as being unfairly dismissed or suppressed. Some commentators have drawn connections between contested legitimacy in Australia and the poor efficacy of state interventions in Indigenous affairs (e.g. the Northern Territory 'Intervention') (Altman 2007; Watson 2009a). Many constitutional legitimacy crises even engender concerted violence. Violence by the state has been a recurring feature of legitimacy disputes in settled states, including Australia (Mills 2016).

How is a constitutional legitimacy crisis, however, different from more ordinary constitutional disputes? After all, other kinds of constitutional disputes raise disagreements between foundational normative assumptions. For example, in debates about implying the freedom of political communication, underlying questions included what values the constitution rests upon (*Nationwide News Pty Ltd v Wills* (1992) 177 CLR 1). However, in such constitutional cases, it is plausible (if never quite easy) for a political community to achieve at least a working agreement, full perhaps of compromise but still sufficient to allow the parties eventually to move on to other matters. A sense of grievance, or outright 'normative fracture' (Levy, O'Flynn and Kong 2021, 98; Levy 2018), does not arise. The differing positions may either reconcile or persist, but these divisions over substantive policy do not cause a more basic rupture over the legitimacy of the state. A decision maker enjoying undisputed legitimacy generally remains capable of umpiring the dispute effectively: a court or other body provides an answer that will ultimately satisfy all of the parties, provided they have been adequately heard in the process (Tyler and Jackson 2014).

In a constitutional legitimacy crisis, these various expectations cannot be taken for granted. In a dispute over sovereignty, for example, a material question is whether the people or institutions purporting to resolve the matter may do so legitimately. Shared assumptions are elusive in this kind of case. The very matter in dispute is who possesses sovereignty and who, in turn, can serve as a legitimate umpire of the dispute. It is the uncertainty over who possesses the normative capacity to bring the dispute to an end that distinguishes a constitutional legitimacy crisis most of all.

We may be tempted to describe the competing parties' arguments as self-serving. After all, each party happens to identify a normative constitutional foundation that justifies its own preferred outcome. Those who speak on behalf of the state often assume the state's sovereignty is ultimate and exclusive, which would straightforwardly settle in their favour both the main question of sovereignty and the further question of who is authorised to answer the question. Many Indigenous groups believe, in turn, that their own unceded sovereignty serves as a counterweight or exception to state sovereignty. Yet, rather than self-serving, we could describe these differing positions more charitably as reflections of distinct experiences. Many non-Indigenous people develop their ideas of the monolithic nature and authority of the state in a milieu where such ideas are taken for granted. While distinct Indigenous experiences and histories clearly contest these ideas, these distinctive perspectives still have limited exposure within schools and popular culture in Australia and elsewhere (Hickling-Hudson and Ahlquist 2003; Hradsky 2022).

Whatever the cause, normative bootstrapping describes the key logical fault that often arises when parties to the crisis press their own competing visions of legitimacy. Some parties favour outcomes to the crisis that presuppose the picture of legitimacy they favour. The argument, therefore, relies on itself for support. Notably, the statist argument (as we will see) distils to the pattern: 'the state has exclusive sovereignty, therefore Indigenous sovereignty is excluded'. This is weak reasoning based on a selective normative claim, whose selectivity would make wide consensus about the claim unlikely. The normative requirement here of reasonable acceptability to all affected parties is rooted in 'public reason' and related assumptions of liberal theory (Rawls 1996, 1997; Gaus 2011). Absent wide acceptance, including among the Indigenous people most affected, selective normative argumentation cannot give rise to stable constitutional arrangements willingly adhered to by all groups.

Prior to the Voice debate, the most prominent historical Australian example of normative bootstrapping involving sovereignty had been the portion of the Mabo decision (*Mabo v Queensland [No 2]* (1992) 175 CLR 1) in which the High Court, having recognised native title, nevertheless said it was barred from recognising the Indigenous sovereignty that native title seems to entail (31–32, Brennan J; 81–82, Deane and Gaudron JJ). (See also *New South Wales v Commonwealth* (1975) 135 CLR 337.) Native title is no mere property right in land or water – that is, relatively thin and akin to basic freehold rights. It is, rather, an elaborate bundle of entitlements to particular spaces, uses and power relations. As one of us has written elsewhere, '[n]ative title is based on the recognition of Indigenous traditional law and custom, prompting legal scholars to argue the recognition of native title is inherently the recognition of Indigenous polities, their sovereignty and capacity for self-government' (McCaul 2023a; see also Dodson 1995; McCaul 2023b). Indeed, Strelein describes native title as 'a right or title of a group to order their own affairs, at least in relation to land' (Strelein 2009, 123). Entailed in this view is that a political community establishes and governs native title in numerous aspects. However, the *Mabo* Court held that it could not judicially recognise Indigenous sovereignty because the Court itself is empowered under the authority of the sovereign Australian state.

In sum, in a constitutional legitimacy crisis, we see those purporting to settle the crisis relying on deeply subjective and partial normative claims – indeed, on the very claims that are contested in the crisis. When we turn to analysing Voice campaign rhetoric in the third and fourth sections, we will see similar bootstrapping patterns in many of the normative claims – especially on behalf of exclusionary statist views of sovereignty.

Contested Visions of Sovereignty: Statist Perspectives

Amidst the public discourse of the Voice referendum campaign, Janet Albrechtsen was one of the leading voices on the right presenting conclusory claims that Indigenous people do not and cannot enjoy their own sovereignty. Albrechtsen, a commentator for *The Australian* newspaper, engaged with academic writing in the area by Voice advocates. She correctly discerned that some such writing claimed the Voice would assume or instantiate Indigenous sovereignty (Appleby, Levy and Whalan 2023, cited in Albrechtsen 2023a). Yet Albrechtsen's view was that the sovereignty of the Australian state is exclusive, inviolable and plainly incompatible with Indigenous sovereignty. She denied that, as she put it, 'black sovereignty has not been ceded'. Arguments similar to hers have indeed been made in courts (e.g. *Love v Commonwealth* (2020) 270 CLR 152; *Coe v Commonwealth* (1979) 53 ALJR 403) and frequently over time in the political arena (e.g. John Howard, cited in Harris 2023).

However, such arguments demonstrate a first kind of normative bootstrapping, which leaves the basis for the assumption of exclusive state sovereignty simply undefended. Presumably, Albrechtsen and others do not believe it needs defending; it is self-evident, even axiomatic. Bare conclusory statements asserting the state's exclusive sovereignty, or an absence of Indigenous sovereignty, appeared in media commentary, submissions to a Voice Parliamentary inquiry and the official Voice Pamphlet. For instance:

- 'Changes on how Australia is governed by a concept of dual sovereignty, or "co-government" will further divide our nation based on the false assertion of an Aboriginal nation that has never surrendered sovereignty to British Settlement' (submission of Robert S. Nixon to Joint Select Committee 2023, 1).
- 'Australians need to understand that the Voice will be used to support the demands for recognition of coexisting sovereignty, a Makarrata commission designed to produce a treaty and monetary compensation, and a rewriting of Australian history' (Terence Cole, cited in Australian Electoral Commission 2023, 13).
- 'I reject the idea of Aboriginal sovereignty as legally and historically unsustainable' (submission of Joe Stella to Joint Select Committee 2023, 29).

In light of our criticisms above regarding self-serving or perspectivally narrow reasons, this genre of argument is problematic. As a descriptive matter, Indigenous people and their supporters in Australia clearly understand Indigenous sovereignty as having persisted since colonisation began. The matter cannot be settled solely from the settler state's perspective. Even majority opinion or dominant state institutions cannot dispose of a minority's sovereignty claims, either in normative terms or as a practical political matter. Failing to resolve a constitutional legitimacy crisis to the satisfaction of all affected parties is, as we saw, liable only to cause the crisis to linger – along with its societal consequences.

On the left side of opposition to the Voice, critics such as Lidia Thorpe, a Gunnai, Gunditjmara and Djab Wurrung woman who sits in the Australian Senate, relied on conclusory arguments in certain respects similar to those of critics on the right. Thorpe's argument against the Voice (and in favour of a treaty) rested partly on the proposition that recognising Indigenous political power in the Australian Constitution amounted to co-opting Indigenous power and an implicit surrender of sovereignty (Lino 2023, 96). In her words, 'we need to be 100% satisfied that we're not ceding our sovereign rights by going into the colonisers "sovereign" rule book' (Thorpe cited in Gregoire 2022). Senator Thorpe was not alone in raising such concerns (see e.g. additional statements quoted in Berry 2024; Davis and Williams 2023, 164–65; and submissions by Feminist Legal Clinic Inc., Teela Reid, and Treaty Before Voice to Joint Select Committee 2023).

But this position perhaps cedes too much ground. The Voice's constitutional entrenchment would have directly declared nothing in law about sovereignty. The claim that it indirectly entailed the giving up of sovereignty was more plausible, but ultimately still doubtful (Davis 2012; Lino 2023). Yet, in any case, as we have seen, those who agree that Indigenous sovereignty remains alive and robust see such sovereignty as having an existence independent of positive laws. These perspectives would understand even an explicit and formal constitutional denial of Indigenous sovereignty as ineffective (Lino 2023; Davis and Williams 2023, 165–66). This point has often been made by Indigenous and other scholars and activists, noting, for example, the 'inalienable relationship to the land' of Indigenous people (Moreton-Robinson 2015, 11; Graham 1999). Nevertheless, some leaders in the Blak Sovereign Movement (BSM) seemed to concede a key position of Voice opponents on the right, who understood Indigenous sovereignty as a ready subject of state power – and state extinguishment.

Granted, the critical positions on the left were often stronger than those on the right in a key sense. The former could be read as making pragmatic rather than conceptual or legal arguments. While constitutional recognition would not have formally extinguished sovereignty, it could plausibly have diminished Indigenous power in effect by subjecting Indigenous power to state control. For instance, the efficacy of the Voice was to be conditional on Parliament's or the executive's willingness to hear it (Lindell 2021). The Voice arguably may also have taken some of the energy out of the movement for Indigenous sovereignty. Empirically, however, these predictions were far from settled prospects. Rather than lose steam, autonomy movements ranging from Quebec to Catalonia have appeared to draw momentum, or to solidify a sense of ethnonational distinctiveness, when boosted through stable constitutional voices allowing for the expression of distinct views (i.e. Quebec's formal status as a province and Catalonia's as an autonomous region: Fenwick 1981, 199; Guibernau 2013, 376). Thus, the empirical claims were at best tendentious and unresolved.

Some of the normative arguments presented in support of state sovereign exclusivity during the referendum campaign were not wholly conclusory but instead sought to support the claim. For instance, some parliamentary submissions explained that the proof of exclusive state sovereignty lies in the judicial acknowledgement or affirmation of this principle:

- '[F]our of the paragraphs of the Uluru Statement from the Heart relate to sovereignty which was "never ceded" and "co-exists with the sovereignty of the Crown"; this is a fiction already dealt with by the High Court' (submission of David Scown to Joint Select Committee 2023, 32; see also submission of Terence Rhoderic Hudson Cole AO RFD KC, 128).

This type of contribution tries to show its work and defend its conclusions and thus improves on conclusory claims. However, the reasons given ultimately recap the bootstrapping problem. It remains unclear whether the formal decisions of judges should count towards settling a constitutional legitimacy crisis. From one perspective, the High Court is indeed the constitution's ultimate legitimate arbiter – but only from one perspective. There remain strong differences over this conclusion among the parties at odds in the crisis. As long as a robust and widespread view persists that Indigenous sovereignty precedes (or coexists with) state sovereignty and state institutions, then the disagreement at the core of the crisis endures.

Thus, even the more sophisticated conceptions raised themselves up by their own bootstraps, albeit through multiple steps. At root, the argument remained that state sovereignty is exclusive, in this case, because the institutions of the state declare it as such. However, a constitutional legitimacy crisis definitionally involves parties who are situated outside of this normative perspective; they disagree with – and are unlikely to be swayed by – this self-referential vision.

Other perspectives also implicitly sought to avoid conclusory arguments by tying claims of exclusionary sovereignty to further values. For instance, Hobbs and Jones identify a 'proprietary' concept of sovereignty in some rhetoric opposing the Voice. The argument put forward was that conquest yields a form of exclusive ownership. Thus, 'the justification of Australian nationhood is tied to the legitimacy of colonisation and the denial of Aboriginal and Torres Strait Islander peoples' inherent sovereignty' (Hobbs and Jones 2022, 135). However, this perspective ultimately fails to explain its own legitimacy – how it differs, for example, from a basic might-makes-right conception rejected in liberal thought. Indeed, this particular value seems to rest on what, in public reason theory, is called a 'comprehensive doctrine' (Rawls 1996, 54–56) – a set of subjective ideals and reasons particular to a given group and tending to serve the group's interests in a selective way. Such ideals are not 'public' – they cannot be reasonably extended to all groups – and other groups are unlikely to accede to their exclusionary assumptions.

Each of the exclusionary statist views of sovereignty that we have seen shares this deficiency. None accounts for its assumption of exclusive rather than shared state sovereignty. Each fails to explain why contrary normative claims, such as assertions of continuing Indigenous sovereignties, lack legitimacy. When multiple values contend for a spot among the value foundations of the constitutional system (or systems), none alone can unproblematically claim pre-eminence in a normative or practical political sense. We will see this more vividly as we turn next to review a set of Indigenous perspectives on sovereignty that were raised in the lead-up to the Voice referendum and that call state sovereign exclusivity into question.

Contested Visions of Sovereignty: Indigenous Perspectives

The constitutional legitimacy crisis central to this chapter begins, of course, with the British assertions of sovereignty in 1770/1788 over the lands now known as Australia. Contrary claims of unceded Indigenous sovereignty are united by the rejection of *terra nullius* that, until the *Mabo* decision, designated Australia as vacant or empty, without a system of law (or at least one recognisable to Europeans) (Miller 2010, 10). However, beyond this, at least three types of Indigenous sovereignty claims can be located: the first is premised upon a deep spiritual connection to land, the second is that of prior occupation and the third asserts that Indigenous sovereignty should lead to forms of separation from the state. Each offers a partly unique yet also frequently overlapping articulation of Indigenous sovereignty claims. All agree that Indigenous sovereignty has never been ceded.

Senior Yolngu leader Galarrwuy Yunupingu describes his connection to country in spiritual terms: the Yolngu have their own laws, which are retold through ceremonial songs to ensure all members of the Yolngu clan know them. Law is possessed, practised and passed on from parents to other generations through speaking language, shared spiritual beliefs and living lives bound together (Yunupingu 2008).

This notion of Indigenous claims to sovereignty as tied to, or emanating from, the deep spiritual connection that Aboriginal and Torres Strait Islander people have to their traditional lands is also expressed in the Uluru Statement from the Heart, which preceded the Voice campaign. In part, it states, that 'Aboriginal and Torres Strait Islander tribes were the first sovereign Nations of the Australian continent and its adjacent islands and possessed it under our own laws and customs' (2017). The Statement continues:

> This sovereignty is a spiritual notion: the ancestral tie between the land, or 'mother nature', and the Aboriginal and Torres Strait Islander peoples who were born therefrom, remain attached thereto, and must one day return thither to be united with our ancestors. This link is the basis of the ownership of the soil, or better, of sovereignty. It has never been ceded or extinguished, and co-exists with the sovereignty of the Crown. (Referendum Council 2017)

Irene Watson, a member of the Tanganekald, Meintangk Boandik First Nations Peoples and legal scholar, explains that Indigenous people hold a cultural and spiritual view of the world and land and of their place in the landscape. For Watson, First Nations law and sovereignty represent 'Raw Law' that is devoid of the baggage of colonialism. The colonial legal system is one imposed upon Indigenous people; by contrast, Raw Law is not imposed but rather lived: 'in the beginning was the country of my peoples, the Coorong in South Australia, *ruwi* to the Tanganekald people that was sung by the ancestors, who sang our beginnings, from *Kaldowinyer*' (Watson 2009b, 37).

Emphasising the spiritual basis of land in Indigenous sovereignty claims, Watson argues that Indigenous peoples hold a different understanding about the origins of law: 'we know that law is everywhere in the land and the natural world. We are belonging to and surrounded by law. We are in relationships with law and all of those relationships are by humans as beings of law and all living things are beings of law' (Watson 2017, 110). Professor Marcia Langton, a descendant of the Yiman and Bidjara nations, explains that the spiritual character of Indigenous sovereignty claims is both recognition of the legal personality of Indigenous polities and the complex social and emotional attachment to land: 'it is this attachment to places through ancestors and traditions that enables us (Indigenous people) to claim a sovereignty that pre-dates the British Crown'

(Langton and Corn 2023, 20). Indeed, in the 2020 *Love/Thoms* case *(Love v Commonwealth of Australia; Thoms v Commonwealth of Australia* (2020) 270 CLR 152), all seven justices made reference to the 'special spiritual and cultural connection' Indigenous people have to their 'country' (Lavery 2020, 168).

Related to the claims of sovereignty based on deep spiritual attachment to land are assertions of Indigenous sovereignty on the basis of prior occupation. As McHugh (2011, 1) notes, '[c]ommon law aboriginal [native] title is concerned with the effect of Crown sovereignty of the pre-existing property rights of the tribal inhabitants.' Much has been made of Justice Gordon's words in Love/Thoms defining the connection of Indigenous people to their traditional lands and waters as having existed and persisted before and after (British) settlement and federation: 'it is older and deeper than the Constitution' (*Love v Commonwealth of Australia; Thoms v Commonwealth of Australia* (2020) 270 CLR 152, 124).

The first Indigenous challenge to *terra nullius* was the 1971 Gove Peninsula land rights case (*Milirrpum v Nabalco Pty Ltd* (1971) 17 FLR 141) in the Northern Territory. In this case, the Yolngu Traditional Owners claimed to possess native title rights over their entire traditional land estate. The Yolngu were responding to a decision of the Australian government in 1963 to grant a 40-year mining lease to Nabalco to mine bauxite, near Gove in Arnhem Land. Justice Blackburn rejected the Yolngu claim of native title as having no existence within Australian common law. Yet he recognized that the Yolngu did possess a system of law: 'if ever a system could be called "a government of law, and not of men"', it was in the evidence before him (*Milirrpum v Nabalco Pty Ltd* (1971) 17 FLR 141, 266–67). This law began many millennia before the arrival of the British in 1770/1788. Through law, Indigenous people express their humanity; honour ancestors; care for their homeland, families and communities; understand the past and present; and build for the future (Langton and Corn 2023, 29).

The recognition of native title in the *Mabo* judgment and *Native Title Act 1993* (Cth) acknowledges that Indigenous people, as holders of property rights, have in effect long had those rights, though they were disregarded by Australian law until 1992. As we said earlier, by recognising native title on the basis of ongoing adherence to Indigenous law and custom, the recognition of native title in Australia creates an inconsistency in the doctrine of the monopoly of Crown sovereignty by recognising the existence of Indigenous 'law' (Anker 2008).

The final expression of Indigenous sovereignty that gained prominence during the Voice referendum debates is the BSM, which to varying degrees has a secessionist aspect. As we saw, Lidia Thorpe has been a leading advocate of BSM, which asserts that Indigenous sovereignty has never been ceded and does not coexist with the sovereignty of the Crown. Speaking in the Senate, Thorpe criticised the Voice referendum for framing Indigenous sovereignty as a simple Yes or No binary, although a No outcome would be a win for the BSM: 'our sovereignty has never been ceded. We have not successfully and sustainably governed our own affairs for over 80,000 years to now hand it all over to an illegal occupation' (Commonwealth, Parliamentary Debates, The Senate, 21 June 2023, 2815, Lidia Thorpe).

Michael Mansell, a Palawa man and lawyer from Tasmania, has been another advocate of greater separation between Indigenous groups and the state. According to Mansell, only the granting of a new and separate Indigenous state for Aboriginal and Torres Strait Islander people within the Australian federation would give proper expression to Indigenous sovereignty (Mansell 2016; see also Grant 2017). Mansell argues for the creation of a seventh state under section 121 of the Constitution. His preferred option thus draws upon Australia's federal system of governance, which distributes power among the levels of government (Mansell 2016, 198).

Mansell, like Thorpe, was critical of the Voice to Parliament as a form of recognition relying on the settler state and ultimately incorporating rather than giving a distinct status to Indigenous sovereignty within the Australian legal and political system. To BSM advocates, resolution of the situation of coexisting sovereignty claims requires that Indigenous people be afforded some form of secession or separateness from the state. BSM arguments during the course of the Voice campaign asserted that Indigenous sovereignty is heterogeneous, inherent to each individual group and not dependent upon recognition from or extinguished by the settler state.

Each expression of Indigenous sovereignty incorporates elements of spiritual connection, prior occupation and unceded sovereignty. Each rejects *terra nullius*, and each also rejects statist perspectives purporting to displace Indigenous sovereignty. Among the rejected positions are those of the Australian courts, which, as we saw, have repeatedly denied any Indigenous sovereignty coexisting with that of the Crown. This is clearly at odds with the position of those Indigenous Australians who maintain their sovereignties are deeply spiritual, heterogeneous and never ceded (Aird and Ardill 2023).

What Is to Be Done? Managing Incommensurable Sovereignty Claims

Given the bootstrapping problem that a constitutional legitimacy crisis over sovereignty may raise, is there a better way to approach a referendum campaign? Given the groundwork of the previous sections, we argue that at a minimum the Yes campaign for the Voice frequently was hobbled by insufficient deliberation about Indigenous peoples' sovereignty. Exactly how much this factor affected the national vote is beyond our scope; our aim is to identify a distinct conceptual species of problem, which the polling studies after the vote did not (and perhaps could not ever precisely) quantify (Biddle et al. 2023). In light of the previous two sections, we think it plausible that competing visions of sovereignty were often influential in the referendum debate. As we saw, Indigenous people themselves have often discussed their own sovereignty. In the long lead-up to the Voice referendum, sovereignty talk was ubiquitous – including in the Uluru Statement from the Heart itself. As we also saw, the No campaign frequently neglected nuanced analyses of Indigenous sovereignty and often fell back instead upon conclusory and self-referential claims. The campaign, therefore, often lacked deliberation adhering to principles of public reason and incorporating genuine knowledge of, and concern for, Indigenous people's claims.

What could have been done differently? There are distinctly better and worse ways to approach referendum design. Referendums fall along a spectrum from more deliberative democratic (e.g. the 2014 Scottish independence referendum; see Tierney 2016) to less deliberative democratic (e.g. the 2016 Brexit referendum; see Marshall and Drieschova 2018). Deliberative democratic ideals that better referendums pursue include mutual engagement between the parties' normative arguments (the ideal of *other-regarding discussion*). The parties should also give reasons, such that the merits of each position can be considered (*reason-giving*). Reasons given should in turn be public in nature, that is, reasonably accessible and agreeable to multiple parties (*public reason*). And any deliberations should proceed with a minimum of prejudgment (*flexibility*). Also importantly, all reasonable normative propositions held by all affected groups should be tabled for discussion (*inclusivity*). Finally, and relatedly, participants in the deliberative process must be presented with the historical and current societal contexts that may make normative claims salient (*information exposure*). (On these various ideals, see Levy and Orr 2016, 21–23.)

These are undeniably high ideals. They pose challenging requirements for any democracy – not least in a referendum campaign, which tends if anything to be a rhetorical free-for-all rather than an opportunity for considered and inclusive deliberation. Yet, a vast canon of institutionalist deliberative democracy research outlines means by which at least some deliberative ideals can be realised at least some of the time. More particularly, conscious design for a 'deliberative referendum' has many of the objectives just noted, with a range of specific models trialled around the world (Levy, O'Flynn and Kong 2021; Tierney 2013; Leib 2006).

We do not aim to catalogue all available institutional options for deliberative referendum design. We focus here, instead, on one especially apt approach used around the world thousands of times thus far, both on its own and in connection with referendums. The 'deliberative mini-public' is a randomly chosen decision-making body selected from the voting population, but demographically representative of that wider population. After an extended period of learning and facilitated deliberation across demographic and ideological lines, these small bodies are often able to bridge normative divides between groups otherwise at odds. They have been used successfully many times, including on deeply divisive matters (e.g. abortion and armed conflict; Suiter et al. 2022; Khuri 2004).

A mini-public could serve as an authoritative, neutral (yet descriptively representative) body capable of generating trusted guidance for voters in a referendum campaign. The model may widen exposure of voters to information and normative claims on matters such as Indigenous sovereignty. In the lead-up to the Voice campaign, a group of academic deliberative democrats and public lawyers from across Australia (including the present authors) devised a detailed plan for mini-public-led provision of information. This initiative would have seen a mini-public write technically accurate, accessible and non-partisan official information to be distributed to voters. This mini-public would not have (re)written the Voice referendum question; that question was the result of years of deliberation leading up to 2023 (including the Uluru process itself and the Regional Dialogues; Appleby and Davis 2018). The mini-public envisaged would instead have been a 'Citizens' Referendum Review' charged with providing accurate and trusted background information during the campaign. This might have offered a counterweight to the factual misstatements that were rife in the campaign, and which can undermine the democratic ideal of informed consent (Levy 2013, 563–64).

The Commonwealth government declined to use this deliberative democratic approach. Instead, members of parliament drawn from across the partisan spectrum wrote the official Yes/No pamphlet, inevitably producing an amalgam of both accurate and tendentious or misleading points and partisan normative claims. The pamphlet was incapable of providing a convincing fix to a key problem that many voters reported: that they possessed too little information about the reform (Biddle et al. 2023, 39, 53–54). In reality, there may have been a great deal of information available. But much of it (including the pamphlet) likely left voters only more confused, given the directly contradictory points contained within it, the varying quality of the information and the basic problem that many voters simply did not know which self-styled experts to believe. Indeed, polling studies showed that low trust tended to associate with a higher incidence of voting No (Biddle et al. 2023, 54).

After all of the funds, time and hope invested in the Voice, this significant constitutional proposal was unfortunately not given all of the institutional support it needed to succeed. At a minimum, the Commonwealth government should have provided voters with an unbiased source of information to help cast informed votes. The sovereignty issue, in particular, provided both context and a rationale for the Voice proposal (Appleby, Levy and Whalan 2023). Understanding the origins and nature of Indigenous sovereignty claims – for instance, their cultural, linguistic, historic and worldview bases – may have helped voters to understand the Voice proposal in context. As polling analysis has revealed, the prospect of division was top of many voters' minds (Biddle et al. 2023, 78). Yet as we have noted, many Voice proponents argue that divisions based on Indigenous sovereignty have already long existed; a more mature deliberation about sovereignty could have provided this missing perspective that challenges the narrative of a unified Australian public threatened by the Voice.

If, as we also noted above, some of the opposition to Indigenous sovereignty can be explained by insufficient exposure to issues of sovereignty, then the use of deliberative democratic mechanisms to prompt perspectival change and a broadening of views or understandings of sovereignty may have been a key missed opportunity. Voters whose political views first formed in milieus that largely ignored Indigenous sovereignty or its underpinnings could not be expected to have sympathy for the concept of Indigenous sovereignty. They may have seen it as a foreign or self-evidently absurd concept. In this light, empirical studies showing that deliberative mini-publics may engender trust and greater mutual awareness between distinct groups (e.g. Suiter, Farrell and O'Malley 2016) are especially relevant.

However, there are limits to the efficacy of deliberative referendum design. One is that seeking to prompt a greater understanding of sovereignty during the short duration of a referendum campaign may be too little, too late. The success of deliberative democratic institutional measures depends partly on the *deliberative capacities* of individual voters: their theoretical ability to reason in open-minded ways and to understand information and values pertinent to people other than themselves. Deliberative capacity is likely a function of early exposure to diverse perspectives and critical ideas through parenting or schooling (Nishiyama 2021; Englund 2016). Polling in the four decades before the Voice referendum indirectly suggested that deliberative capacity had been changing over time (Levy and McAllister 2022) – perhaps as instruction on Indigenous issues became more widespread. General Australian attitudes towards Indigenous people thus saw a long-rising trend of liberalisation. However, despite such rises, deliberative capacity and liberalisation on Indigenous matters differed between younger (more liberal) and older (less liberal) generations (Levy and McAllister 2022, 80).

In addition to questions of capacity, we must also acknowledge that overall citizen support for reforms such as the Voice may face another hard ceiling, given the further subset of voters who stubbornly subscribe to *comprehensive doctrines* (often variations on 'might makes right'), in spite of any contrary information or normative arguments they encounter. Indeed, this subset may include some who possess ample information about the 'other side' but refuse to adopt a wider moral view. Some may be 'motivated reasoners' (Kahan 2013), who argue strenuously for the policy positions that their own identity group espouses, hoping to remain a member of the group in good standing. Motivated reasoners are often adept at using factually selective claims or logical sophistry to achieve a 'win' against others in a policy contest. They do not consider in a genuine way – that is, from first principles and without preconception – the normative stakes at issue.

Nevertheless, despite these real limitations, in any referendum campaign there remain those who are open to taking the wider view, as well as those who are not so new to the matter that they lack adequate deliberative capacity. This is a potentially sizeable subgroup of voters open to considering first-principle normative questions on an inclusive basis. As Parkinson notes in relation to such 'ordinary people', 'it is not that [they] cannot deliberate, but that existing liberal democratic structures do not allow them the chance to develop those deliberative capacities' (Parkinson 2003, 186–87). Institutional design must often meet these voters halfway. Mini-publics could perhaps have provided more trusted and accurate information and arguments to help those voters widen and nuance their reasoning. Should a constitutional referendum connected to Indigenous sovereignty arise again, the old approaches to public information – including the partisan information pamphlet – must be retired. Instead, deliberative referendum design features may help voters understand the full spectrum of the reform's social, historical and normative origins and aims.

Conclusion

We have shown how a fundamental disagreement between the sides of the Voice referendum campaign over sovereignty instantiated a constitutional legitimacy crisis. Such a crisis is distinguished by its apparent intractability. The parties each base their arguments for a given constitutional outcome on distinct normative foundations drawn from their distinct experiences. Bridging the divide between these views is especially difficult, in turn, given the absence of an authoritative umpire to settle the crisis. The putative umpires that some parties turn to may 'play for one of the teams' (Tokaji 2010, 433), taking their authority from just one side of the normative debate. Under these circumstances, a constitutional legitimacy crisis can persist indefinitely and undermine the efficacy and claims to normative legitimacy of the dominant legal order.

Convincing the parties in a referendum to adopt a more deliberative approach is essential if the crisis – and its ongoing and often caustic societal effects – are to have any realistic chance of resolving. A genuinely impartial and deliberative, yet also representative, body such as a mini-public may have helped to umpire normative claims and other information in the Voice campaign. It could indeed have encouraged wider public consideration of claims on their merits without favouring a given outcome. While far from guaranteed, globally this model has had many successes at engendering deliberation and even at setting deliberative cues later picked up in wider public conversations (Warren and Gastil 2015). Though it can offer at best an incremental deliberative improvement, such deliberative referendum design must be considered in relation to any future constitutional reforms, particularly if those reforms implicate Indigenous sovereignties.

References

Aird, J. and Ardill, A. 2023. 'A "Kind of Sovereignty": Towards a Framework for the Recognition of First Nations Sovereignties at Common Law'. *Melbourne University Law Review* 46 (2): 330–371.

Albrechtsen, J. 2023a. 'Thorpe Wants Separatism Rather Than Reconciliation'. *The Weekend Australian*, 11 February: 21.

Albrechtsen, J. 2023b. 'Dear Voters, Please Read This Letter to Appreciate What "Yes" Will Mean'. *The Weekend Australian*, 8 April: 20.

Altman, J. C. 2007. 'The Howard Government's Northern Territory Intervention: Are Neo-Paternalism and Indigenous Development Compatible?'. Topical Issue No 16, Centre for Aboriginal Economic Policy Research.

Anker, K. 2008. 'The Law of the Other: Exploring the Paradox of Legal Pluralism in Australian Native Title'. In *Dealing with the Other: Australia's Faces and Interfaces*, edited by P. Lagayette. Paris: Sorbonne University Press.

Appleby, G. and Davis, M. 2018. 'The Uluru Statement and the Promises of Truth'. *Australian Historical Studies* 49 (1): 501–509.

Appleby, G., Levy, R. and Whalan, H. 2023. 'Voice Versus Rights: A First Nations Voice and the Australian Constitutional Crisis of Legitimacy'. *UNSW Law Journal* 46 (3): 761–790.

Australian Electoral Commission. 2023. 'Your Official YES|NO Referendum Pamphlet'.

Bedford, N. 2023. 'The Aftermath: What if The Voice Referendum Does Not Succeed?'. *Public Law Review* 34: 156–164.

Berry, M. 2024. 'The Voice Referendum'. *Journal of Australian Political Economy* 92: 240–248.

Biddle, N., Gray, M., McAllister, I. and Qvortrup, M. 2023. 'Detailed Analysis of the 2023 Voice to Parliament Referendum and Related Social and Political Attitudes'. ANU Centre for Social Research and Methods.

Cobb, A. J. 2005. 'Understanding Tribal Sovereignty: Definitions, Conceptualizations, and Interpretations'. *American Studies* 46 (3/4): 115–132.

Coe v Commonwealth (1979) 53 ALJR 403.

Commonwealth, 'Parliamentary Debates', The Senate, 23 June 2023.

Commonwealth of Australia. 2012. Recognising Aboriginal and Torres Strait Islander Peoples in the Constitution: Report of the Expert Panel.

Davis, M. 2012. 'Constitutional Reform Does Not Foreclose on Aboriginal Sovereignty'. *Indigenous Law Bulletin* 8 (1): 12–14.

Davis, M. and Williams, G. 2023. *Everything You Need to Know About the Voice.* Sydney: UNSW Press.

Dodson, M. 1995. 'From "Lore" to "Law": Indigenous Rights and Australian Legal Systems'. *Aboriginal Law Bulletin* 3 (72): 2–3.

Englund, T. 2016. 'On Moral Education through Deliberative Communication'. *Journal of Curriculum Studies* 48 (1): 58–76.

Fenwick, R. 1981. 'Social Change and Ethnic Nationalism: An Historical Analysis of the Separatist Movement in Quebec'. *Comparative Studies in Society and History* 23 (2): 196–216.

Gaus, G. F. 2011. *The Order of Public Reason: A Theory of Freedom and Morality in a Diverse and Bounded World.* New York: Cambridge University Press.

Graham, M. 1999. 'Some Thoughts about the Philosophical Underpinnings of Aboriginal Worldviews'. *Global Religions, Culture, and Ecology* 3 (2): 105–118.

Grant, S. 2017. 'An Indigenous Seventh State: A Radical Idea from a Constitutional Conservative'. *ABC News*, 2 June. [Online]

Gregoire, P. 2022. 'Analysis: Greens Senator Lidia Thorpe: "Voice to Parliament may Threaten First Nations Sovereignty"', 16 August, Issue 1357.

Guibernau, M. 2013. 'Secessionism in Catalonia: After Democracy'. *Ethnopolitics* 12 (4): 368–393.

Habermas, J. 1998. *Between Facts and Norms.* Maiden: MIT Press.

Harris, B. 2023. *Treaty-Making and Its Limitations. In Indigenous Peoples and Constitutional Reform in Australia: Beyond Mere Recognition*, 87–118. Singapore: Springer Nature.

Hickling-Hudson, A. and Ahlquist, R. 2003. 'Contesting the Curriculum in the Schooling of Indigenous Children in Australia and the United States: From Eurocentrism to Culturally Powerful Pedagogies'. *Comparative Education Review* 47 (1): 64–89.

Hobbs, H. 2020. 'The Road to Uluru: Constitutional Recognition and the UN Declaration on the Rights of Indigenous Peoples'. *Australian Journal of Politics & History* 66 (4): 613–632.

Hobbs, H. and Jones, B. T. 2022. 'Egalitarian Nationhoods: A Political Theory in Defence of the Voice to Parliament in the Uluru Statement from the Heart'. *Australian Journal of Political Science* 57 (2): 129–144.

Hradsky, D. 2022. 'Education for Reconciliation? Understanding and Acknowledging the History of Teaching First Nations Content in Victoria, Australia'. *History of Education* 51 (1): 135–155.

Joint Select Committee on the Aboriginal and Torres Strait Islander Voice Referendum inquiry into Constitution Alteration (Aboriginal and Torres Strait Islander Voice) 2023.

Kahan, D. M. 2013. 'Ideology, Motivated Reasoning, and Cognitive Reflection'. *Judgment and Decision Making* 8 (4): 407–424.

Khuri, M. L. 2004. 'Facilitating Arab-Jewish Intergroup Dialogue in the College Setting'. *Race Ethnicity and Education.* 7 (3): 229–250.

Langton, M. and Corn, A. 2023. *First Knowledges Law: The Way of the Ancestors.* Port Melbourne: Thames & Hudson Australia Pty Ltd.

Lavery, D. 2020. 'Judicial Distancing in the High Court: *Love/Thoms v Commonwealth*'. *James Cook University Law Review* 26: 159–174.

Leib, E. J. 2006. 'Can Direct Democracy Be Made Deliberative?' *Buffalo Law Review* 54: 903–925.

Levy, R. 2013. '"Deliberative Voting": Realising Constitutional Referendum Democracy'. *Public Law* 555: 563–564.

Levy, R. 2018. '"Shotgun Referendums": Popular Deliberation and Constitutional Settlement in Conflict Societies'. *Melbourne University Law Review* 41 (3): 1237–1277.

Levy, R. 2025. 'Right to a Referendum, or Duty to Deliberate? Rethinking Normative Entitlements to Secession'. *Politics and Governance*, 13.

Levy, R., Kong, H., Orr, G. and King, J. (eds.). 2018. *The Cambridge Handbook of Deliberative Constitutionalism.* Cambridge: Cambridge University Press.

Levy, R. and McAllister, I. 2022. 'Public Opinion on Indigenous Issues and Constitutional Recognition: Three Decades of Liberalisation'. *Australian Journal of Political Science* 57 (1): 75–92.

Levy, R., O'Flynn, I. and Kong, H. L. 2021. *Deliberative Peace Referendums.* Oxford: Oxford University Press.

Levy, R. and Orr, G. 2016. *The Law of Deliberative Democracy.* London: Routledge.

Lindell, G. 2021. 'The Relationship between Parliament and the Voice and the Importance of Enshrinement'. AUSPUBLAW, 2 March. https://www.auspublaw.org/blog/2021/03/the-relationship-between-parliament-and-the-voice-and-the-importance-of-enshrinement.

Lino, D. 2023. 'Why a First Nations Voice Will Not Extinguish Indigenous Sovereignty'. *Public Law Review* 34 (2): 95–102.

Love v Commonwealth (2020) 270 CLR 152.

Mabo v Queensland [No 2] (1992) 175 CLR 1.

Mansell, M. 2016. *Treaty and Statehood: Aboriginal Self Determination.* Sydney: The Federation Press.

Marshall, H. and Drieschova, A. 2018. 'Post-Truth Politics in the UK's Brexit Referendum'. JSTOR 26 (3): 89–106.

McCaul, J. 2023a. 'Deliberating Native Title: Deliberative Democracy and Native Title'. Doctoral Thesis, Australian National University.

McCaul, J. 2023b. *Caring for Country as Deliberative Policymaking' in Public Policy and Indigenous Futures.* Singapore: Springer Nature.

McHugh, P. G. 2011. *Aboriginal Title: The Modern Jurisprudence of Tribal Land Rights.* Oxford: Oxford University Press.

Milirrpum v Nabalco Pty Ltd (1971) 17 FLR 141.

Miller, R. J. et al. 2010. *Discovering Indigenous Lands: The Doctrine of Discovery in the English Colonies.* Oxford: Oxford University Press.

Mills, A., 2016. 'The Lifeworlds of Law: On Revitalizing Indigenous Legal Orders Today'. *McGill Law Journal* 61 (4): 847–884.

Moreton-Robinson, A. 2015. *The White Possessive: Property, Power and Indigenous Sovereignty.* Minneapolis: University of Minnesota Press.

National Constitutional Convention. 2017. 26 May. Uluru Statement from the Heart.

Nationwide News v Wills (1992) 177 CLR 1.

New South Wales v Commonwealth (1975) 135 CLR 337.

Nishiyama, K. 2021. 'Democratic Education in the Fourth Generation of Deliberative Democracy'. *Theory and Research in Education.* 19 (2): 109–126.

Parkinson, J. 2003. 'Legitimacy Problems in Deliberative Democracy'. *Political Studies* 51: 180–196.

Rawls, J. 1996. *Political Liberalism.* New York: Colombia University Press.

Rawls, J. 1997. 'The Idea of Public Reason Revisited'. *University of Chicago Law Review* 64 (3): 765–807.

Referendum Council. 2017. Final Report of the Referendum Council.

Strelein, L. 2009. *Compromised Jurisprudence: Native Title Cases Since Mabo.* Canberra: Aboriginal Studies Press.

Suiter, J., Farrell, D. M., Harris, C. and Murphy, P. 2022. 'Measuring Epistemic Deliberation on Polarized Issues: The Case of Abortion Provision in Ireland'. *Political Studies Review* 20 (4): 630–647.

Suiter, J., Farrell, D. M. and O'Malley, E. 2016. 'When do Deliberative Citizens Change their Opinions? Evidence from the Irish Citizens' Assembly'. *International Political Science Review* 37 (2): 198–212.

Tierney, S. 2013. 'Using Electoral Law to Construct a Deliberative Referendum Moving Beyond the Democratic Paradox'. *Election Law Journal* 12 (4): 509–523.
Tierney, S. 2016. 'The Scottish Independence Referendum: A Model of Good Practice in Direct Democracy'. In *The Scottish Independence Referendum: Constitutional and Political Implications*, edited by A. McHarg, T. Mullen, A. Page, and N. Walker, 53–73. Oxford: Oxford University Press.
Tokaji, D. P. 2010. 'Lowenstein Contra Lowenstein: Conflicts of Interest in Election Administration'. *Election Law Journal* 9 (4): 421–441.
Tyler, T. R., and Jackson, J. 2014. 'Popular Legitimacy and the Exercise of Legal Authority: Motivating Compliance, Cooperation, and Engagement'. Psychology, Public Policy, and Law 20 (1): 78–95. https://doi.org/10.1037/a0034514.
Warren, M. E. and Gastil, J. 2015. 'Can Deliberative Minipublics Address the Cognitive Challenges of Democratic Citizenship?' *Journal of Politics* 77 (2): 562–574.
Watson, I. 2009a. 'In the Northern Territory Intervention: What Is Saved or Rescued and at What Cost?'. *Cultural Studies Review* 15 (2): 45–60.
Watson, I. 2009b. 'Sovereign Spaces, Caring for Country, and the Homeless Position of Aboriginal Peoples'. *South Atlantic Quarterly* 108 (1): 27–51.
Watson, I. 2017. 'Civilizing Missions and Humanitarian Interventions'. In *Legal Violence and the Limits of the Law*, edited by A. Swiffen and J. Nichols, 110–121. London: Routledge.
Young, K. 2014. 'American Exceptionalism and Government Shutdowns: A Comparative Constitutional Reflection on the 2013 Lapse in Appropriations'. *Boston University Law Review* 94 (99): 991–1027.
Yunupingu, G. 2008. 'Tradition, Truth & Tomorrow'. *The Monthly*, December: 32–40.

Chapter 8

AUSTRALIAN CIVIC ENGAGEMENT: A CASE STUDY OF THE 2023 VOICE TO PARLIAMENT REFERENDUM

Andrea Carson, Phoebe Hayman and Justin Phillips

Introduction

A healthy democracy relies on an engaged citizenry able to freely elect their political representatives based on quality information in a diverse public sphere (McNair et al. 2017, 3). In Australia, compulsory voting ensures broad participation in elections. Beyond voting, civic engagement is supported by the media, which traditionally included print, TV and radio, in informing the public and fostering democratic involvement.

Since the commercialisation of the internet in the mid-1990s, however, the media landscape has transformed, both expanding and fragmenting at the same time. The development and proliferation of social media platforms, together with the lowered barriers to entry for news production – meaning you do not need to be a journalist or own an expensive printing press or broadcast licence to produce news – have enabled anyone with an internet connection and keyboard (or voice activation) to both consume and contribute media content.

The digital age is maturing, and the first wave of social media platforms are now being described as legacy platforms as new entrants arrive (Newman et al. 2024, 5). This high-choice, hybrid media environment that Van Aelst and colleagues (2017) describe, which combines legacy and social media, is reshaping civic engagement in Australian democracy. Political communication occurs across multiple mediums in order to target specific voters with key messages and, at the same time, reach the largest audience possible (Carson and Simon 2024). Like never before, Australians can access news from across the globe in real time. Social media platforms have made it easier for audiences to get information and for anyone to produce information and reach audiences. Access to news transcends old constraints that limited legacy media, such as time (e.g. radio bulletins), space (e.g. printed newspapers) and geography (e.g. broadcast signals). Digital and online platforms are central to how Australians send and receive information. Search aggregators such as Google and Bing are an intrinsic part of how Australians prioritise that information. As we move deeper into the twenty-first century, generative AI is supplementing search platforms to further shape Australians' news production and use and what are now termed legacy social media sites, such as X (formerly Twitter), Facebook and Instagram.

To highlight the crucial role of digital access in Australians' news consumption, the *2024 Digital News Report* finds most Australians (75 per cent) get their information online. In terms of the devices Australians use to access news online, the mobile phone is the most popular method (67 per cent) followed by the desktop (50 per cent) and less so the iPad (29 per cent) (Newman et al. 2024, 133). One-quarter of Australians rely on social media platforms as their main source of news (Park et al. 2024, 10). This means that online information is ubiquitous and easily accessible through the mobile devices in people's pockets and handbags. At the same time, traditional news outlets are using technology and deploying generative AI to produce journalism, with Australia's major news proprietor, News Corp, reportedly producing 3,000 articles a week using artificial intelligence (Newman et al. 2024, 133).

As this chapter will show, the change in the way Australians access news and how it is produced has weakened the once-powerful, traditional gatekeeping role of professional news organisations. In doing so, it liberates political actors and others from relying on journalists to mediate their message, instead enabling them to bypass mainstream media and speak directly to audiences through social media. This affordance widens the pool of influencers in Australian society beyond traditional politicians and other authority figures like business leaders, unions and subject-matter experts. Theoretically, it enables anyone who can build an online following or master how to draft a viral social media post to influence public opinion.

The 2023 Voice to Parliament referendum provides an excellent case study to illustrate the changing nature of civic engagement in Australian democracy and to provide further evidence for some of the features of the transformed information environment. This analysis draws on 3.3 million social media posts and mainstream stories relating to the Voice referendum[1] from media monitoring company Meltwater and complements this with Meta's CrowdTangle data, as well as YouTube and TikTok data, to better understand civic engagement in Australian democracy. The chapter proceeds as follows: it elaborates on the contemporary media landscape and discusses the role of negative campaigning and agenda-setting. It then provides background details about the Voice referendum, outlining key actors and messages of the major campaigns, before taking a closer look at civic engagement on specific social media platforms.

---

1. In consultation with Meltwater, we created a Boolean search query to identify Voice-specific discourse from their data sources. Our collection period spanned from 1 January 2023 to the referendum on 14 October 2023, capturing over 3.3 million mainstream and social media records referencing the Voice referendum.

Background and Literature

The Australian Media and Information Ecosystem

As stated, in the contemporary Australian media landscape, audience fragmentation is occurring as the information ecosystem expands. While Facebook remains the most used digital platform in Australia in 2024, Australians' reliance on Facebook for news is declining. This can be partly explained by Meta's decision to deprioritise news on its platforms (Riga 2024). Meanwhile, the use of video platforms (e.g. YouTube, TikTok) and encrypted apps (e.g. WhatsApp) for news is rising globally (Newman et al. 2024, 5).

Younger Australians, particularly Gen Z (those aged 18–26), are the heaviest users of social media to access news, according to 2024 survey findings. Sixty per cent of Gen Z say social media is their main news source (Park et al. 2024, 10). Yet, the most popular sources of news for people on social media still come from mainstream news brands and journalists; however, this is shifting with younger Australians, especially TikTok and Instagram users, accessing their news from 'ordinary' people explaining news events or by seeking alternative news sources on X (Park et al. 2024, 11). Meanwhile, older Australians are most likely to maintain life-long habits and turn on the television to get their news updates.

This shift to social media for news consumption compounds an already difficult problem for legacy media: news outlets are losing revenue and direct audience share to online competitors. The introduction of the world first legislation, the News Media Bargaining Code (NMBC) in 2021, provided short-term relief for traditional news providers when it directed Facebook and Google to enter deals to pay news providers for third-party news content that appeared on their sites in Australia (Bossio, Carson and Meese 2024). However, the platforms were not officially designated, meaning all deals were voluntary and unenforceable without designation. Three years later, as the deals have expired, Meta announced it would not renew the media contracts (Facebook 2024), leaving at least 13 of Australia's big news outlets with funding shortfalls (see Bossio, Carson and Meese 2024). While Google has renewed its deals, the withdrawal of Meta funding to media outlets estimated to be worth 70 million a year (Buckingham-Jones and Kehoe 2024) coincides with the slowing of the Australian economy and shrinking advertising revenues. This confluence of events has since triggered hundreds of editorial job cuts across Australian newsrooms (Verrender 2024) with implications for future news production.

At the same time as mainstream media face ongoing financial duress, trust in mainstream media is declining, and news distrust is continually increasing since 2016, climbing 8 points to 33 per cent in 2024 (Park et al. 2024, 9).[2] The report authors find this increase in distrust is growing faster than the falling rate of trust (trust fell 3 per cent

2. Distrust is a measure in the 2024 Digital News Report from survey respondents (N = 2,003) who say they disagree with the statement 'I can trust most news most of the time' (for more details, see Park et al. 2024, 113). Trust is a measure of those who answer affirmatively to this question.

over the same time period), suggesting active distrust in the news is a growing problem. It occurs amidst increasing public concern about information quality, particularly misinformation, with three out of four Australians expressing worry – an 11 per cent rise from 2022 – placing Australian concern about misinformation among the highest globally (Park et al. 2024, 9, 15, 19). Further, interest in the news is falling across countries, including Australia. Termed news avoidance, it is most common in women and young people according to cross-national surveys (Newman et al. 2024, 26).

Political Communication: Agenda-setting and the Role of Negative Campaigning

The evolving information environment not only disrupts mainstream media and news interests but also presents challenges and opportunities for political actors and those aiming to influence public opinion. These actors have adapted by crafting political communications across various media and digital platforms (see Carson and Jackman 2023). Social media has become an important part of any communication strategy and influences the dissemination and format of campaign materials (Stier et al. 2018). Moreover, as was shown with the 'No' campaign during the Voice to Parliament, often these messages are negative, as negativity can enhance the viral spread of a message (Klinger, Koc-Michalska and Russmann 2023).

Despite the digital affordances that make possible greater public interaction and engagement online, findings are mixed on the role negative campaigning plays in voter engagement and behaviour. Some researchers have shown incivility can dampen online engagement and interactivity, leading to unidirectional communication flow (Tenove et al. 2023).

On the other hand, researchers have consistently identified a negativity bias in public engagement (Fournier, Soroka and Nir 2020; Soroka 2014). Negative and politically charged messages can lead to greater dissemination across social media platforms, creating an incentive to employ negativity in messaging (Fine and Hunt 2023). It can extend beyond mere oppositional arguments and may encompass campaigning that spreads fear, anger, distrust or other negative affective responses (Klinger, Koc-Michalska and Russmann 2023). Incivility can be a feature of negativity and can vary from mildly rude to overtly threatening, and disproportionately targets women and people of colour (Tenove et al. 2023).

Further, social norms may shape the extent and visibility of engagement, as individuals consider whether it is socially acceptable to 'like' certain messages online (Phillips 2023). These are important factors to consider when discussing message virality and understanding how people engage with online content.

Negativity aside, social media also opens up opportunities for broader public engagement, allowing citizens to respond to debates and produce their own content online that can influence and set the public agenda. Scholars contend that this agenda-setting power, however, is somewhat flattened online, as campaigners, media, and users' political agendas may influence one another (Gilardi et al. 2022).

In addition to the growth of alternative news sources, such as Australia's 6 News, online personalities who create content focused on news and politics are a growing aspect of the digital media landscape, and many users regularly turn to these influential figures for news and analysis. This content is particularly popular on video-based platforms, such as YouTube and TikTok, and whether partisan or educational, it attracts large followings because it is often entertaining and critical of mainstream media (Fischer, Kolo and Mothes 2022). It is also defined by its appeal to 'authenticity' – a point of distinction with mainstream media, even as social media creators become increasingly professionalised (Lewis 2020). The next section reflects on the literature above concerning agenda-setting, negativity and distinctions between social and mainstream media content style with consideration of the 2023 Australian referendum. While this case enables us to analyse the impact of newer communication platforms on Australian democratic engagement, this analysis does not aim to establish a causative link that engagement changed voting behaviour. People vote the way they do for many reasons, and political campaigns are just one aspect of the influences on Australian political attitudes.

The 2023 Voice to Parliament Referendum

The Aboriginal and Torres Strait Islander Voice referendum held on 14 October 2023 was an historic milestone in Australian history, years in the making. The referendum aimed to amend the Australian Constitution to enshrine an Indigenous Voice to Parliament, enabling Aboriginal and Torres Strait Islanders to 'make representations to the Parliament and the Executive Government of the Commonwealth on matters relating to Aboriginal and Torres Strait Islander peoples' (Parliament of Australia 2023).

A year earlier, on the night of the Australian federal election in May 2022, the newly elected prime minister Anthony Albanese had committed his Labor government to the referendum arising out of the wishes of Indigenous Australians formalised in the 2017 Uluru Statement from the Heart (ABC News 2022).

Initially, the referendum had majority public support. Two-thirds of Australians surveyed said they would vote 'Yes' to the proposition (The Australia Institute 2022). A year later, the final outcome saw 60.1 per cent voting 'No' and 39.9 per cent voting 'Yes' at the national level. To pass, the referendum required a double majority, meaning a majority of voters nationwide and a majority in at least four of the six states. However, none of the states returned a majority 'Yes' vote, leading to the referendum's resounding failure.

What led to a 25 per cent drop in public support for the Voice to Parliament within a year – one of the largest falls in public opinion in any political context? (Carson et al. 2024, 34). Some commentators explained the fall by citing coarse public discourse during the campaign that featured both incivility and misinformation and disinformation (Wellauer, Williams and Brennan 2023). Researchers suggest the referendum failed as a result of institutional, structural and campaign effects (Carson et al. 2024, iii).

Referendum Campaigns

Typically, referenda are not apex campaigns such as elections that rely on centralised and disciplined messaging from opposing political parties. Rather, referendum campaigns can include a wide array of political actors and civil society actors (Udris and Eisenegger 2023). Before the referendum campaign begins, voters and the media often lack a prior understanding of which political actors will participate in the campaign or the stances they will take (Udris and Eisenegger 2023). Normatively speaking, the campaign and media's roles are to inform voters as they evaluate the proposal so they can make an informed choice. Typically, referenda do not map directly onto partisan lines and therefore campaign effects have been found to be stronger in referenda (De Vreese 2015; Udris and Eisenegger 2023). Turning to the major campaigns of the Australian 2023 referendum and its key actors, we also see that the 'Yes' and 'No' sides of Australia's 2023 referendum featured multiple campaigns and actors and did not fall directly down partisan lines.

Findings: Voice to Parliament – Campaigns, Actors and Social Media Use

'Yes' Campaign

Prominent campaigns for the 'Yes' side (each with multiple spokespersons) included 'Yes23', 'Liberals for Yes' and 'Uluru Statement from the Heart' – a group of First Nations people from the Uluru Dialogue who developed the Uluru Statement from the Heart in 2017 and who are hosted by the UNSW Indigenous Law Centre. Australians for Indigenous Constitutional Recognition was the formal title of a loose coalition of business, union advocates and grassroots campaigners that advocated for constitutional change under the banner Yes23. Across the campaigns, prominent 'Yes' Indigenous campaigners included Professor Megan Davis, Pat Anderson, Noel Pearson, Thomas Mayo and Rachel Perkin and Dean Parkin. Additionally, ALP politicians Linda Burney and the prime minister were key political voices advocating 'Yes' (see Figure 8.1).

'No' Campaign

Unlike the 'Yes' side, which featured multiple spokespersons, 'No' was predominantly represented in the media by Indigenous political figures Nyunggai Warren Mundine (former ALP national president turned Liberal Party federal candidate) and Jacinta Nampijinpa Price (a federal Senator with the Northern Territory's Country Liberal Party and affiliated with the Coalition), with Price leading the 'Fair Australia' campaign and Mundine fronting the 'Not my Voice' movement. Both were supported by the conservative lobby group Advance Australia (later known simply as Advance) and funded by its nonprofit arm Australians for Unity (AFU).

Advance came to prominence in the 2019 election as Advance Australia, claiming to represent 'mainstream Australia' by 'removing the far-left's control' and attacking the progressive activist group GetUp!. Advance's executive director, Matthew Sheahan, of

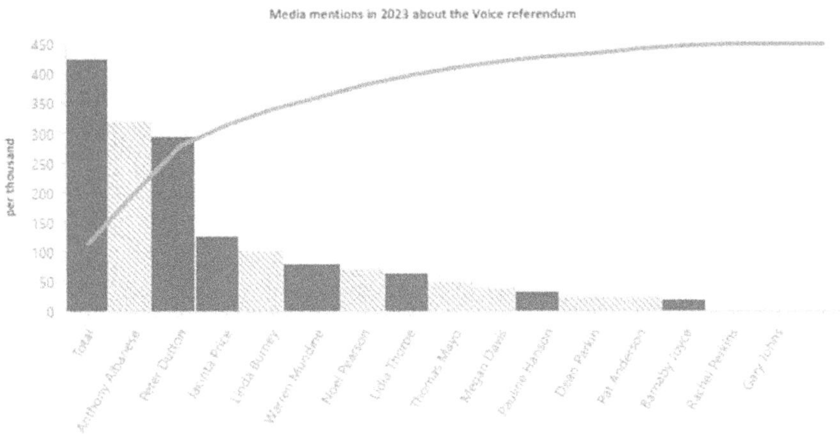

Figure 8.1 Share of mainstream and social media mentions of key Voice campaigners during the 2023 referendum. Source: Authors used Meltwater data and Boolean operators for the Voice, reproduced from data in Carson et al. (2024, 10). Note: Patterned represents 'Yes' campaigners and solid represents 'No' campaigners.

whom little is known and other Advance staff are registered as directors of 'Australians for Unity', along with Nyunggai Warren Mundine and former Labor federal politician Gary Johns (Carson et al. 2024, 12). Advance's 'Fair Australia' campaign was led by Jacinta Nampijinpa Price and its 'Not My Voice' campaign by Nyunggai Warren Mundine. Nampijinpa Price was a former spokesperson for Advance before entering politics (Carson et al. 2024, 12). Advance is closely aligned with conservative politics and backed by some wealthy businesspeople who crop up in AEC political donations records. AEC political donations data in February 2024 showed Advance received $5.2 million in donations and other receipts in the year following the 2022 federal election, more than double what it received the year before (Basford Canales and Evershed 2024).

Conservative politicians, including the Coalition leader Peter Dutton, also advocated publicly for the 'No' case. To potentially add to public confusion, 'The Blak sovereignty movement' was another campaign opposing the Voice proposition, but for diametrically opposite reasons to Advance. Former Australian Greens Party Senator turned Independent Lidia Thorpe led the Indigenous Blak Sovereignty campaign, which was described as a 'progressive No' vote, arguing the Voice mechanism was inadequate to deliver sovereignty to First Nations people. By contrast, Advance opposed the referendum on 'division' grounds, claiming the Voice gave Indigenous Australians privileged access to the parliament over other Australians, thereby dividing the Australian people into two groups. Advance's polling and focus groups identified early on that its 'division' message was strategically potent, claiming 'it was clear that division was the big, big factor for people voting "No"' (see Seccombe 2023).

The 'Yes' and 'No' cases were portrayed in mainstream media coverage and had large followings across social media platforms, exemplifying the complex hybrid media ecosystem in which political communication occurs. The next section analyses the discourse of the referendum campaign across key social media platforms: X (formerly Twitter), TikTok, YouTube and Meta: Facebook and Instagram. We analyse Meltwater data together with the social media content of the major campaigns and actors. We examine the affordances of these platforms, user demographics, campaign messages, public engagement and the tone and content of the referendum debate. Drawing on these results, we find that consistency of messaging across online spaces was a feature of the successful 'No' campaign. We also find that the 'Yes' campaign achieved greater audience reach across the platforms than 'No'. However, its messaging and advocates were more disparate. We also find that across platforms, the 'No' campaign adapted more obviously to the platform-specific norms and interactivity of online spaces than 'Yes', revealing a sophisticated understanding of how to craft effective campaigns on social media.

X (Formerly Known as Twitter)

In Australia, X users represent approximately 27 per cent of the population aged over 13, and the user base skews towards men (Kemp 2024). Despite recent declines in mainstream news' dominance of the platform, Australian politicians, journalists, academics and other key figures remain active and influential users (Park et al. 2024, 14), ensuring X's relevance as a site for agenda-setting and boosting issue salience.

The use of X for campaign communications was evident in the lead-up to the referendum. However, conspicuously, Advance did not campaign directly on X through its own account but instead relied on 'No' advocates Jacinta Nampijinpa Price and Nyunggai Warren Mundine to be the faces of the 'No' campaign on the platform, allowing them to attract many followers (about 120,000 followers between them) while Advance funded their campaigns. Price and Mundine overlapped in their key messages and at times appeared in the media together, indicating the strategic co-operation between them and Advance. The key actors of the 'Yes' campaign were also well represented on social media, although the accounts of the Uluru Statement and Yes23 did not attract the same number of followers as those of Price or Mundine (about 50,000 followers between them).

Hashtags associated with the 'Yes' campaign were more common on X than 'No' hashtags. Our analysis found hashtagged 'Yes' campaign tweets outnumbered self-labelled 'No' tweets by more than 3:1. 'Yes' hashtags were also more common than 'No' on Facebook and Instagram but less so than on X. However, it should be noted that posts associated with the 'No' campaign (and its well-known campaigners) sometimes included 'Yes' hashtags. As an example, Mundine tweeted in May 2023: 'Read my article busting 10 myths about the Indigenous Voice. #notmyvoice #yes23', and his subsequent re-tweet asking '#VoteNoAustralia or #VoteYesAustralia?' Similar attempts by 'Yes' campaigners to 'hijack' 'No' hashtags seemed less common. This suggests a deliberate strategy of disruption and negativity from the 'No' campaign that used the interactive elements of the platform to disseminate campaign messages to a broader audience beyond its base – including to get its message to pro-Voice supporters. Beyond the campaign actors, journalists, commentators, politicians and the public discussed the referendum on X.

Of the 2.34 million posts on X that mentioned the Voice from January 2023 to the close of the polls on October 14, we found X activity aligned closely with key campaigning moments and major news stories, confirming an interconnectedness between legacy media and social media use. Peak topics on X included the release of the question wording, the Constitution Alteration Bill passing through parliament and the referendum date announcement. The majority of high-performing topics about the referendum on X were usually in response to media coverage of campaign events. These were more commonly coordinated campaign events from the 'Yes' camp and included its release of Australian singer John Farnham starring in a television advertisement advocating 'Yes' and the 'Walk for Yes' rallies (see Figure 8.2). Clearly, these events attracted attention across both traditional and social media spheres.

Further, the aggregate data reveals that 'Yes' and 'No' supporters commented on common topics throughout the referendum, sometimes robustly, showing an exchange between the two camps rather than isolated echo chambers (see Phillips et al. 2024). In the latter stages of the campaign, this media coverage and the debate itself became a discussion topic on X. Users criticised referendum reporting variously, describing it as uncivil, negative, containing misinformation and racist. This focus on the negative

Figure 8.2 Peaks on X (Authors using Meltwater data 2024). Source: Carson et al. 2024, 15.

dynamics of the discourse served 'No's key message that the Voice was 'divisive' and added salience to its argument. As expected, as polling day neared, public engagement with the campaigns and referendum news increased, peaking on polling day.

Both sides of the referendum debate responded to campaign events and media coverage, indicating not only the enduring role of legacy media in agenda-setting but also the role of platforms in amplifying some narratives over others.

YouTube

YouTube attracts 82.5 per cent of Australian internet users with 26 per cent using it to access news content (Kemp 2024). Using YouTube for news is a growing global trend, with mainstream news providers facing significant competition from alternative news producers and online personalities (Newman et al. 2024, 53). The average user is likely younger, but the platform does not provide detailed information on user demographics.

During the referendum, content from mainstream news sources dominated the discussion across YouTube. *Sky News*, *ABC*, *Nine* and *Guardian Australia*, along with the government-funded 'Civics Australia' account, which provided information on referenda in satirical cartoon form, were notable YouTube news contributors. YouTube personalities also featured prominently. Many of these accounts, such as 'Aussie Law' or 'Auspol Explained', are framed as educational and 'unbiased' resources, expressing their intention to promote information rather than opinion or argument. The popularity of their content explaining the Australian Constitution, the referendum process and the proposed Voice to Parliament indicates users' interest in alternative information sources. Other accounts, such as 'Danger Dan', 'The Podcast of the Lotus Eaters' or 'Australian Agenda', were overtly critical of the referendum and attracted views ranging from 154 thousand down to 20 thousand.

The official campaigns all had active YouTube accounts during the referendum (see Table 8.1). Yes23 ran a popular series of videos featuring 'Local Voices' – with a combination of prominent Indigenous figures such as Australian Olympian Cathy Freeman and AFL football great Adam Goodes as well as everyday Indigenous Australians expressing their views and motivations for voting 'Yes'. These short-form videos, alongside most of the content posted by Yes23 on YouTube, were typically less than 30 seconds and appear to have been primarily produced as advertisements – as production values were high, and they featured Yes23 branding and official authorisations.

The Uluru Statement's YouTube account exclusively featured advertisements for the 'Yes' campaign and extended versions of these ads. These videos, such as the John Farnham advertisement, were played across media platforms including television.

This approach was reflected in some of Advance's content, which included longer versions of material used elsewhere. Although posting far less content on the referendum in total (just four videos), some of Advance's content was more platform-specific, including exposés or the 'secrets' behind the 'Yes' campaign and its activists. This use of longer-form content and tone aligns with YouTube video essay formats.

Table 8.1 Top five YouTube videos by campaign accounts.

Account	*Video Title*	*Length*	*Date*	*Views*	*Likes*	*Comments*
Yes23	Yes Makes It Possible	00:30	16/9/23	3,719,138	177	93
	'Why We're Voting Yes' – Christine	00:18	10/9/23	2,619,535	14	1
	Cathy Freeman Supports a Voice	00:19	11/10/23	2,605,205	15	1
	'Why We're Voting Yes!' – Matilda	00:17	10/9/23	2,351,014	12	5
	Join Us	00:30	26/4/23	2,080,639	78	17
Uluru Statement	History Is Calling	00:30	10/5/23	1,879,550	46	NA
	HISTORY IS CALLING	01:00	26/9/23	950,801	946	NA
	You're the Voice That Will Make History Vote Yes. The Uluru Dialogue | John Farnham (full)	02:47	27/9/23	409,632	115	47
	You're the Voice That Will Make History Vote Yes. The Uluru Dialogue | John Farnham 15"	00:15	27/9/23	263,338	18	7
	You're the Voice That Will Make History Vote Yes. The Uluru Dialogue | John Farnham 60"	01:00	27/9/23	82,495	50	26
Advance Australia	Meet the Architect behind the 'Voice' … Who Literally Wrote the Book	01:26	19/6/23	70,655	586	373
	We're Voting No	04:39	21/9/23	23,263	2.5K	466
	Meet Voice Activist Teela Reid	01:03	10/7/23	10,215	101	116
	One, Together – Fair Australia Full Documentary	08:59	19/4/23	4,391	150	26

Source: Authors, using data from YouTube.

In many ways, YouTube was a key medium in the digital campaign strategies of campaign actors and online discourse surrounding the Voice. Online personalities and interactivity featured here, but less prominently than on newer video platforms such as TikTok. Campaigns, particularly the 'No' campaign, adopted some of the style and tone of opinion content created for YouTube and the format of video essays. However, it should be noted that this analysis is drawn from the aggregate. YouTube is shaped by micro-celebrity, and throughout the campaign, videos supporting a 'No' vote from various perspectives achieved substantial, if niche, audiences.

TikTok

Like in other countries, TikTok use has grown substantially in Australia; its user base exceeds that of X. Forty per cent of Australians use it for around double the number of hours spent on any other platform (Kemp 2024). The majority (71 per cent) of adult TikTok users globally are between 18 and 34 years old. This demographic is reflected in the form of TikTok's content, which prioritises interactivity and authenticity and has been effectively used as a campaigning tool, most commonly by left-wing political leaders (Leon and Cully 2023; Moir 2023). The value of interactivity is built into the language and form of TikTok, in which users add to, respond to and build upon other creators' contributions to gain visibility. TikTok's algorithm supports and encourages these norms through the 'For You' page, which rewards engagement with content rather than preferring posts from accounts with more followers (Hern 2022). Despite this, most political campaigns on TikTok embody a standard, top-down approach to political communication, albeit with more poli-tainment (political content presented as entertainment) compared to other forms of political communication (Cervi, Tejedor and Blesa 2023; Cervi, Tejedor and Marín Load 2021).

Researchers and users find the most successful TikToks are characterised by simplicity, humour and the potential for re-creation (Pérez et al. 2023, 12). As seen in New Zealand's 2023 elections, political actors who embrace TikTok's interactive features can gain significant followings and engagement. For example, despite not historically appealing to young voters, the New Zealand National Party amassed more than 10 times Labour's TikTok views during the campaign through an interactive game run through their posts (Topham Guerin 2024). Negative campaigning on TikTok is not a new development and appears to have been a successful tactic for the Australian Labor Party in the 2022 federal election (Grantham 2024). Unlike elections, the 'Yes' and 'No' campaigns were not seeking to develop a public profile or sense of authenticity for a political figure, but instead their primary goal was to spread a message to persuade voters.

The major Voice campaigns used TikTok in different ways. Our analysis of Advance, Yes23 and Uluru Statement found significant distinctions in the frequency, form, and tone of posts and use of interactive affordances, especially in the campaign's final month. Advance posted the most, at least daily, while the 'Yes' campaigns posted more sporadically, particularly the Uluru Statement account. As a result, Advance posted as many times on TikTok in the campaign's final month as Yes23 and the Uluru Statement combined (see Figure 8.3). Advance recycled and remixed content, while the 'Yes' campaigns tended to post unique offerings each time. As TikTok's algorithm evaluates and promotes content over creators, Advance's strategy was more effective and likely contributed to their substantially higher views, likes and shares (see Appendix).

The reuse of Advance content contributed to its consistent messaging, tone and form of its posts. These were – as might be expected of a 'No' campaign – negative messages, claiming the referendum was 'divisive'. To lend credibility to its message, most of Advance's posts featured Indigenous Australians, mostly everyday people sharing their views on the Voice to Parliament and the referendum. Featuring such persons

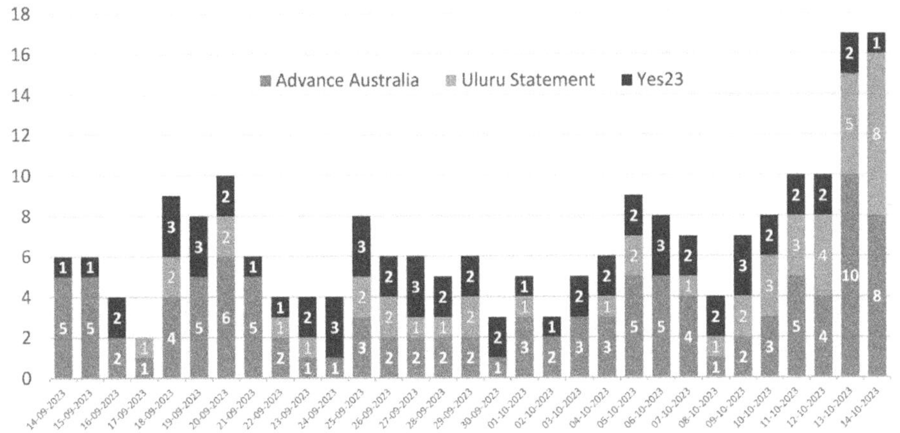

Figure 8.3 TikTok posts in the final month of the campaign. Source: Carson et al., 2024, 54.

prominently *likely* had the effect of signalling to non-Indigenous Australians that opposition to the Voice was OK, and Advance was *likely* quite aware of this. Yes23 and Uluru Statement also featured Indigenous Australians. The tone of these videos was primarily informative and entertaining. These videos were often framed as 'myth-busting' and a response to alleged misinformation about the referendum and the Voice to Parliament, essentially responding to the 'No' agenda. There was much greater variation in both the message and the tone of posts from the 'Yes' campaigns on TikTok, ranging from professional advertisements to 'home-made' content. Unlike Advance, both Yes23 and Uluru Statement rarely recycled or remixed content across multiple posts, likely contributing to the greater variation in production, messaging and tone.

TikTok users and creators outside of the official campaign also posted referendum videos. Some content featured figures from formal campaign efforts, such as Freya Leach's video with Jacinta Nampijinpa Price, while others offered commentary, critique and satire. These videos, and the comments and interactions they prompted, made up a notable portion of the broader discussion of the referendum on TikTok, and those that gained significant views embodied the platform's norms of engagement and interaction. Advance used TikTok's features to great effect, including hashtags associated with both 'Yes' and 'No' in each of their posts; engaging with comments, adopting trends, employing humour and framing their posts as replies to other users. This approach aligns with other effective political campaigns on TikTok (Pérez et al. 2023) and likely contributed to Advance's large audience and engagement. Conversely, Yes23 did not allow comments on their posts and neither of the 'Yes'-associated accounts employed interactivity or regularly included hashtags associated with the 'No' campaign (see Table 8.3).

These differences in the form, content, and strategy of TikTok posts likely contributed to significant variations in visibility and engagement between the major campaign accounts. The primary distinction lay not in the content itself but in the use of interactivity, trends, and posting strategies. The 'No' campaigns' success on the platform (see

Table 8.2 Overview of campaign TikTok accounts.

Campaign	*Posts about the Referendum*	*Followers*	*Likes*
Advance Australia	226*	80,000	2,600,000
Yes23	88*	8182	197,100
Uluru Statement	213	7044	111,000

Note: * Yes23 has no posts prior to 10 August 2023, Advance had none prior to 5 May 2023.

Table 8.2) supports the argument that campaigners must adapt to platform norms to excel in these spaces (Leon and Cully 2023).

Meta: Facebook and Instagram

Of course, while Twitter is popular among a smaller segment of Australia (26 per cent), it pales in comparison to Meta's Facebook user base within the country – roughly 80 per cent. Our search for Voice-specific discourse on Meta produced a much smaller dataset though: with over 100 thousand Facebook and 16 thousand Instagram posts. This discrepancy results from Meta's data restrictions, which only provide access to posts from public accounts, and not from arguably the most valuable material: Facebook private comments. Still, the smaller Meta sample partially reflects what we already know from our analysis of the Meltwater data. That is, #Yes considerably outnumbered #No posts (around 8:1), as well as among total subscribers (13:1), and total engagements (2:1). Indeed, the #Yes campaign prompted more comments (3.5:1) and shares (2:1) as well. Given Facebook's more extensive reaction set, we can also compare emoji reactions to the #Yes and #No self-labelled posts: that is, #Yes had a 9:1 advantage in loves, 1.25:1 wows, 7.4:1 hahas, 3.5:1 sads, 2.4:1 angries and 12:1 cares. In turn, our data continues to suggest the #Yes campaign on Facebook and Instagram dwarfed the #No campaign, much like occurred on Twitter. Only about 17 thousand posts were captured by our hashtag estimates though – perhaps reflecting the platform's less intensive use of hashtags compared to Twitter.

So, given the outperformance of 'Yes' hashtags over 'No' hashtags and evidence of greater public engagement with 'Yes' messages on social media, how do we make sense of the Voice outcome – a resounding 'No' victory? It would seem that public engagement and social media reach are only part of the equation of political influence and voter behaviour. Alongside audience reach, the agenda-setting power and issue salience of messages also matter. In many instances, 'Yes' was responding to the 'No' camp's negative framing of the Voice as 'divisive'. There are also other non-campaigning factors that contributed to the Voice's failure that are not explored here.

Our primary focus was to investigate the role of social media as a site for political communication using the case study of the referendum. In doing so, we have identified that X largely reflected and amplified the formal news cycle. It operated primarily as a space in which news and information were disseminated and discussed, revolving around key campaign events, significant actors and media coverage. In most cases, this coverage focused on the 'Yes' campaign's efforts, which successfully garnered attention from traditional media. This may be expected of a platform with a limited but politically astute audience and highlights the entwined relationship between mainstream and social media. We also found Voice-specific public discourse on Meta was smaller than X, a finding that suggests Voice discourse more likely occurred in private pages and posts outside our and the wider public's purview. In contrast, TikTok was very public. We saw how TikTok enabled the 'No' campaign to amass millions of views when campaigners adapted to its logic and norms: utilising politainment and maximising the platform's interactivity features to increase message visibility and user engagement. YouTube offered a middle ground, featuring both mainstream news media that attracts information-seeking audiences while also hosting more niche influencers with often negative perspectives. The official 'Yes' and 'No' campaigns were less prominent here, and only Advance produced content specifically for the platform in very limited quantities. Both TikTok and YouTube demonstrate audiences affinity for consuming short-form video content, as identified by others (Newman et al. 2024, 5).

Despite some notable differences between the platforms and the form and tone of posts, the 'No' campaign's message was consistent across channels. Its repeated and consistent negative messaging contrasts with the disparate messages (of varied tone and form) coming from the 'Yes' accounts. Building on Biddle and McAllister's (2024) findings on Australian referendums, which show that voters generally avoid risk in ambiguous political situations, the 'No' campaign's consistent negative messaging and portrayal of the Voice as divisive was an effective strategy to urge Australians to retain the status quo and vote 'No'. Both sides of the campaign prominently featured Indigenous figures explaining their reasons for voting 'Yes' or 'No', which further complicated voters' efforts to hear a clear and unified Indigenous perspective. In this noisy environment, the consistency and negativity of the 'No' campaign's message and the campaign's nimble adaptation to the norms of various platforms appear to have cut through the noise.

Conclusion

This chapter explored the Voice referendum to investigate contemporary Australian civic engagement, comparing the strategies of the 'Yes' and 'No' campaigns and underscoring social media's pivotal role in shaping modern public discourse. The case study reveals at least five key lessons about the relationship between social media and democratic engagement in Australia.

The first is that the media landscape has irreversibly transformed from the dominant days of mainstream media setting the news agenda. The information environment is both expanding and fragmenting with lowered barriers to entry for Australians to consume and produce news.

Second, this transformation highlights the digital dominance and central role of social media platforms with most Australians now getting news online and the majority of younger Australians relying on social media as their main news source, typically accessed on a mobile phone.

Third, these changes have altered approaches to political communication. Political actors use social media to bypass traditional gatekeepers and directly reach audiences, favouring visual content like short-form videos on TikTok and YouTube.

Fourth, while research findings are mixed on the efficacy of employing negative campaigning, it can enhance message spread. In the case of the 'No' campaign, negativity seems to have helped it dominate the issue agenda, consistently framing the Voice as divisive for Australians.

Fifth, while social media is certainly ascendant, the most effective campaigners also recognise the complex hybrid nature of the media environment that they operate in and will thus use the affordances of digital platforms and media to tailor their message to different audience demographics and sensibilities.

On a final note, as we consider the future of political engagement in Australia within a complex information environment, it is important to note that the referendum took place at the onset of the rapid development of generative AI technologies. Although there was little evidence of its use in the Voice campaigns, generative AI presents both an opportunity and a challenge for future political communication and democratic engagement. Public concerns about misinformation in Australia, already significant, are unlikely to diminish as these technologies become more sophisticated and pervasive in news production and the broader information landscape. Its use for both beneficial and harmful purposes poses new challenges for Australians trying to locate quality and trustworthy information. This situation becomes more complex if Meta proceeds with completely removing news from its platforms in response to the demands of the NMBC, resulting in popular platforms lacking professional news sources to help users distinguish between low-quality and credible information. Such communication challenges are likely to impact future public engagement in Australian democracy.

References

ABC News. 2022. 'Anthony Albanese's Victory Speech Paid Homage to His Roots and Australia. Read the Full Speech'. *ABC*, 21 May 2022. https://www.abc.net.au/news/2022-05-22/anthony-albanese-acceptance-speech-full-transcript/101088736.

Basford Canales, Sarah and Evershed, Nick. 2024. 'Rightwing Lobby Group Advance Australia Doubles Donation Revenue but Half of Donors Unknown'. *The Guardian*, 3 February. https://www.theguardian.com/australia-news/2024/feb/03/rightwing-lobby-group-advance-australia-doubles-donation-revenue-but-half-of-donors-unknown.

Bossio, Diana, Carson, Andrea and Meese, James. 2024. 'A Different Playbook for the Same Outcome? Examining Google's and Meta's Strategic Responses to Australia's News Media Bargaining Code'. *New Media & Society*. https://doi.org/14614448241232296.

Buckingham-Jones, Sam and Kehoe, John. 2024, 1 March. 'It's War – Meta Pulls Out of News Deal'. *Australian Financial Review*. https://www.afr.com/companies/media-and-marketing/meta-refuses-to-pay-for-news-setting-up-war-with-publishers-20240301-p5f93l.

Carson, Andrea and Jackman, Simon. 2023 'Media Coverage of the Campaign and the Electorate's Responses'. In *Watershed: The 2022 Australian Federal Election*, edited by Anika Gauja, Marian Sawer and Jill Sheppard, 121–144. Canberra: ANU Press.

Carson, Andrea and Simon, Felix M. 2024. 'Facebook's Role in the General Election: Still Relevant in a More Fragmented Information Environment'. *UK Election Analysis 2024: Media, Voters and the Campaign*, 104–105. https://www.electionanalysis.uk/uk-election-analysis-2024

/section-6-the-digital-campaign/facebooks-role-in-the-general-election-still-relevant-in-a-more-fragmented-information-environment/.

Carson, A., Strating, R., Jackman, S., Grömping, M., Hayman, P. and Gravelle, T. (2024). *Influencers and Messages: Analysing the 2023 Voice to Parliament Referendum Campaign*. La Trobe University: Melbourne. https://doi.org/10.17605/OSF.IO/N2H5A.

Cervi, Laura, Tejedor, Santiago and Blesa, Fernando García. 2023. 'TikTok and Political Communication: The Latest Frontier of Politainment? A Case Study'. *Media and Communication* 11 (2). https://doi.org/10.17645/mac.v11i2.6390.

Cervi, Laura, Tejedor, Santiago and Marín Lladó, Carles. 2021. 'TikTok and the New Language of Political Communication'. *Cultura, Lenguaje y Representación* 26 (November): 267–287. https://doi.org/10.6035/clr.5817.

De Vreese, C. H. (2015). 'Referendum'. In *The International Encyclopedia of Political Communication*, edited by Gianpietro Mazzoleni, 1–5. Wiley Blackwell.

Facebook. 2024, 29 February. 'An Update on Facebook News'. Meta. https://about.fb.com/news/2024/02/update-on-facebook-news-us-australia/.

Fine, Jeffrey A., and Megan F. Hunt. 2023. "Negativity and Elite Message Diffusion on Social Media." *Political Behavior* 45 (3): 955–973. https://doi.org/10.1007/s11109-021-09740-8.

Fischer, Tasja-Selina, Kolo, Castulus and Mothes, Cornelia. 2022. 'Political Influencers on YouTube: Business Strategies and Content Characteristics'. *Media and Communication* 10 (1): 259–271. https://doi.org/10.17645/mac.v10i1.4767.

Fournier, Patrick, Soroka, Stuart N. and Nir, Lilach. 2020. 'Negativity Biases and Political Ideology: A Comparative Test across 17 Countries'. *American Political Science Review* 114 (3): 775–791.

Gilardi, Fabrizio, Gessler, Theresa, Kubli, Maël and Müller, Stefan. 2022. 'Social Media and Political Agenda Setting'. *Political Communication* 39 (1): 39–60. https://doi.org/10.1080/10584609.2021.1910390.

Grantham, Susan. 2024. 'The Rise of TikTok Elections: The Australian Labor Party's Use of TikTok in the 2022 Federal Election Campaigning'. *Communication Research and Practice*, May: 1–19. https://doi.org/10.1080/22041451.2024.2349451.

Hern, Alex. 2022. 'How TikTok's Algorithm Made It a Success: "It Pushes the Boundaries"'. *The Guardian*, 24 October 2022, sec. Technology. https://www.theguardian.com/technology/2022/oct/23/tiktok-rise-algorithm-popularity.

Kemp, Simon. 2024. 'Digital 2024: Australia'. *DataReportal – Global Digital Insights*, 21 February 2024. https://datareportal.com/reports/digital-2024-australia.

Klinger, Ulrike, Koc-Michalska, Karolina and Russmann, Uta. 2023. 'Are Campaigns Getting Uglier, and Who Is to Blame? Negativity, Dramatization and Populism on Facebook in the 2014 and 2019 EP Election Campaigns'. *Political Communication* 40 (3): 263–282. https://doi.org/10.1080/10584609.2022.2133198.

Leon, Lucien and Cully, Richard. 2023. 'Talking Pictures (and Cartoons, Videos, Memes, Etcetera)'. In *Watershed: The 2022 Australian Federal Election*, edited by Anika Gauja, Marian Sawer and Jill Sheppard, 145–178. Canberra: ANU Press.

Lewis, Rebecca. 2020. '"This Is What the News Won't Show You": YouTube Creators and the Reactionary Politics of Micro-Celebrity'. *Television & New Media* 21 (2): 201–217. https://doi.org/10.1177/1527476419879919.

McAllister, Ian and Biddle, Nicholas. 2024. 'Safety or Change? The 2023 Australian Voice Referendum'. *Australian Journal of Political Science*, May: 1–20. https://doi.org/10.1080/10361146.2024.2351018.

McNair, Brian, Terry Flew, Stephen Harrington, and Adam Swift. 2017. *Politics, Media and Democracy in Australia: Public and Producer Perceptions of the Political Public Sphere*. New York: Routledge.

Moir, Aidan. 2023. 'The Use of TikTok for Political Campaigning in Canada: The Case of Jagmeet Singh'. *Social Media + Society* 9 (1): 20563051231157604. https://doi.org/10.1177/20563051231157604.

Newman, Nic, Fletcher, Richard, Robertson, Craig T., Ross Arguedas, Amy and Kleis Nielsen, Rasmus. 2024. 'Reuters Institute Digital News Report 2024'. https://reutersinstitute.politics.ox.ac.uk/sites/default/files/2024-06/RISJ_DNR_2024_Digital_v10%20lr.pdf.

Park, Sora, Fisher, Caroline, McGuinness, Kieran and Young Lee, Jee. 2024. *Digital News Report: Australia 2024*. News and Media Research Centre. https://doi.org/10.60836/FXCR-XQ72.

Parliament of Australia. 2023. *Constitution Alteration (Aboriginal and Torres Strait Islander Voice, 2023.* https://www.aph.gov.au/Parliamentary_Business/Bills_Legislation/Bills_Search_Results/Result?bId=r7019.

Pérez Rastrilla, Laura, Sapag M., Pablo and Recio García, Armando (eds.). 2023. *Fast Politics: Propaganda in the Age of TikTok*. The Language of Politics Series. Singapore: Springer Nature Singapore. https://doi.org/10.1007/978-981-99-5110-9.

Phillips, Justin B. 2023. "Laughing at Death: Facebook, the 'Haha' Reaction, and Death Coverage on Local US News Pages." *Popular Communication* 22 (1): 17–32. https://doi.org/10.1080/ 15405702.2023.2287738.

Phillips, Justin B., Carson, Andrea and Simon Jackman. 2024. "Issue Agenda-Setting in the Voice to Parliament Referendum: Using Big Data to Explain Voice Discourse on Traditional and Social Media." *Australian Journal of Political Science*, 59 (3): 344–359, https://doi.org/10.1080/10361146.2024.2409113.

Riga, Jessica. 'Seeing Less Political Content on Instagram? It's a Deliberate Move from Meta, Which Experts Say Could Impact Democracy'. *ABC News*, 25 March 2024. https://www.abc.net.au/news/2024-03-26/instagram-limiting-political-content-threatens-democracy/103629990.

Seccombe, M. 2023, 11 April. 'The Man behind Advance's Far-right Campaign'. *The Saturday Paper*. https://www.thesaturdaypaper.com.au/news/2023/11/04/the-man-behind-advances-far-right-campaign.

Soroka, Stuart N. 2014. *Negativity in Democratic Politics: Causes and Consequences*. Cambridge: Cambridge University Press.

Stier, Sebastian, Bleier, Arnim, Lietz, Haiko and Strohmaier, Markus. 2018. 'Election Campaigning on Social Media: Politicians, Audiences, and the Mediation of Political Communication on Facebook and Twitter'. *Political Communication* 35 (1): 50–74. https://doi.org/10.1080/10584609.2017.1334728.

Tenove, Chris, Tworek, Heidi, Lore, Grace, Buffie, Jordan and Deley, Trevor. 2023. 'Damage Control: How Campaign Teams Interpret and Respond to Online Incivility'. *Political Communication* 40 (3): 283–303. https://doi.org/10.1080/10584609.2022.2137743.

The Australia Institute. 2022. 'Polling – Voice to Parliament in the Constitution'. *The Australia Institute*. https://australiainstitute.org.au/report/polling-voice-to-parliament-in-the-constitution/.

Topham Guerin. 2024. 'The Digital Campaign That Rewrote NZ's Political Playbook'. *Topham Guerin*. https://www.tophamguerin.com/work/the-digital-campaign-that-rewrote-nzs-political-playbook.

Udris, Linards and Eisenegger, Mark. 2023. 'Referendum Campaigns in the Digital Age: Towards (More) Comparative Analyses in Hybrid Media Systems'. *Media and Communication* 11 (1): 1–5. https://doi.org/10.17645/mac.v11i1.6703.

Van Aelst, P. et al. 2017. 'Political Communication in a High-Choice Media Environment: A Challenge for Democracy?' *Annals of the International Communication Association* 41 (1): 3–27.

Verrender, Ian. 2024, 28 June. 'Nine Entertainment's Job Cuts are the Latest in a Line of Commercial Media Outlets Feeling the Economic Chill'. *ABC News*. https://www.abc.net.au/news/2024-06-28/nine-entertainment-job-cuts-commercial-media-slowing-economy/104036502.

Wellauer, Kirstie, Williams, Carly and Brennan, Bridget. 2023, 16 October. 'Why the Voice Failed'. *ABC News*. https://www.abc.net.au/news/2023-10-16/why-the-voice-failed/102978962.

Appendix: Table 8.3

Table 8.3 Top five TikTok posts from campaign actors.

	Post	*Views*	*Likes*	*Comments*	*Shares*
Yes23	Have you googled it? #yes23 #voicetoparliament #referendum #voteyes #australia #FirstNations #auspol #australianreferendum #ulurustatement #closingthegap #briggs #fromtheheart	784,800	58,400	0*	1,092
	We need action now, and planning for the future. That's why John Harding is voting Yes. #yes23 #voice #thevoice #voicetoparliament #australia #tiktokaustralia #fyp #garma	444,900	47,300	0*	2,369
	Rachel Perkins answering questions on the Voice to Parliament 🖤🤍🖤 #yes23 #voicetoparliament #referendum #voteyes #australia #FirstNations #auspol #australianpolitics #ulurustatement #closethegap ##fromtheheart# #australianreferendum	271,600	15,600	0*	353
	Rachel Perkins talking about one of the biggest misconceptions! Also, if you're worried about money, the Voice is very likely to make things more efficient! #yes23 #voicetoparliament #referendum #voteyes #australia #FirstNations #auspol #australianpolitics #ulurustatement #australianreferendum #referendum #fromtheheart	198,400	11,900	0*	392
	We as parents want to give a better version of life than we've all had. On Saturday stand with 80% of Aboriginal and Torres Strait Islander People and vote YES! 🖤 #yes23 #voteyes #voicetoparliament #referendum #FirstNations #auspol #closingthegap #australianpolitics #australianreferendum #australia #fromtheheart #ulurustatement #closingthegap	121,900	16,000	0*	652

(*Continued*)

Table 8.3 (Continued)

	Post	*Views*	*Likes*	*Comments*	*Shares*
Uluru Statement	If you don't know, here you go ✅ #TheVoice #UluruStatement #VoteYes	342,500	33,900	127	1,509
	It's time for a history lesson on the Australian Constitution. #VoteYes #UluruStatement #VoiceReferendum	86,500	9,143	60	380
	OUR NEW AD IS LIVE! You're the Voice that will make history. On 14 October, we know we all can stand together with the power to be powerful. #HistoryIsCalling, so #VoteYes. Are you in? John Farnham is. #UluruStatement #StayTrue2Uluru #YoureTheVoice #voteyes	55,700	5,598	734	248
	The Voice will improve the lives of First Peoples and all Australians, now and for future generations. Check our FAQs page to learn more about the referendum for a First Nations Voice to Parliament enshrined in the Constitution https://ulurustatement.org/education/faqs/ (link in bio) #ulurustatement #historyiscalling #voicetoparliment #auspol #auspolitics	37,700	3,772	274	46
	Couldn't have said it better ourselves @Jessica Mauboy 👊👊👊	21,500	2,624	50	25
Advance Australia	Replying to @McLovin What is the Indigenous Voice to Parliament? These Indigenous Australians are voting 'No' because the Voice will divide us. #votenoaustralia #voicetoparliament #australia🇦🇺 #auspol #yes23 #fyp #foryoupage #blowthisup #referendum #indigenous #aboriginal #australia #australian #tiktokaustralia	2600,000	209,600	2,714	17,100
	#votenotodivision #votenoaustralia #voiceofdivision #yes23 #thevoice #referendum #auspol #voteno #voicetoparliament #voice #indigenousvoicetoparliament	2,200,000	120,300	4,311	25,300
	Replying to @joey_tulips We are ALL Australians! The Voice will divide us. Vote No to the Voice of Division. #voicetoparliament #votenoaustralia #tiktokaustralia #fyp #voicetoparliamentexplained #voteno #notothevoice #referendum #voteyes #voteyesaustralia #yes23 #australian #auspol #thevoiceaustralia #viral #blowthisup #referendum2023 #thevoicereferendum #notmyvoice #parliament #indigenous #aboriginal #australia🇦🇺	2,100,000	197.3K	2,600	5,424

	If you don't understand the Voice to Parliament, listen to this Indigenous woman. 😟 #earlyvoting #earlyvoting2023 #voteno #voicetoparliament	1,900,000	120,400	2,561	14,800
	'I don't want others to look at me differently.' These Indigenous Australians don't want to be divided along the lines of race. Vote No to the Voice of Division. #voicetoparliament #votenoaustralia #tiktokaustralia #fyp #voicetoparliamentexplained #referendum #voteyes #voteyesaustralia #yes23 #yes23au #australian #auspol #thevoiceaustralia #foryoupage #viral #blowthisup #voteno #notothevoice #referendum2023 #thevoicereferendum #australians #indigenousvoicetoparliament #indigenous #australia #aboriginal	1,700,000	159,700	1,948	6,643

Source: Authors using TikTok data: Note: * indicates comments were turned off on Yes23 posts.

Chapter 9

THE UNSTABLE FOUNDATIONS OF THE IMPLIED FREEDOM OF POLITICAL COMMUNICATION

Murray Wesson

Introduction

The Australian Constitution ('the Constitution') does not include a right to freedom of expression. However, the Constitution's express commitment to representative government in sections 7 and 24 is regarded as giving rise to an implied freedom of political communication ('implied freedom'). The implied freedom is not a right but rather a limit on legislative competence at all levels of government in Australia. Sourced in the political sovereignty of the people, the implied freedom plays an important role in fostering and safeguarding civic engagement. As Deane and Toohey JJ observe in the foundational case of *Nationwide News Pty Ltd v Wills* (1992) 177 CLR 1 (*Nationwide News*), representative government and hence the implied freedom entails 'an ability of represented and representatives to communicate information, needs, views, explanations and advice. It also presupposes an ability of the people of the Commonwealth as a whole to communicate among themselves, information and opinions about matters relevant to the exercise and discharge of government powers and functions on their behalf' (1992, 72).

On the basis of the implied freedom, in *Brown v Tasmania* (2017) 261 CLR 328 (*Brown*) the High Court invalidated provisions of the *Workplaces (Protection from Protestors) Act 2014* (Tas) (*Protestor's Act*), noting that historically protests have been an important 'means of bringing about political and legislative change on environmental issues' (2017, 346). Conversely, in *Farm Transparency International Ltd v State of New South Wales* (2022) 96 ALJR 655 (*Farm Transparency*) the High Court upheld provisions of the *Surveillance Devices Act 2007* (NSW) (*Surveillance Devices Act*). The *Surveillance Devices Act* is an example of *ag gag* legislation that prohibits the publication or communication of records of agricultural practices where these have been obtained through the installation of a surveillance device without the express or implied consent of the owner or occupier. Farm Transparency International Ltd is a company and not-for-profit charity whose civic engagement takes the form of advocacy for the rights of non-human animals in agriculture by publishing photos, videos and audio-video recordings of agricultural practices on their website. By exposing the realities of modern agriculture their objective is to end commercialised non-human animal abuse and exploitation, including through changes to law, policy and practice.

The High Court's approach to the implied freedom plays a crucial role in shaping the legal environment within which civic engagement is pursued. However, the implied freedom has also been a perennial source of contention in Australian constitutional law. In recent years, there have been widely discussed differences on the High Court about whether the implied freedom should be enforced through a 'structured proportionality' test derived from German constitutional law, a 'categorical' approach influenced by United States constitutional law, or the established 'reasonably appropriate and adapted' standard. Even more fundamentally, divisions have emerged on the High Court about the existence and normative status of the implied freedom. Broadly speaking, it is possible to identify three positions. At one end of the spectrum, there is the approach of Gageler CJ, whose 'representation-reinforcing' conception of the implied freedom is influenced by the work of John Hart Ely (1980). Combined with a 'calibrated approach' to judicial review, Gageler CJ adopts a normatively robust approach to the implied freedom where legislation jeopardises the system of representative government established by the Constitution. At the other end, there is the extreme scepticism of Steward J, who applies a structured proportionality test with a high level of deference but also doubts the very existence of the implied freedom and has sought to open the door to argument on this point in future litigation. A possible compromise position is represented by the moderate scepticism of Edelman J, who does not doubt the existence of the implied freedom but likewise applies the structured proportionality test with a high level of restraint. The chapter develops an analogy suggested by Stephen Gageler in a speech given as Commonwealth Solicitor-General (2009), to argue that Gageler CJ's conception of the judicial role may be likened to a 'referee', Steward J to a 'spectator' and Edelman J to a 'linesman' in the processes of representative democracy.

This chapter outlines, explores and critiques each of these positions. It does so against the backdrop of the rationale for the implied freedom. There is a compelling argument that free political communication is essential to the effective operation of representative government and is necessarily implied by the terms of the Constitution. This understanding of the rationale for the implied freedom provides support for the approach of Gageler CJ, whose representation-reinforcing conception of the implied freedom seeks to ensure the effective functioning of representative government. The difficulty is that, even narrowly construed, this rationale for the implied freedom supports the implication of further freedoms essential to representative government, such as freedom of assembly, freedom of association, freedom of movement, and regular, free and fair elections (Kirk 1995, 50). Apart from a right to vote (*Roach v Electoral Commissioner* (2007) 233 CLR 162 (*Roach*)), the High Court has steadfastly declined to imply further freedoms since its unanimous decision in *Lange v Australian Broadcasting Corporation* (1997) 189 CLR 520 (*Lange*). From this perspective, the implied freedom can equally be viewed as an anomaly in Australian constitutional law or a wrong turn on a path not ultimately taken by the High Court. This provides support for Steward J's extreme scepticism regarding the existence of the implied freedom.

That leaves the moderate scepticism of Edelman J, who urges a restrained approach to the implied freedom. Edelman J accepts the existence of the implied freedom but is willing to invalidate legislation only in extreme scenarios that threaten the fundamentals of representative democracy. The attraction of Edelman J's position is that it promises to reconcile the existence of the implied freedom and the political constitutionalist orientation of the Constitution on issues of rights and freedoms. There are indications that a majority of the High Court may be gravitating towards Edelman J's position. Yet Edelman J's approach is difficult to square with dicta in foundational cases, such as *Lange*, that the implied freedom should ensure not merely the existence but also the 'effective operation of the mandated system of representative government' (1997, 546). Edelman J's approach also holds the potential to weaken the legal protections for free political communication and hence civic engagement in Australia, especially where matters of public concern are pursued through methods such as protests.

The paradoxical conclusion that emerges from this analysis is that the unstable foundations of the implied freedom are capable of supporting multiple, sharply divergent conceptions of the judicial role – none of which are fully satisfactory or coherent with those foundations. It follows that the implied freedom is likely to remain a site of contest regarding both its existence and enforcement. Absent a willingness by a High Court majority to revisit the foundations of the implied freedom, uncertainty regarding the constitutional protection for free political communication is likely to persist. Freedom of expression would be more coherently protected in Australia through human rights legislation that safeguards freedom of expression alongside a range of other rights and freedoms (Australian Human Rights Commission 2022).

The first part of the chapter revisits the foundations of the implied freedom. Thereafter, the chapter outlines and critiques the approaches of Gageler CJ, Steward J and Edelman J. The chapter concludes by considering the repercussions of this analysis for the future of the implied freedom, freedom of expression and civic engagement in Australia.

Revisiting the Foundations of the Implied Freedom

The implied freedom was introduced in the seminal cases of *Nationwide News* and *Australian Capital Television Pty Ltd v Commonwealth* (1992) 177 CLR 106 (*ACTV*). In *Nationwide News*, Deane and Toohey JJ identified 'representative government' as a doctrine that underlies the Constitution and is implemented by its provisions. The joint judgment finds that the people of the Commonwealth would 'be unable responsibly to discharge and exercise the powers of governmental control which the Constitution reserves to them if each person was an island, unable to communicate with any other person' (1992, 72). Similarly, in *ACTV*, Mason CJ holds that absent the implied freedom, 'representative government would fail to achieve its purpose, namely, government by the people through their elected representatives; government would cease to be responsive to the needs and wishes of the people and, in that sense, would cease to be truly representative' (1992, 139). As Kirk observes, the argument for the implied freedom can be broken into three steps: first, the Constitution establishes representative government;

second, freedom of political communication is an essential element of representative government; and third, freedom of political communication is impliedly protected by the Constitution (Kirk 1995, 40–41).

The difficulty is that representative government is an amorphous concept. Broadly construed, the Constitution's commitment to representative democracy entails not simply majority rule and free political communication but also a range of civil and political rights. Ronald Dworkin, for example, distinguishes the 'majoritarian premise' (meaning that democracy entails decisions that would be supported by a majority of citizens) from the 'constitutional conception of democracy' (which holds that democracy requires majority rule subject to the condition of equal status for all citizens). Dworkin endorses the constitutional conception of democracy and argues that the defining aim of democracy is that collective decisions should be made by political institutions 'whose structure, composition, and practices treat all members of the community, as individuals, with equal respect and concern' (Dworkin 1999, 17). Even more broadly, it might be argued that a 'social minimum' providing for the basic needs of citizens is a prerequisite for effective democratic participation. Meaningful participation in political decision-making requires access to education, healthcare, social security and the like. On this view, a constitutional commitment to representative government also entails recognition of social and economic rights (King 2012, 25). In short, notwithstanding its deceptively simple structure, the logic of the implied freedom is capable of generating an entire judicially developed bill of rights.

There are intimations in the early case law on the implied freedom that some members of the High Court are open to implying a broad range of rights and freedoms. In *ACTV*, for example, Gaudron J states that the provisions of the Constitution establishing representative government 'predicate and, in turn, are predicated upon a free society governed in accordance with the principles of representative parliamentary democracy' (1992, 210). The reference to a 'free society' alludes to Murphy J's suggestion in a series of earlier judgments that the Constitution entails a range of freedoms 'so elementary that it was not necessary to mention them in the Constitution' (*Ansett Transport Industries (Operations) Pty Ltd v Commonwealth* (1977) 139 CLR 54, 88). Given the potential ramifications of this approach, it is perhaps unsurprising that Gaudron J's intimations are not developed in the subsequent case law. At the time, some academic commentators also sought to constrain the rationale for the implied freedom. Kirk, for instance, distinguishes between a broad, substantive conception of democracy that would entail various rights and freedoms and a narrow, process-oriented conception of democracy focused upon ensuring the minimum essential conditions of majority rule. These include freedom of speech, freedom of assembly, freedom of association, freedom of movement, access to government, and regular, free and fair elections (Kirk 1995, 50). On this approach, the High Court's discovery of the implied freedom opened the door to protection of these minimum essential requirements of representative government but not a judicially implied bill of rights.

Importantly, *Nationwide News* and *ACTV* were decided during the 'Mason Court' (1987–1995), a period during which, under the leadership of Sir Anthony Mason, the High Court sought to depart from its traditional 'textualism' and 'legalism' and develop more values-based forms of reasoning (Mason 1986). But even at the time, there were members of the High Court who were sceptical of the Mason Court's new reasoning methods and the implied freedom. In *Theophanous v Herald & Weekly Times Ltd* (1994) 182 CLR 104 (*Theophanous*), for example, Dawson J held that a constitutional guarantee of free political communication could only be drawn from outside the terms of the Constitution and could not be done so 'consistently with established principles of interpretation' (1994, 193). Similarly, in *McGinty v Western Australia* (1996) 186 CLR 140, McHugh J characterised the concept of representative government as a 'free-standing principle' (1996, 234) and stated that in the implied freedom cases 'the text and structure of the Constitution have receded into the background and it is the concept of representative democracy, not the text or structure of the Constitution, that governs the application of the Constitution in such cases' (1996, 234).

The eventual result of this period of division was the High Court's unanimous decision in *Lange*. Written in the name of 'the Court', *Lange* is clearly a product of compromise. On the one hand, the Court affirms the existence of the implied freedom as an 'indispensable incident' (1997, 559) of the system of representative government established by the Constitution. The judgment also introduces the '*Lange* test' for enforcement of the implied freedom. As developed in *Brown*, the *Lange* test provides as follows:

1. 'Does the law effectively burden the freedom in its terms, operation or effect?
2. Is the purpose of the law legitimate, in the sense that it is compatible with the maintenance of the constitutionally prescribed system of representative and responsible government?
3. Is the law reasonably appropriate and adapted to advance that legitimate object in a manner that is compatible with the maintenance of the constitutionally prescribed system of representative and responsible government'? (2017, 376)

On the other hand, in contrast to *Nationwide News* and *ACTV*, in *Lange* the implied freedom is no longer derived from a broad conception of representative government underlying the terms of the Constitution. The focus is instead more narrowly on specific provisions of the Constitution, particularly sections 7 and 24 (which respectively provide that the Senate and House of Representatives should be directly chosen by the people). This difference in emphasis may seem inconsequential. However, notwithstanding its affirmation of the implied freedom, *Lange* appears to have drawn a line under the implication of further freedoms in the terms of the Constitution. Apart from recognising a right to vote in *Roach*, the High Court has since consistently held that freedom of association (*Wainohu v New South Wales* (2011) 243 CLR 181, 230 (*Wainohu*)) and freedom of movement (*Gerner v Victoria* (2020) 270 CLR 412, 421 (*Gerner*)) exist only as corollaries to the implied freedom. This means that these freedoms have no independent life. They are protected only to the extent that it is necessary to protect free political communication. It follows that the same test of infringement applies as the implied freedom. Roux observes that in *Lange* 'the reform-minded judges on the Mason Court were forced to trade victory in respect of one aspect of the desired role transformation for defeat in respect of the new reasoning methods they sought to introduce' (Roux 2015, 22).

The result is an instability in the foundations of the implied freedom. While following from the constitutional commitment to representative democracy, the implied freedom is also the product of an incomplete revolution. As the remainder of this chapter explores, this instability is capable of generating radically divergent approaches to the existence and enforcement of the implied freedom.

The Judge as Referee: Gageler CJ's 'Representation-Reinforcing' Conception of the Implied Freedom

Appointed to the High Court in 2012, Gageler CJ has heard 10 cases involving the implied freedom and found that legislation is incompatible with the implied freedom in 6 judgments: *Unions NSW v New South Wales* (2013) 252 CLR 530 (*Unions NSW [No 1]*), *Brown*, *Unions NSW v New South Wales* (2019) 264 CLR 595 (*Unions NSW [No 2]*), *LibertyWorks Inc v Commonwealth of Australia* (2021) 274 CLR 1 (*LibertyWorks*), *Ruddick v Commonwealth* (2022) 399 ALR 476 (*Ruddick*) and *Farm Transparency*. Notably, Gageler CJ was in dissent in the three most recent decisions: *LibertyWorks*, *Ruddick* and *Farm Transparency*. This suggests that Gageler CJ's approach to the implied freedom is normatively stronger than the majority of the High Court, and the case law on the implied freedom may be moving towards a more restrained approach to its enforcement.

Gageler CJ's approach to the implied freedom needs to be understood in light of the influence of Ely's 'process-based' theory of constitutional review on his conception of the judicial role under the Constitution. Writing from a US perspective, Ely argued in *Democracy and Distrust* that the determination of 'substantive values' should generally be left in the hands of the legislature but that courts should play an active role in protecting the mechanisms of political accountability. Ely argued that the judicial role is to facilitate citizen participation in the processes of government by applying strict judicial scrutiny where the 'channels of political change' (1980, 103) are choked by the majority in power or where minorities are systemically disadvantaged by majoritarian political processes. *Democracy and Distrust* envisages a restrained role for the courts in cases involving disputes about substantive values and a more active role when upholding the mechanisms of political accountability established by the US Constitution.

Dixon and Loughland (2021) explain that Gageler was exposed to theories of process-based judicial review while studying for his LLM at Harvard Law School. He read *Democracy and Distrust* while writing his LLM thesis and 'regarded it as an articulation of his nascent position as to the appropriate role of a federal judge undertaking constitutional review' (Dixon and Loughland 2021, 462). The influence of Ely is evident in the published version of Gageler's thesis (1987) and in a lecture delivered as Commonwealth Solicitor-General, 'Beyond the Text: A Vision of the Structure and Function of the Constitution' (2009). There, Gageler argues that the underlying purpose of the Constitution is to enlarge the self-government powers of the Australian people. Judicial deference is due when political accountability is strong, but judicial vigilance is required when political accountability is weak or endangered. The Constitution should be seen as 'creating a political system whose ordinary constitutional working will be through the political process, and to see the role of the judicial power within that political system as akin to that of a referee whose extraordinary constitutional responsibility is for the game itself rather than a linesman whose only responsibility is to call in or out' (2009, 37).

Gageler's analogy of the representation-reinforcing judge to a 'referee' is illuminating. When the processes of representative democracy are working effectively, the role of the judge will be limited. But when these processes start to break down, the judge will be required to assume a more activist role and ensure that the rules are upheld. This may require the judge to shape the operation of the system in light of its fundamental objectives. In other words, the judge may be required to make contested judgments about the values and aims underlying the rules (Dworkin 1975). Indeed, as Laurence Tribe notes, process-based theories of judicial review are inevitably intertwined with consideration of substantive rights and values. These inform both the nature of procedural norms and questions about which minority groups the courts should protect from systemic disadvantage (Tribe 1980). The role of the judge as a representation-reinforcing referee is distinct from the judge as 'spectator' and 'linesman'. These analogies are developed further in the discussions of Steward J and Edelman J, respectively.

Dixon and Loughland (2021) note that Gageler was key in bringing Ely's ideas before the High Court in *ACTV*. The case involved a challenge to the *Political Broadcasts and Political Disclosures Act 1991* (Cth), which imposed a blanket prohibition on political advertisements on radio or television during federal election periods, while also establishing a scheme of 'free time' for political advertising on the public broadcaster. Sir Maurice Byers QC and Gageler as junior counsel submitted that the 'fundamental premise of the structure of the Constitution [...] is the continuous ability of the Australian people as a whole to make informed judgments on matters of political significance' (1992, 110). This necessarily 'involves the capacity at all times for free and unhindered public discussion on all such matters, subject to traditional and proportional limitations' (1992, 110). These themes are reflected in the High Court's judgment in *ACTV*. Deane and Toohey JJ hold that freedom of political communication is 'implicit in, and of fundamental importance to, the effective working of the doctrine of representative government which is embodied in our Constitution' (1992, 174). Mason CJ expresses particular concern about the potential for the Commonwealth legislation – which reserved 90 per cent of the free advertising time for parties represented in the previous Parliament and fielding a prescribed number of candidates – to distort the democratic process in favour of incumbent parties: '[the Act] severely restricts freedom of communication in relation to the political process, particularly the electoral process, in such a way as to discriminate against potential participants in that process' (1992, 145).

As a Justice of the High Court, Gageler CJ's judgments continue to demonstrate the influence of Ely's theory. This is combined with an approach that 'calibrates' the intensity with which the *Lange* test is applied according to the nature and intensity of the burden on the system of representative government. *Ruddick*, for example, concerned Commonwealth legislation which provides that the Australian Electoral Commission must refuse an application for registration of a political party if the name of the party contains a word in the name of an existing registered political party unless that party consents to the use of the word. Gageler J quotes Laurence Tribe (1988) to the effect that 'few prospects are so antithetical to the notion of rule by the people as that of a temporary majority entrenching itself by cleverly manipulating the system through which the voters, in theory, can register their dissatisfaction by choosing new leadership' (2022, 368). A test of 'strict necessity' consistent with the need for a 'compelling justification' is 'especially appropriate to be applied to a law which discriminates in favour of incumbency' (2022, 370). On this basis, Gageler J dissented in finding that the law was incompatible with the implied freedom.

These themes are further developed in Gageler J's dissenting judgment in *Farm Transparency*, where *ag gag* legislation in the form of the *Surveillance Devices Act* prohibited the publication or communication of records of agricultural practices where these have been obtained through the installation of a surveillance device without the express or implied consent of the owner or occupier. Gageler J held that the implied freedom protects against the inherent risk of legislative or executive impairment of 'the capacity of, or the opportunity for, the Australian people to form the political judgments required for the exercise of their constitutional functions' (2022, 674). An aspect of that risk is that 'political communications unhelpful or inconvenient or uninteresting to a current majority might be unduly impeded' (2022, 674). The implied freedom, therefore, functions as a 'structural implication serving to safeguard the efficacy of the system against realisation of that systemic risk' (2022, 674). Of particular concern to Gageler J was that the *Surveillance Devices Act* threatened to dry up the constitutionally protected 'marketplace of ideas' (2022, 675) where 'factual information bearing on matters of political and governmental concern known to its possessor and potential communication to be true is all too often in short supply' (2022, 675). The indiscriminate nature of the *Surveillance Devices Act*, particularly the absence of the type of public interest exceptions found in similar legislation in other States and Territories, meant that it imposed a 'greater burden on political communication than can in all circumstances be justified as appropriate and adapted to the protection of privacy of activities on private property' (2022, 675).

Gageler CJ's approach to the implied freedom is sourced in a sophisticated theoretical and doctrinal framework. It is also supported by dicta in the foundational cases on the implied freedom, especially the pre-*Lange* decisions such as *Nationwide News* and *ACTV*. The difficulty is that if Gageler CJ's conception of the implied freedom follows from the constitutional commitment to representative democracy, then it is not apparent why a range of other freedoms – such as freedom of assembly, freedom of association, and regular, free and fair elections (Kirk 1995, 50) – should not also follow from these provisions. In other words, an understanding of the Constitution that takes seriously the idea of the judge as a representation-reinforcing referee who maintains and, where necessary, directs the processes of representative government would seem to commit the High Court to a broader and more ambitious project than the implied freedom. Yet, apart from recognising a right to vote in *Roach*, the High Court has since *Lange* declined to uphold further constitutional implications such as freedom of association (*Wainohu*) and freedom of movement (*Gerner*), except as adjuncts to the implied freedom.

In *Tajjour v New South Wales* (2014) 254 CLR 508 (*Tajjour*), the High Court considered the constitutionality of section 93X of the *Crimes Act 1900* (NSW) which makes it an offence for a person to habitually consort with two or more convicted offenders after being warned by a police officer that they are convicted offenders and that consorting with a convicted offender is an offence. The plaintiffs challenged the law on various grounds, including an implied freedom of association that was said to exist in the Constitution independently of the implied freedom of political communication. Gageler J acknowledged previous High Court decisions finding that freedom of association does not have this status but took care to emphasise that these 'should not be read as suggesting that the constitutional protection of freedom of association for governmental or political purposes is in doubt. They should not be read as suggesting that it is secondary or derivative. Association for the purpose of engaging in communication on governmental or political matter is part and parcel of the protected freedom' (2014, 578).

Nevertheless, in the absence of a clear rationale for why freedom of association and other such freedoms protecting representative government are not more than 'part and parcel of the protected freedom', the implied freedom remains vulnerable to more sceptical approaches.

The Judge as Spectator: Steward J's Extreme Scepticism of the Implied Freedom

Steward J was appointed to the High Court in 2020 and has heard three cases involving the implied freedom: *LibertyWorks*, *Ruddick* and *Farm Transparency*. Unlike Gageler CJ, who found that legislation was incompatible with the implied freedom in each of these cases, Steward J is yet to find a violation of the implied freedom. In *LibertyWorks*, Steward J also stated that 'it is arguable that the implied freedom does not exist' (2021, 95) and sought to open the door to submissions on this point in future litigation. Steward J reiterated his scepticism regarding the implied freedom in *Ruddick* and *Farm Transparency* by referring to his reasons in *LibertyWorks*. In contrast to Gageler CJ's conception of the judge as a representation-reinforcing referee, Steward J's view of the judge may be likened to a spectator: observing but also trusting the participants to maintain the integrity of the essentials of representative government.

Steward J's remarks in *LibertyWorks* caused some consternation in academic circles. However, scepticism about the existence of the implied freedom is not novel on the High Court and has antecedents in the judgments of Dawson J in *Theophanous*, Callinan J in *Australian Broadcasting Corporation v Lenah Game Meats Pty Ltd* (2001) 208 CLR 199 and Heydon J in *Monis v The Queen* (2013) 249 CLR 92. The existence of the implied freedom has also been the subject of academic critique (Goldsworthy 2011). Steward J is simply the most recent torchbearer in this sceptical tradition.

To justify his scepticism, in *LibertyWorks*, Steward J pointed to the ongoing division on the High Court about the role of structured proportionality in enforcing the implied freedom. For Steward J, the

> divergence of views in this Court concerning the test for the application of the implied freedom may perhaps illustrate the tenuous nature of that implication. If the content of the implied freedom cannot even now be agreed upon, then, for my part, that may demonstrate that it was never justified. (2021, 111)

As it stands, this argument is clearly unpersuasive. In *Palmer v Western Australia* (2021) 272 CLR 505, there is a parallel disagreement about the role of structured proportionality in enforcing section 92, the guarantee of freedom of trade, commerce and intercourse among the states. It would be absurd to infer from the fact of this disagreement that section 92 does not exist. It is also quite possible that a future High Court will converge on structured proportionality, or another test, for enforcement of the implied freedom just as the 'reasonably appropriate and adapted' standard was used without controversy from *Lange* until the adoption by a majority of structured proportionality in *McCloy v New South Wales* (2015) 257 CLR 178 (*McCloy*). The logic of Steward J's position would then be that the implied freedom does exist.

It follows that disagreement about the enforcement of constitutional doctrines does not shed much light on their existential status. Indeed, commenting on the implied freedom in *LibertyWorks*, Steward J observes that 'whilst implying a legal guarantee of such a freedom from the text and structure of the Constitution may be understandable, that text and structure may not supply a clear answer for when and how that freedom may permissibly be limited' (2021, 113). This is true of many, if not most, constitutional rights and freedoms.

However, disagreement about the existence of the implied freedom is not the only basis of Steward J's scepticism. In *LibertyWorks*, Steward J also quotes Dawson J in *Theophanous*:

> If a constitutional guarantee of freedom of speech or of communication is to be implied, the implication must be drawn from outside the Constitution by reference to some such concept as 'the nature of our society'. That is not an implication which can be drawn consistently with the established principles of interpretation. (1994, 193)

Dawson J goes on to explain that the implications that might properly be drawn from the text and structure of the Constitution are those which are 'necessary or obvious having regard to the express provisions of the Constitution itself' (1994, 194). Steward J agrees with Dawson J that the implied freedom does not follow necessarily or obviously from sections 7 and 24 of the Constitution and is inconsistent with the textualist interpretative methodology established in the High Court's decision in *Amalgamated Society of Engineers v Adelaide Steamship Co Ltd* (1920) 28 CLR 129.

Of course, one's view about whether the implied freedom follows necessarily or obviously from the text of the Constitution is likely to be determined by deeper theoretical commitments about the nature of the Constitution and the role of the courts. A judge committed to a representation-reinforcing conception of the judge as referee will more easily conclude that the efficacy of the Constitution depends critically upon the implied freedom and indeed other essentials of representative democracy. In contrast, Steward J's extreme scepticism of the implied freedom is best understood within the theory of political constitutionalism. Waldron, for example, argues that rights are subject to reasonable disagreement and in a democratic society the legislature provides a more legitimate process for settling rights disagreements than the judiciary (2006). This extends to rights that constitute the political process such as freedom of expression and freedom of association: '[d]emocracy is in part *about* democracy: one of the first things on which the people demand a voice about, and concerning which they claim a competence, is the procedural character of their own political arrangements' (Waldron 1999, 296). Waldron's emphasis upon the amenability of our key political concepts to reasonable disagreement is echoed by Steward J in *Ruddick* where he remarks that 'this Court has traditionally deferred to the legislative branch in the case of laws regulating federal elections. This is because the concept of "representative democracy" comprehends a large range of virtues and possibilities' (1999, 398). This contrasts with Gageler CJ's greater willingness to make contested judgments about the rights and values underlying the processes of representative government, where these are threatened by legislative action.

Similarly to Gageler CJ, the foundations of the implied freedom provide some support for the extreme scepticism of Steward J. From Steward J's perspective, the reluctance of the High Court post-*Lange* to recognise further key democratic freedoms means that the implied freedom can be viewed as an anomaly in the Australian constitutional universe. The anomalous nature of the implied freedom is underscored by the political constitutionalist orientation of the Constitution, which entrusts rights disagreements overwhelmingly to the political process. Yet the High Court is extremely unlikely to revisit its unanimous decision in *Lange* that the implied freedom is an 'indispensable incident' (559) of the system of representative government established by the Constitution. Rather than dispensing with the implied freedom, Steward J's extreme scepticism is more likely to fuel moderate forms of scepticism. In *Ruddick*, Steward J observes that the invalidation of legislation must be 'reserved to those more extreme laws which offend the most essential of democratic values and systems' (2022, 398). This moderately sceptical approach to the implied freedom finds fuller expression in the judgments of Edelman J.

The Judge as Linesman: Edelman J's Moderate Scepticism of the Implied Freedom

Edelman J does not doubt the existence of the implied freedom, but he has sought to diminish its normative status. In *Clubb v Edwards; Preston v Avery* (2019) 267 CLR 171 (*Clubb/Preston*), Edelman J explains that a restrained approach to the implied freedom is required because 'the freedom of political communication is a limited implication from the Constitution that applies only where it is necessary to ensure the existence and effective operation of the scheme of representative and responsible government protected by the terms of the Constitution' (2019, 311). For Edelman J, the relatively weak nature of the implied freedom follows from the absence of a federal bill of rights. This leads Edelman J to emphasise in *Farm Transparency* that the implied freedom is capable of accommodating a wide range of legislative choices and is not a constitutional 'trump card' over legislative goals (2022, 705). In the same judgment, Edelman J contrasts the implied freedom with the First Amendment of the US Constitution to emphasise the relatively weak normative status of the implied freedom (2022, 346).

Edelman J does not employ Gageler CJ's calibrated approach to judicial review but instead applies the structured proportionality test adopted by a majority of the

High Court in *McCloy*. The effect of structured proportionality is to disaggregate the third step of the *Lange* test – whether the law is reasonably appropriate and adapted to advance the legitimate object in a manner that is compatible with the maintenance of the constitutionally prescribed system of representative and responsible government – into a further three steps. As stated in *McCloy*, these steps are whether the law is *suitable* (rationally connected to the purpose of the provision); *necessary* (in the sense that there is no obvious and compelling alternative, reasonably practicable means of achieving the same purpose which has a less restrictive effect on the freedom); and *adequate in its balance* (a criterion requiring a value judgment, consistent with the limits on the judicial function, describing the balance between the importance of the purpose served by the restrictive measure and the extent of the restriction it imposes on the freedom).

Edelman J's moderate scepticism of the implied freedom is evident in his approach to the structured proportionality test. In *LibertyWorks*, Edelman J rightly describes the necessity stage of structured proportionality as 'the heartland of the dispute in the application of structured proportionality' (2021, 78). It is at this stage of the test that legislation is most likely to be invalidated. However, there are different approaches to the necessity stage. In *McCloy*, the joint judgment characterises their approach to necessity as follows: there should be no 'obvious and compelling alternative, reasonably practicable means of achieving the same purpose which has a less restrictive effect on the freedom' (2015, 195). An advantage of this approach to necessity is that it does not insist that hypothetical measures should be *equally* effective as the impugned law. As David Bilchitz notes, alternative measures will normally entail some disadvantage and not be considered equally effective (Bilchitz 2014, 14). A 'strict' approach to necessity that insists that alternative measures should be equally effective may mean that impugned laws are very rarely invalidated at the necessity stage.

Yet Edelman J has increasingly adopted a strict approach to necessity. In *Farm Transparency*, for example, Edelman J states that 'an alternative choice that imposes a lesser burden on the freedom of communication must be "obvious and compelling" such that it must be clearly expected to achieve the same purposes to at least the same extent, and to do so with significantly lesser burden' (2022, 704). In contrast to Gageler J's concern about the indiscriminate nature of the *Surveillance Devices Act*, Edelman J employs a strict conception of necessity to reject the relevance of similar legislation in other States and Territories that includes public interest exceptions for publication of recordings obtained through surveillance devices installed without the consent of the owner or occupier: 'the alternative models might not be expected to achieve the same purposes, to at least the same extent, and to do so with a significantly lesser burden' (2022, 704).

There are indications that other members of the High Court may be gravitating to a strict conception of necessity. In *Brown*, Kiefel CJ, Bell and Keane JJ compared the impugned provisions of the *Protestors Act* with the pre-existing *Forest Management Act 2013* (Tas) (*Forest Management Act*). The joint judgment did not seek to establish that the *Forest Management Act* was equally effective as the *Protestors Act*. Instead, the joint judgment held that the 'special case contains no indication that, generally speaking, the provisions of the *Forest Management Act* have been ineffective to prevent the disruption of forest operations or damage to property associated with those operations' (2017, 372) – a far less stringent approach. This was coupled with the observation that the measures under the Forest Management Act were 'substantially less restrictive of the freedom' (2017, 373). On this basis, the joint judgment found that the relevant provisions of the *Protestors Act* failed the necessity test and did not proceed to the balancing stage. In contrast, in the more recent case of *Farm Transparency*, Kiefel CJ and Keane J's approach to the necessity stage is very similar to Edelman J: to be 'equally practicable as the impugned provision, the alternative must achieve the same legislative purpose to the same degree, which is to say it must be possible to conclude that the alternative legislative measure is equally as effective' (2022, 670). Applying this strict conception of necessity, the joint judgment also rejected the relevance of the public interest exceptions found in other State and Territory laws for the publication of recordings obtained through surveillance devices installed without the consent of the owner or occupier. For Kiefel CJ and Keane J, it cannot 'be said that such measure would made the [impugned] Act equally efficacious in the protections it seeks to provide' (2022, 671).

Edelman J also favours a highly constrained approach to the balancing stage of structured proportionality. In *Clubb/Preston*, Edelman J explains that this is because the 'Australian foundations of the implied freedom of political communication are inconsistent with an open-ended assessment at the adequacy in the balance stage [...] This is, in part, because the freedom of political communication arises only as an implication to secure the effective operation of the constitutional system of representative and responsible government' (2019, 343). In the same judgment, Edelman J emphasises that in balancing the importance of the purpose against the cost to the implied freedom, the 'assessment of the importance of purpose is not the judge's idiosyncratic policy preference. Instead, the [...] constraint directs attention to the importance that Parliament has given to the purpose' (2019, 343).

Edelman J was appointed to the High Court in 2017 and has heard seven cases involving the implied freedom. During this time, Edelman J has invalidated legislation for inconsistency with the implied freedom in one case: *Unions NSW [No 2]*. Even in *Brown*, where six judges of the High Court invalidated provisions of the *Protestors Act*, Edelman J upheld the *Protestors Act* by interpreting the legislation so that it applied to conduct that was already unlawful under the pre-existing *Forest Management Act*. Edelman J acknowledged that this approach would impose 'additional consequences' (2017, 507) on protestors, given that the '*Protestor's Act* still imposes penalties and other consequences on protestors for their unlawful conduct which go beyond the burdens imposed by the *Forest Management Act*' (2017, 507). *Unions NSW [No 2]* may therefore provide an indication of the threshold that must be reached for Edelman J to determine that the implied freedom has been breached. In *Unions NSW [No 2]*, New South Wales legislation limited electoral expenditure by third-party campaigners in a manner that curbed, in particular, the campaigning activities of trade unions, thereby disadvantaging the Australian Labor Party. The justification provided by New South Wales for the legislation was threadbare, if not non-existent, but possibly motivated by a politically partisan agenda (Wesson 2019). In other words, the legislation not only lacked a clear justification but threatened to fundamentally distort the processes of representative government in a manner that would have undermined the existence of the scheme of representative government established by the Constitution.

Edelman J's moderate scepticism of the implied freedom can be regarded as charting a middle course between the representation-reinforcing approach of Gageler CJ and the extreme scepticism of Steward J. If Gageler CJ's conception of the judge may be likened to a referee and Steward J to a spectator, then Edelman J regards the judge as a linesman: generally observing the democratic process but willing to raise a flag in the face of fundamental threats to representative government or when play proceeds entirely out of bounds. These types of cases arise infrequently and only at the margins of Australian politics. Outside these extreme scenarios, it will generally be for legislatures to determine the limits that may justifiably be imposed on free political communication.

The most compelling rejoinder to Edelman J's approach is that it marks a retreat from the foundational cases on the implied freedom in a manner that weakens the constitutional protection for freedom of expression and hence civic engagement in Australia. In *Lange*, which itself marks a retreat from *Nationwide News* and *ACTV*, the Court stated that implicit in the Constitution is a 'requirement of freedom of communication among Australians to the extent that such freedom is necessary to the effective operation of the mandated system of representative government' (1997, 546). While Edelman J's conception of the implied freedom ensures the existence of a system of representative government, it is doubtful that it is sufficient to ensure its effective operation. An approach to the implied freedom that seeks to ensure the efficacy of the system of representative government would be more aligned with Gageler CJ's representation-reinforcing conception of the implied freedom as a safeguard against systemic risks to democratic governance. Yet, this returns us to the difficulties inherent in justifying Gageler CJ's approach absent a broader and more coherent doctrinal framework protecting the essentials of representative government. Edelman J's approach enjoys some support from the foundations of the implied freedom but cannot be made fully coherent with those foundations.

Conclusion

The implied freedom is a key constitutional safeguard for freedom of expression in Australia. Accordingly, the implied freedom plays a crucial role in shaping the legal environment for civic engagement. As the *Brown* case illustrates, the High Court's approach to the implied freedom has repercussions for the extent to which legislatures can curb protest activities. The implied freedom is also relevant to other forms of civic engagement, such as those pursued by Farm Transparency International Ltd. In this light, it is concerning that there are continued divisions on the High Court about the existence and enforcement of the implied freedom.

Unfortunately, the instability inherent in the foundations of the implied freedom means that these divisions are likely to persist. Indeed, Gageler CJ's representation-reinforcing conception of the implied freedom, Steward J's extreme scepticism and Edelman J's moderate scepticism can each be viewed as tacit calls to reshape the foundations of the implied freedom in line with their preferred approach. For Gageler CJ, this would mean locating the implied freedom within a broader and more coherent framework of constitutional protections for the essential processes of representative government. Steward J's view is that the seminal cases on the implied freedom such as *Nationwide News*, *ACTV* and *Lange* should be viewed as wrong turns or the anomalous products of a path not ultimately taken by the High Court. In contrast, Edelman J's approach involves an implicit retreat from these foundational cases.

The sceptical approaches of Steward J and Edelman J also both threaten to weaken the legal foundations for freedom of expression in Australia. In the absence of a High Court majority for Gageler CJ's approach, freedom of expression would be more coherently protected through federal human rights legislation protecting freedom of expression alongside a range of other rights and freedoms (Australian Human Rights Commission 2022). This would also provide a more secure legal environment for civic engagement by groups and individuals.

References

Amalgamated Society of Engineers v Adelaide Steamship Co Ltd (1920) 28 CLR 129.

Ansett Transport Industries (Operations) Pty Ltd v Commonwealth (1977) 139 CLR 54.

Australian Broadcasting Corporation v Lenah Game Meats Pty Ltd (2001) 208 CLR 199.

Australian Capital Television Pty Ltd v Commonwealth (1992) 177 CLR 106.

Australian Human Rights Commission. 2022. 'Free and Equal. Position Paper: A Human Rights Act for Australia', 1–380.

Bilchitz, David 2014. 'Necessity and Proportionality: Towards a Balanced Approach'. In *Reasoning Rights: Comparative Judicial Engagement*, edited by Liora Lazarus, Christopher McCrudden and Nigel Bowles (pp. 41–62). Oxford: Hart Publishing.

Brown v Tasmania (2017) 261 CLR 328.

Clubb v Edwards; Preston v Avery (2019) 267 CLR 171.

Dixon, Rosallind and Loughland, Amelia. 2021. 'Comparative Constitutional Adaptation: Democracy and Distrust in the High Court of Australia'. *International Journal of Constitutional Law* 19 (2): 455–475.

Dworkin, Ronald. 1975. 'Hard Cases'. *Harvard Law Review* 88 (6): 1057–1109.

Dworkin, Ronald. 1999. *Freedom's Law: The Moral Reading of the American Constitution*. Oxford: Oxford University Press.

Ely, John Hart. 1980. *Democracy and Distrust*. Cambridge, MA: Harvard University Press.

Farm Transparency International Ltd v State of New South Wales (2022) 96 ALJR 655.

Gageler, Stephen. 1987. 'Foundations of Australian Federalism and the Role of Judicial Review'. *Federal Law Review* 17 (3): 162–198.

Gageler, Stephen. 2009. 'Beyond the Text: A Vision of the Structure and Function of the Constitution'. *Bar News*, Winter: 30–41.

Gerner v Victoria (2020) 270 CLR 412.

Goldsworthy, Jeffrey. 2011. 'Constitutional Implications Revisited'. *University of Queensland Law Journal* 30 (1): 9–34.

King, Jeff. 2012. *Judging Social Rights*. Cambridge: Cambridge University Press.

Kirk, Jeff. 1995. 'Constitutional Implications from Representative Democracy'. *Federal Law Review* 23 (1): 37–76.

Lange v Australian Broadcasting Corporation (1997) 189 CLR 520.

LibertyWorks Inc v Commonwealth of Australia (2021) 274 CLR 1.

Mason, Anthony. 1986. 'The Role of a Constitutional Court in a Federation: A Comparison of the Australian and United States Experience'. *Federal Law Review* 16 (1): 1–28.

McCloy v New South Wales (2015) 257 CLR 178.

McGinty v Western Australia (1996) 186 CLR 140.

Monis v The Queen (2013) 249 CLR 92.

Nationwide News Pty Ltd v Wills (1992) 177 CLR 1.

Palmer v Western Australia (2021) 272 CLR 505.

Roach v Electoral Commissioner (2007) 233 CLR 162.

Roux, Theunis. 2015. '"Reinterpreting 'the Mason Court Revolution'": An Historical Institutionalist Account of Judge-Driven Constitutional Transformation in Australia'. *Federal Law Review* 43 (1): 1–25.

Tajjour v New South Wales (2014) 254 CLR 508.

Theophanous v Herald & Weekly Times Ltd (1994) 182 CLR 104.

Tribe, Laurence. 1980. 'The Puzzling Persistence of Process-Based Constitutional Theories'. *The Yale Law Journal* 89: 1063–1080.

Tribe, Laurence. 1988. *American Constitutional Law*, 2nd edn. Mineola: Foundation Press.

Unions NSW v New South Wales (2013) 252 CLR 530.

Unions NSW v New South Wales (2019) 264 CLR 595.

Wainohu v New South Wales (2011) 243 CLR 181.

Waldron, Jeremy. 1999. 'The Constitutional Conception of Democracy'. In *Law and Disagreement* (pp. 282–312). Oxford: Oxford University Press.

Waldron, Jeremy. 2006. 'The Core of the Case Against Judicial Review'. *Yale Law Journal* 115: 1346–1406.

Wesson, Murray 2019. '*Unions NSW v New South Wales [No 2]*: Unresolved Issues for the Implied Freedom of Political Communication'. *Media and Arts Law Review* 23 (1): 93–104.

Chapter 10

INCREASING THIRD-SECTOR GOVERNANCE EXPECTATIONS AS A BARRIER TO CIVIC ENGAGEMENT IN AUSTRALIA

Ian Murray and Sarah Murray

Introduction

Ever more is being expected from not-for-profits and their directors, trustees and managers. In part, higher anticipated standards of managerial professionalism have resulted from the adoption of market sector practices in the charity sector and changing social norms emphasising greater accountability across all sectors (Anheier and Toepler 2023, 421–22; Productivity Commission 2010, xxx–xxxii; Kurti 2013). This reflects – in many liberal democracies – the adoption of new public management approaches by government (Anheier, Lang and Toepler 2020, 673–74; Brinkerhoff and Brinkerhoff 2002, 5) and more sophisticated and strategic approaches to giving on the part of donors (Anheier and Toepler 2023, 200, 213–15; Horvath and Powell 2020, 117; Considine, O'Sullivan and Nguyen 2014, 93–94). These trends have been amplified by the creation of a regulator focused on the not-for-profit sector in Australia in 2012 known as the Australian Charities and Not-for-profits Commission (ACNC).

Tougher governance requirements serve a purpose: improved systems to measure, report and ensure accountability such that not-for-profit sector assets are used for civil society purposes and not carelessly risked or captured for the enrichment of managers. These heightened governance demands may promote public confidence in the sector in some ways, but they also risk a range of unintended consequences,[1] including disincentivising people from being involved in not-for-profits, whether as volunteers, employees, directors/trustees or as members.

Building on evidence that increased governance expectations may decrease participation, this chapter highlights some of the ways in which increased governance builds false confidence in the sector. That is, reducing participation or changing the form of participation to paid employment has major negative ramifications for the maintenance

1. As to the ambivalent relationship between accountability auditing and trust and confidence, see Power (1999, 134–36).

of social capital (Putnam [2000] 2020; Leigh 2014). Beyond a certain point, there are significant questions about the level of effectiveness of governance and accountability checks and the diversion of scarce resources to undertake those checks (Power 1999), especially if the governance requirements skew activities to game the governance and accountability metrics and divert attention from a not-for-profit's mission (Power 1999; Nel De Koker 2022).[2] Importantly, for this chapter, declining participation in the third sector in Australia can also affect the role of not-for-profits as sites of collective action and political expression as well as civic participation more generally.[3] This chapter explores the trend towards hyper-regulation of the third sector and the concomitant impact this may have on the vibrancy of engagement and civic participation in Australian democracy.

Terminological Insights

There is significant overlap between the terms 'not-for-profit sector', 'third sector' and 'organised civil society', and we use each of these terms to distinguish a sector from government, business and personal households (as to such use, see e.g., Anheier and Toepler 2023, 62–74, 81–84; Garton 2009, 19–20). It should nevertheless be borne in mind that the borders between these sectors are porous and in flux, for instance, as a result of government outsourcing and the rise of social enterprises. The term 'not-for-profit sector' (or non-profit sector) focuses on what this sector cannot do – distribute profits to owners (Anheier and Toepler 2023, 63; Garton 2009, 38–39). 'Third sector' highlights the distinction from the government and business sectors (Anheier and Toepler 2023, 63; Garton 2009, 20). 'Organised civil society' focuses more positively on what this sector involves – voluntary association to pursue common interests independent of compulsion from the state (Anheier and Toepler 2023, 82; Garton 2009, 35–37).

Many writers might conceive more broadly of 'civil society' as a social sphere beyond the market and the state that includes not only associations that have sufficient formality to be treated as organisations but also fluctuating groups of individuals, interpersonal connections and informal networks, which would fall beyond the not-for-profit sector (Lechterman and Reich 2020, 172; Anheier and Toepler 2023, 82–84). However, not-for-profit organisations and the not-for-profit sector are widely seen as an important component of civil society (Anheier and Toepler 2023, 81; Clemens 2020, 192), and the benefit of examining civil society from an organisational perspective has been emphasised by writers such as Garton (2009) and Skocpol (2003, 15–17).

The 'charity sector' is a subset of the not-for-profit sector (Garton 2009, 24–27). In broad terms, in addition to being not-for-profit, charities must be non-governmental, have worthy purposes that fall within the accepted categories of charitable purposes

2. As to skewed activities as a result of the adoption of for-profit governance practices in the UK university system, see Synge (2023, ch. 6).
3. As to professionalization of not-for-profits and the impacts of decreased participation, see Clemens (2006, 207–11) and Skocpol (2003).

(such as the advancement of social welfare, advancement of education, advancement of religion, etc.), have purposes that are for the public benefit and not have any purposes against public policy (Murray 2018, 2). In Australia, many charities choose to register with a federal regulator, the ACNC, in order to gain state endorsement on a public register of charities and to be eligible for a range of tax concessions, over and above those available to most other not-for-profit organisations.

When we refer to 'governance', we mean 'the framework of rules, relationships, systems and processes within and by which authority is exercised and controlled in [organisations]' (Owen 2003, xxxiv, adopted in ASX Corporate Governance Council 2019, 2).[4] It thus incorporates the formal and informal means and practices by which authority is exercised and those with authority are held to account. As noted by Farrar and Hanrahan in relation to corporate governance, this means that accountability arises not just as a result of direct legal requirements but also self-regulation and institutional codes and guidelines (like accounting standards and ASX governance principles) and broader industry practices that might not all directly impose legal obligations but might inform the content of organisational controller duties (Farrar and Hanrahan 2017, 4–5).[5] 'Governance expectations' are then the formal and informal rules, relationships and systems that hold not-for-profit directors and trustees to account for their decisions and for the actions of the not-for-profit organisation. It covers, among other things, the reporting obligations that apply to not-for-profits, the duties applying to not-for-profit trustees and directors and broader expectations of managerial professionalisms that are reflected across legal duties, institutional codes and industry practices.

Declining Participation

Putnam ([2000] 2020) argued in the classic American work *Bowling Alone: The Collapse and Revival of American Community* that community and neighbourhoods are fracturing. He concluded that American citizens were more and more isolated from civil society organisations and other traditional social structures, carrying implications for democracy more generally. Recent Australian research suggests involvement in civil society is in a period of significant deterioration and that engagement, where it still exists, is more tangential. Andrew Leigh (2014, 2–3) applied his experience as a researcher for Putnam to the Australian context in *Disconnected*. Leigh suggested that Australian 'social capital' was in decline, something he defined as 'networks of trust and reciprocity that link multiple individuals together'.[6] Where community participation in civil society occurs, it tends to be less concentrated on membership and direct participation in civil society organisations and instead is channelled through citizens contributing to funding campaigns or petition-based appeals (Productivity Commission (Cth) 2023, 106–10;

4. See also ACNC (Cth) (nd a).
5. Noting that some institutional codes and guidelines are adopted and applied by legislation, such as the accounting standards set by the Australian Accounting Standards Board.
6. See also Hendriks, Ercan and Boswell (2020). As to social capital, see also Bourdieu and Wacquant (1992, 119); Coleman (1988).

Nicholas 2023). As Ariadne Vromen notes from her research, 'people [...] have ad hoc involvements based on particular issues or events or campaigns that draw them in' (cited in Nicholas 2023). But these more transitory involvements are not the same thing and result in a degree of decline in community participation.

These broad trends are reflected in volunteering statistics for the Australian charity sector (a decline of just under 600,000 volunteers from 2018, leaving 3,200,000 volunteers in 2021) (ACNC (Cth) 2023a, 19) and civil society volunteering more generally, with general volunteering figures indicating a drop of 20 per cent in formal volunteering between 2010 and 2018 and a further drop as a result of COVID-19 (Biddle and Gray 2023, 4). While COVID-19 has clearly impacted the drop in volunteering, the underlying trend already reflected significant decline before COVID-19 (Biddle and Gray 2023, 4). The trends are also reflected at the board level. The percentage of not-for-profit board members who are paid rather than volunteers has increased from 14 per cent in 2018 to 22 per cent in 2023 (AICD 2023, 16). Concern about the increasing difficulties in finding directors, trustees or management committee members who can meet governance requirements has also been expressed in surveys or interviews with Australian not-for-profits (Chelliah, Boersma and Klettner 2016, 12–13; Murray, Fardin and O'Hara 2019, 79–80; Mex 2018, 82–84; Cornish 2013, 68–69; Nel 2024). Indeed, Mex's research on grassroots not-for-profit associations identified 'red tape' (defined as 'obligations that are excessive, unnecessary or confusing') as the third largest of four major barriers to members volunteering to join boards (Mex 2018, 82). Further research by Mex, involving an expanded data set, indicated five major reasons that people did not join association committees. Three of those reasons related to increased governance expectations, being 'fear of responsibility', 'perceived lack of skills' and 'red tape'; the other two being board politics and 'lack of time' (Mex 2022, 9). Even over a decade ago in 2008, research by the Centre for Corporate Public Affairs highlighted concerns of business and not-for-profit leaders that for-profit governance requirements developed for large trading entities were being applied to not-for-profits, acting as 'a current and potential inhibitor to business [person] participation on not-for-profit boards' (Centre for Corporate Public Affairs 2008, 84). Difficulty in attracting such responsible persons can frequently have a direct impact on retention and attraction of members and volunteers if this results in a less capable or less diverse set of responsible persons, or at the extreme, in too few responsible persons to govern the not-for-profit (Mex 2022, 7).

Increased Governance Expectations

There are a range of factors contributing to the decreasing participation trends outlined above. These include the impact of COVID-19, higher female labour market participation than in the past and the role of social media and the internet in enabling the formation of specific interest groups as needed, rather than relying on multi-purpose organisations (Productivity Commission (Cth) 2023, 110; Nicholas 2023; Biddle et al. 2022). We argue that increased governance expectations are one of those factors (and our focus for the purposes of this chapter). Clearly, focusing on one among a number of factors means that addressing governance may not alone reverse participation trends; however, its importance in its own right justifies the concentration on it here. Additionally, to the extent that increased governance expectations involve more top-down professional managerial practices, there is a link to particular modes of acting that de-emphasise more voluntaristic participatory bottom-up processes that may be connected with volunteering rather than expectations of a paid professional role.

Until 2012 and the creation of the ACNC, large sections of the not-for-profit sector were effectively left to their own devices. Prior to the ACNC, unless engaged in fundraising, most charitable trusts and many unincorporated associations and specific Act of Parliament religious organisations had no reporting obligations (Murray 2014). Even for charities required to report, the depth of information that had to be provided was typically very low (Murray 2014). Unsurprisingly, given the limited information base, enforcement activity was sporadic and relied largely on the interest of the Australian Taxation Office (Treasury (Cth) 2011, 58; Murray 2014). The formation of the ACNC represents a watershed moment. Not-for-profit organisations in the form of charities that wished to access tax concessions had to register with the ACNC. Registration obliges charities to maintain financial records, to annually provide financial and non-financial information, as well as to comply with a series of governance standards and (for those that operate outside Australia or that work with third parties that operate outside Australia) external conduct standards.[7] Given the range of legal forms in which charities can exist and the vast diversity in the charity sector, the governance standards and external conduct standards are drafted in a principles-based way that involves interpreting and applying these general principles over the top of existing obligations arising from sources such as legal form, tax endorsement and fundraising registration (Murray 2018; Nel de Koker 2022, 775–76).

However, while it does fill in regulatory gaps for some not-for-profits, the overlay of additional obligations also results in duplication (of regulatory obligations and regulators), complexity and unintended consequences as a result of unanticipated interaction between legislative regimes (Langford and Webster 2023, 349–53; Brand, Fitzpatrick and Lombard 2013).[8] This situation was described in the statutory review of the ACNC legislation as 'an unacceptable level of unnecessary red tape' such that 'the current system of different governance requirements is complex and confusing. It is unreasonable to expect that volunteer directors in the sector understand and comply with the multiple jurisdictional and sometimes inconsistent sets of governance requirements' (Treasury (Cth) 2018, 112–14). Jeanne Nel (2024) has recently completed doctoral research examining the extent and enforcement of the duty of care owed by volunteer directors of charitable corporations. Nel argues that over time (indeed, predating the creation of the ACNC) the duty of care has become increasingly focused on commercial and business skills and standards, without appropriate regard for the charitable and volunteer contexts. Nel (2024, ch. 7) describes the development as leading 'to a strict, objectively

7. Australian Charities and Not-for-profits Commission Act 2012 (Cth).
8. For discussion of some of the competing views on the benefits and burdens of the regulatory framework for charities, see also Productivity Commission (Cth) (2023, 234–35).

measured duty of care responding to a professional relationship, without considering the unique needs of charity organisations'. For instance, as discussed by Nel, the guidance provided by the ACNC to charity responsible persons in fulfilling their reporting obligations and the reporting obligations themselves are relatively finance-focused – with no reporting required on the effectiveness or evaluation of programs, while the required financial reporting does give a sense of the financial resilience of organisations (Nel 2024, ch. 9; ACNC (Cth) 2023b; ACNC(Cth) nd b).

As an example of the overlay of regulators and obligations, trustees of charitable trusts owe general law duties (to avoid conflicts, not to make unauthorised profits, to exercise prudence, to exercise powers in good faith, etc.), are subject to duties under state trusts legislation (which, for instance, typically articulates additional duties for trustees exercising investment powers), and are – indirectly – subject to restated fiduciary duties applying under ACNC Governance Standard 5. Governance Standard 5 requires a registered charity to 'take reasonable steps to ensure that its [trustees] are subject to, and comply with' a list of duties, including to act with care and diligence, to disclose perceived or actual material conflicts of interest, to act in good faith in the registered charity's best interests (whatever that means in the context of a trust) and so on.[9]

An example of duplicated obligations and unintended consequences is also provided by companies limited by guarantee that are registered charities. First, some of the statutory duties imposed directly on directors of charitable companies limited by guarantee are potentially removed by a new section 111L in the Corporations Act 2001 (Cth). However, the precise effect of section 111L is debated by commentators and, even if effective in removing some statutory duties, it leaves in place indirect duties applied via the ACNC governance standards to the registered charity itself, but in a context where the interpretation of this new indirect approach is open to question and where general law duties continue to apply directly to directors (Ramsay and Webster 2017). Second, companies limited by guarantee are obliged to inform the ACNC of changes of directors.[10] They are no longer formally obliged to notify ASIC, but if they do not, currently no director resignation takes effect (so resigning directors remain liable as directors)[11] and third parties cannot rely on Corporations Act 2001 (Cth) statutory assumptions based on the identity of directors. This has resulted in many charities experiencing difficulties opening bank accounts and obtaining loan funding and has resulted in a charity having to seek court orders to confirm the identity of directors (Law Council of Australia 2023, 3–4).[12]

More recently, a series of royal commissions focused on aged care and disability services and institutional responses to child sexual abuse have increased governance expectations, particularly around awareness and accountability of quality of care and

9. Australian Charities and Not-for-profits Commission Regulations 2022 (Cth) r 45-25(2).
10. Australian Charities and Not-for-profits Commission Act 2012 (Cth) section 65-5(1)(c).
11. Corporations Act 2001 (Cth) section 203AA. Note that the Treasury Laws Amendment (Miscellaneous Measures) Bill 2024 (Cth) proposes to amend 203AA to take account of ACNC notification.
12. Re Leeuwin Ocean Adventure Foundation Limited (In Administration) [2023] WASC 480.

safeguarding (AICD 2023, 6). These royal commissions build on what has already been a long process of imposing increasing governance obligations – modelled on for-profit business norms and on public sector accountability norms – via funding legislation and contracts for human services organisations (Steane and Christie 2001, 48, 50).

The ramping up of governance expectations cannot be seen as impact-neutral. Not-for-profits are expected to maintain governance standards and, by design, this has brought about changes in priorities and the way the sector operates. However, at the same time, the impact of these changes on the sector needs to be appraised in a wider sense, particularly, taking account of the maintenance of social capital.

Changing Sector Expectations: The Impact on Social Capital and Collective Action

It is not new to see involvement in civil society organisations as important for a dynamic and strong democracy. Arnstein's (1969, 216) work suggested over half a century ago that citizen participation can vary considerably in its depth but that overall it 'enables the have-not citizens, presently excluded from the political and economic processes, to be deliberately included in the future'.[13] Likewise, Lechterman and Reich describe nonprofits as a 'counterpublic'

> permitting and transmitting the expression of ideas that run counter to official government policy [i.e., those of marginalised groups]. Nonprofit organizations can do more than help protect individual rights; they are in large measure the way citizens exercise their rights. The rights to association, speech, and religious liberty are all exercised in the context of formal (and informal) groups. It is through participation in these groups that people develop their interests and passions and meet others who share them. As a venue for expressive association, a vibrant nonprofit sector is a crucial part of life in a liberal-democratic society. (Lechterman and Reich 2020, 177)

In this way, civil society permits the formation, communication and refinement of political preferences so as to help identify what a political society views as being in the common good (Clemens 2020, 197–98; Lechterman and Reich 2020, 177–78).

Involvement in civil society organizations also supports norms that emphasise different modes of acting compared to market-based modes of acting focused on the maximization of individual well-being. As noted by Vaclav Havel (1992, 18), 'we will never build a democratic state based on rule of law if we do not at the same time build a state that is [...] humane, moral, intellectual and spiritual, and cultural.'

Of course, that is not to suggest that all civil society involvement necessarily supports democratic processes. For instance, racist hate groups that seek to dehumanise and devalue certain peoples, or theocratic or anarchist groups that seek to overturn and replace democratic institutions, might build social capital within these groups but may also have a chilling effect on other people participating in democratic processes

13. See also Clemens (2020, 197) and Andrias and Sachs (2021, 551–52).

or remove their ability to do so and may reduce respect for democratic institutions (Chambers and Kopstein 2001; Clemens 2020, 199–200; Productivity Commission (Cth) 2023, 79; Lechterman and Reich 2020, 182; Putnam 2020, 22–23). Further, those interested in profit-maximising modes of acting might use the halo effect of a nonprofit organisation to mask their extraction of assets by way of inflated salaries, perks and management fees (Clemens 2020, 193–94). Liberal democracies face challenges in how best to discourage such anti-democratic practices while still enabling associational life. For instance, what are the precise boundaries beyond which associational purposes will be judged as unlawful or otherwise against public policy? To what extent should freedom of political communication be curtailed to eliminate hate speech? However, a reduction in participation due to generally onerous governance expectations might be anticipated to affect pro- and anti-democratic not-for-profits in similar ways. Our concern is with the impact on democracy-supporting not-for-profits.

In this section, we explore the impact of decreased participation on society and Australian democracy in terms of a trend away from traditional types of citizen engagement as members and responsible persons of organisations towards more professionalised forms of engagement resulting in a decline in organisational diversity. We also look at the link between increased governance expectations and mission drift from participation as an organizational purpose and charitable endeavour.

Ever Professionalising

Rahman and Gilman, writing in the US context, have reflected on the 'shift in recent decades from mass-member organizing to professionalized advocacy groups that engage "members" in a more superficial form through fundraising, petition, and publicity appeals' (Rahman and Gilman 2019, 82). Also in the United States, Skocpol (2003, 7) has referred to the extraordinary transformation of civic life where 'once cross-class voluntary federations held sway, national public life is now dominated by professionally managed advocacy groups without chapters or members'. In the context of changing governance expectations, this membership transformation makes some sense. It means that not-for-profits are able to 'keep the lights on' while ensuring that there is no slippage in the ability to meet regulators' expectations. But as Rahman and Gilman (2019, 82) recognise, something drops out, and that is an ebbing away at the 'capacities of advocacy organizations and movements to build deep ties with on-the-ground constituencies and communities'. With this, there is also a weakening of democratic tools of citizen engagement when more transitory involvement means that there is a gap in the acquisition of a richer citizenry skill set or 'civic capacity' and missed opportunities to train those engaged citizens to become future leaders (Rahman and Gilman 2019, 52). Fundamentally, there is also a significant lessening of the opportunity for citizens to form social bonds with each other and a lessening of social capital (Putnam [2000] 2020, ch. 1; Leigh 2014, ch. 9). In Australia, we see this in the activities of organisations like GetUp or Greenpeace, which are increasingly social media driven and campaign-based.

There is also a centralisation of organisational power away from regional or grassroots bases to the largest urban environments with the reins of not-for-profit management held by the educated elite more than community-based volunteers (Rahman and Gilman 2019, 62; Nel de Koker 2022, 771). The regulatory burdens have only increased this trend. There is a distancing from the community as well as members with lived experiences of the issues that motivate the formation of the not-for-profits in the first place. It resonates with Arnstein's (1969, 217) focus on 'lower rung' forms of participation that centre more on 'placation' and 'consultation' than 'citizen control'.

Professionalisation has also affected the role (and involvement) of board members and senior managers (Considine, O'Sullivan and Nguyen 2015, 55; Hwang and Powell 2009). Historically, a major governance difference between not-for-profit and for-profit organisations has been that the people on not-for-profit boards are far more diverse than those on for-profit boards (Steane and Christie 2001, 49, 52; Kang and Cnaan 1995).[14] This is for a range of reasons. For instance, a common desire that the board be representative of, and enable participation by, the membership base (Steane and Christie 2001, 52; Hwang and Powell 2009, 270), a wish to also include representatives of those served by the not-for-profit's mission (Steane and Christie 2001, 54),[15] and a desire for specific skill sets such as an ability to fundraise from donors or government (Steane and Christie 2001, 49). Until the last few decades, there has been less focus on building up limited ranges of professional expertise and more focus on a broader range of skill sets and experiences (Brueckner, Holmes and Pick 2017, 30). But the last few decades have seen a narrowing of focus, largely aimed at preventing mismanagement of not-for-profits.[16]

In the human services space, for instance, Ife (1997) has noted a dynamic of more top-down modes of acting involving objectively measurable facts, to the detriment of more bottom-up and human-focused approaches. Ife analyses this as a series of four competing discourses in human service delivery, with managerial or professional discourses viewing human services as products or services, whereas a community discourse 'emphasises welfare as a social activity, or *participation* in a community context. In contrast to the other [discourses], it is more of a process than an outcome' (Ife 1997, 50). The contrast that Ife draws between the 'professional' discourse and the 'community'

14. Though of course the degree of diversity has changed across both types of organisations over time, for instance, in relation to matters such as race and gender, among others.
15. In relation to the effects of a stakeholder focus on board composition.
16. For instance, in Australia, the federal charity regulator was initially proposed to have only one objective focused on policing the sector ('maintain, protect and enhance public trust and confidence in the Australian not-for-profit sector') and was initially only funded to pursue that objective, despite the last-minute inclusion of several additional objectives related to supporting the sector and reducing regulatory duplication (Treasury (Cth) 2019, 24–25). The Productivity Commission (2023, 210–11) recently characterised this regulatory focus on trust and confidence as relating primarily to the principal-agent problem whereby the interests of not-for-profit controllers are not aligned with the interests of the public in the pursuit of the not-for-profit's purposes, resulting in mismanagement. See also Adediran (2022, 368, 376).

discourse is interesting in the context of thinking about what increased professionalisation might do to the participatory modes of acting of not-for-profits:

> The *professional* discourse incorporates a policy direction which emphasises the importance of both the quality and available quantity of human service professionals. The way to solve social problems is seen as being to provide skilled professional services for those affected, in sufficient quantity to meet identified needs. Hence the emphasis is on standards of *professional training*, the adequate *certification* of professional workers [...] Finally, in the *community* discourse, desirable policy directions will include *decentralisation*, the *facilitation* of community-based processes and structures through the provision of resources and expertise, and allowing space for community-based initiatives to develop. (Ife 1997, 55, italics in the original)

These views are consistent with Kreutzer and Jager's (2011, 636–38) research on not-for-profit organisations, which emphasise that increasing professionalisation of organisations is causing a shift in organisational identity from one that emphasises 'basic democratic structures and nonmanagerial logics in which integration is more important than efficiency' to one involving more hierarchical, structured and specialised practices (see also Brueckner, Holmes and Pick 2017; Skocpol 2003, 223–29). This is also consistent with the empirical work of Hwang and Powell (2009, 272–73, 286–90). Adediran (2022, 362–67, 394–403), through a study of US public interest legal organisation charities, notes that a narrow focus on legal and financial skills and connections for directors threatens the ability of not-for-profits to both meaningfully serve and 'empower' the communities they serve by failing to understand the social issues faced by those communities and failing to include members of those communities in decision making.

Such a focus on managerial professionalism poses a threat to the inclusion of community members and service recipients on the board. By way of an example, many universities have historically included student representatives in their governing bodies (see e.g. University of Western Australia Act 1911 (WA) section 8(1)(g)), while some community housing providers have included housing tenants as board members (Alliance Housing 2024). Requirements for managerial professionalism have also impacted the ability of Aboriginal and Torres Strait Islander communities to ensure appropriate cultural experience and application of culture by board members of not-for-profit organisations that serve those communities (Murray, Fardin and O'Hara 2019, 53–58, 61–67, 79–80).

Mission Drift

A second historical major governance difference between not-for-profit and for-profit organisations has been a focus on purpose or mission (and the values underlying that purpose) in not-for-profit organisation decision making (Steane and Christie 2001, 49, 55; Nel 2024; Kang and Cnaan 1995; Sugin 2007, 894–97; King 2017, 242–43). While there is increasing discussion of the role of purpose in shaping governance within business corporations (The British Academy 2021; Langford 2020), the difference still remains. Governance obligations that encourage too great a focus on easily-measured objective facts, such as an organisation's financial performance or even selected results or outcomes metrics, risk encouraging decisions that are good for the organisation's financial return or for achievement of a particular performance indicator, but bad for its purpose (Considine, O'Sullivan and Nguyen 2014, 95; Keevers et al. 2012; Eikenberry and Kluver 2004, 136; Adediran 2022, 368–69; Sugin 2007, 894–97; Synge 2023, ch. 6; Siciliano 1996, 1318; Power 1999; Nel 2024, ch. 9), including to the extent that the purpose involves civic participation. This can result from changes in the relationship between the not-for-profit and its stakeholders, such as its funders, service recipients, members and volunteers (Zimmerman and Dart 1998; Dart 2004; Dees 1998, 58–62; Kim 2005).[17]

For instance, Synge's analysis of governance in English not-for-profit universities highlights that, for the majority of universities, the approach to governance is *not* purpose-based (2023, ch. 6). Instead of facilitating and encouraging education and research for the public good, Synge suggests that most governance models emphasise (inapt) proxies such as university ranking metrics and student numbers. Synge considers that a major reason for this mission drift is a drastic reduction of participation by academics in governance structures (2023, 278).

By way of another example, not-for-profits that focus on raising revenue from contracts for services often do not receive direct funding to cover advocacy activities on behalf of the people who receive that service. They may also be concerned about overtly criticising government funders (Riboldi, Fennis and Steer 2022; Phillips 2007). Focusing on financial returns and cutting unprofitable activities could mean that the expressive dimensions of a not-for-profit are discontinued, even if important to its purpose (Eikenberry and Kluver 2004, 136–37). Likewise, it could also mean cutting programmes focused on community participation, such as volunteer programs (Backman and Rathgeb Smith 2000, 368–69).[18] A focus on financial return from service delivery might even cause not-for-profits to adjust the community to whom they deliver services (so as to exclude hard-to-serve members) and so impact the degree of participation by community members in that way too (Eikenberry and Kluver 2004, 136). Even a focus on acquittal against non-financial outcomes or results might mean cutting or de-emphasising participatory activities that are not considered when the focus is on the delivery and outcome of services. For instance, Keevers et al. refer to the 'foregrounding of service provision in RBA [results based accountability] planning [being] accompanied by a backgrounding of the importance of reciprocity and belonging' to social justice services (Keevers et al. 2012, 110).

17. As to a focus on purpose and values indicating a stakeholder-focussed approach, see Steane and Christie (2001, 55).
18. Or putting off volunteers due to the new emphasis on business-like activities rather than social mission (Dees 1998, 58).

Conclusion

As Miller (2018, 7) has indicated:

> Perhaps, as Tocqueville and others have argued, democracy isn't merely a form of government, it is also a way of life, and shared faith, instantiated in other forms of association, in modes of thought and belief, in the attitudes and inclinations of individuals who have absorbed a kind of democratic temperament.

This chapter has suggested that the changing 'corporatisation' or hyper-regulation of the not-for-profit sector is having unintended consequences for participation in the third sector as well as the role of not-for-profits as sites of collective action and for civic participation more generally. While increasing regulatory expectations may improve confidence in the sector in some senses, it also can deplete it of the participatory life force that has historically contributed to the vigour of the not-for-profit sector as a whole. While this tension is not easily resolved, it is an important discussion to ensure that civil society can retain its diversity and vibrancy and to keep citizens from 'bowling alone'.

References

ACNC (Cth). 2023a. *Australian Charities Report – 9th Edition*. Melbourne: ACNC.

ACNC (Cth). 2023b. '2023 Annual Information Statement Guide'. https://www.acnc.gov.au/tools/guides/2023-annual-information-statement-guide (accessed 31 May 2024).

ACNC (Cth). nd a. 'Governance for Good: A Guide for Responsible People'. https://www.acnc.gov.au/tools/guides/governance-for-good-acncs-guide-for-responsible-people (accessed 30 May 2024).

ACNC (Cth). nd b. 'Reporting Annually to the ACNC'. https://www.acnc.gov.au/for-charities/manage-your-charity/obligations-acnc/reporting-annually-acnc (accessed 31 May 2024).

Adediran, A. O. 2022. 'Nonprofit Board Composition'. *Ohio State Law Journal* 83 (2): 357–421.

AICD. 2023. *Not-for-profit Governance and Performance Study 2023*. Sydney: AICD.

Alliance Housing. 2024. 'Our CEO and Board'. https://www.alliancehousing.com.au/our-team (accessed 24 July 2024).

Andrias, K. and Sachs, B. I. 2021. 'Constructing Countervailing Power: Law and Organizing in an Era of Political Inequality'. *Yale Law Journal* 130 (3): 546–635.

Anheier, Helmut K., Lang, M. and Stefan, Toepler S. 2020. 'Comparative Nonprofit Sector Research: A Critical Assessment'. In *The Nonprofit Sector: A Research Handbook*, edited by P. Bromley and W. W. Powell, 3rd edn, 648–676. Stanford: Stanford University Press

Anheier, Helmut K. and Toepler, S. 2023. *Nonprofit Organizations: Theory, Management, Policy*, 3rd edn. Oxon: Routledge.

Arnstein, S. R. 1969. 'A Ladder of Citizen Participation'. *Journal of the American Institute of Planners* 35 (4): 216–224.

ASX Corporate Governance Council. 2019. *ASX Corporate Governance Principles and Recommendations*, 4th edn. Australia: ASX Corporate Governance Council.

Backman, E. V. and Rathgeb Smith, S. 2000. 'Healthy Organizations, Unhealthy Communities?'. *Nonprofit Management & Leadership* 10 (4): 355–373.

Biddle, N., Boyer, C., Gray, M. and Jahromi, M. 2022. *Volunteering in Australia 2022: The Volunteer Perspective*. Canberra: Australian National University Centre for Social Research and Methods.

Biddle, N. and Gray, M. 2023. 'Ongoing Trends in Volunteering in Australia'. ANU Centre for Social Research and Methods. https://csrm.cass.anu.edu.au/sites/default/files/docs/2023/10/Ongoing_trends_in_volunteering_in_Australia.pdf.

Bourdieu, P. and Wacquant, L. P. D. 1992. *An Invitation to Reflexive Sociology*. Chicago: University of Chicago Press.

Brand, V., Fitzpatrick, J. and Lombard, S. 2013. 'Governance and Not-for-profits: Regulatory Reform'. *Flinders Law Journal* 15: 381–409.

Brinkerhoff, J. and Brinkerhoff, D. 2002. 'Government-Nonprofit Relations in Comparative Perspective'. *Public Administration and Development* 22 (1): 3–18.

Brueckner, M., Holmes, K. and Pick, D. 2017. 'Out of Sight: Volunteering in Remote Locations in Western Australia in the Shadow of Managerialism'. *Third Sector Review* 23 (1): 29–49.

Centre for Corporate Public Affairs. 2008. *Relationship Matters: Not-for-profit Community Organisations and Corporate Community Investment*. Sydney: Centre for Corporate Public Affairs.

Chambers, S. and Kopstein, J. 2001. 'Bad Civil Society'. *Political Theory* 29 (6): 837–865.

Chelliah, J., Boersma, M. and Klettner, A. 2016. 'Governance Challenges for Not-for-profit Organisations: Empirical Evidence in Support of a Contingency Approach'. *Contemporary Management Research* 12 (1): 3–24.

Clemens, E. 2006. 'The Constitution of Citizens: Political Theories of Nonprofit Organizations'. In *The Nonprofit Sector: A Research Handbook*, edited by W. Powell and R. Steinberg, 207–220, 2nd edn. New Haven: Yale University Press.

Clemens, E. 2020. 'Nonprofits as Boundary Markers'. In *The Nonprofit Sector: A Research Handbook*, edited by P. Bromley and W. W. Powell, 192–207, 3rd edn. Stanford: Stanford University Press.

Coleman, J. S. 1988. 'Social Capital in the Creation of Human Capital'. *American Journal of Sociology* 94: S95–S120.

Considine, M., O'Sullivan, S. and Nguyen, P. 2014. '"Mission Drift" The Third Sector and the Pressure to be Businesslike: Evidence from Job Services Australia'. *Third Sector Review* 20 (1): 87–107.

Considine, M., O'Sullivan, S. and Nguyen, P. 2015. 'Governance, Boards of Directors and the Impact of Contracting on Not-for-profits Organizations – An Australian Study'. In *Contracting-out Welfare Services: Comparing National Policy Designs for Unemployment Assistance*, edited by Mark Considine and Siobhan O'Sullivan, 55–74. Chichester: Wiley.

Cornish, M. 2013. 'Exploring Social Networks of Non-executive Directors in Australian Third Sector Organisations'. *Third Sector Review* 19 (1): 51–73.

Dart, R. 2004. 'Being "Business-Like" in a Nonprofit Organization: A grounded and Inductive Typology'. *Nonprofit and Voluntary Sector Quarterly* 33 (2): 290–310.

Dees, J. G. 1998. 'Enterprising Nonprofits'. *Harvard Business Review* 76 (1): 54–67.

Eikenberry, A. M. and Kluver, J. D. 2004. 'The Marketization of the Nonprofit Sector: Civil Society at Risk?'. *Public Administration Review* 64 (2): 132–140.

Farrar, J. and Hanrahan, P. 2017. *Corporate Governance*. Chatswood: LexisNexis.

Garton, J. 2009. *The Regulation of Organised Civil Society*. Oxford: Hart Publishing.

Havel, Vaclav. 1992. *Summer Meditations*. New York: Vintage Books.

Hendriks, C. M., Ercan, S. E. and Boswell, J. 2020. *Mending Democracy: Democratic Repair in Disconnected Times*. Cambridge: Cambridge University Press.

Horvath, A. and Powell, W. 2020. 'Seeing Like a Philanthropist'. In *The Nonprofit Sector: A Research Handbook*, edited by W. Powell and P. Bromley, 3rd edn, 81–122. Stanford: Stanford University Press

Hwang, H. and Powell, W. W. 2009. 'The Rationalization of Charity: The Influences of Professionalism in the Nonprofit Sector'. *Administrative Science Quarterly* 54 (2): 268–298.

Ife, J. 1997. *Rethinking Social Work*, 39–76. Frenchs Forest: Pearson Education Australia.

Kang, C. H. and Cnaan, R. A. 1995. 'New Findings on Large Human Service Organization Boards of Trustees'. *Administration in Social Work* 19 (3): 17–44.

Keevers, L., Treleaven, L., Sykes, C. and Darcy, M. 2012. 'Made to Measure: Taming Practices with Results-based Accountability'. *Organization Studies* 33 (1): 97–120.

Kim, S. 2005. 'Balancing Competing Accountability Requirements'. *Public Performance & Management Review* 29 (2): 145–163.

King, D. 2017. 'Becoming Business-Like: Governing the Nonprofit Professional'. *Nonprofit and Voluntary Sector Quarterly* 46 (2): 241–260.

Kreutzer, K. and Jager, U. 2011. 'Volunteering versus Managerialism: Conflict over Organizational Identity in Voluntary Associations'. *Nonprofit and Voluntary Sector Quarterly* 40 (4): 634–661.

Kurti, P. 2013. 'In the Pay of the Piper: Governments, Not-for-Profits, and the Burden of Regulation'. *Issue Analysis* 139: 1–16.

Langford, R. T. 2020. 'Purpose-Based Governance: A New Paradigm'. *University of New South Wales Law Journal* 43 (3): 954–976.

Langford, R. T. and Webster, M. 2023. 'The Australian Charitable Incorporated Organisation: A Reform Proposal'. *Company and Securities Law Journal* 39 (5): 347–374.

Law Council of Australia. 2023. 'Letter to Treasury on Miscellaneous Amendments to Treasury Portfolio Laws 2023', 23 August. https://lawcouncil.au/publicassets/538124aa-d646-ee11-948a-005056be13b5/4411%20-%20S%20-%20Miscellaneous%20Amendments%20to%20Treasury%20Portfolio%20Laws%202023.pdf.

Lechterman, T. and Reich, R. 2020. 'Political Theory and the Nonprofit Sector'. In *The Nonprofit Sector: A Research Handbook*, edited by P. Bromley and W. W. Powell, 171–191, 3rd edn. Stanford: Stanford University Press.

Leigh, A. 2014. *Disconnected*. Sydney: University of New South Wales Press.

Mex, C. L. 2018. 'Stepping Up or Stepping Out? Recruitment and Retention of Volunteer Leaders in Grassroots Associations'. *Third Sector Review* 24 (1): 71–96.

Mex, C. L. 2022. 'The Free-fall of Volunteer Leaders in Australian Grassroots Associations' (National Strategy for Volunteering Research Working Group, Volunteering Research Paper). https://www.volunteeringaustralia.org/wp-content/uploads/VRP_The-free-fall-of-volunteer-leaders-in-Australian-grassroots-associations.pdf.

Miller, J. 2018. *Can Democracy Work?*. London: Oneworld Publications.

Murray, I. 2014–2015. 'The Australian Charities and Not-for-profits Commission: Reform or Un-Reform?'. *The Charity Law & Practice Review* 17: 151–171.

Murray, I. 2018. 'Regulating Charity in a Federated State: The Australian Perspective'. *Nonprofit Policy Forum* 9 (4): 1–17.

Murray, I., Fardin, J. and O'Hara, J. 2019. *Co-designing Benefits Management Structures*. Perth: UWA Centre for Mining, Energy and Natural Resources Law.

Nel, J. Y. 2024. *Regulating the Conduct of Volunteer Directors in the Australian Charity Sector: Aligning Mission and Accountability*. La Trobe University, PhD.

Nel de Koker, J. 2022. 'Regulating Volunteer Directors' Duties in Companies registered with the Australian Charities and Not-For-profits Commission'. *University of New South Wales Law Journal* 45 (2): 764–797.

Nicholas, Josh. 2023. 'Australians aren't Joining in Any More – And it Appears to be having Big Political Consequences'. *Guardian*, 12 November, https://www.theguardian.com/australia-news/2023/nov/12/australians-arent-joining-in-any-more-and-it-appears-to-be-having-big-political-consequences.

Owen, N. 2003. *The HIH Royal Commission – Vol 1*. Canberra: Canberra Publishing and Printing.

Phillips, R. 2007. 'Tamed or Trained? The Co-option and Capture of "Favoured" NGOs'. *Third Sector Review* 13 (2): 27–48.

Power, M. 1999. *The Audit Society: Rituals of Verification*. Oxford: Oxford University Press.

Productivity Commission (Cth). 2010. *Contribution of the Not-for-Profit Sector: Research Report.* Melbourne: Productivity Commission.

Productivity Commission (Cth). 2023. *Future Foundations for Giving: Draft Report.* Canberra: Productivity Commission.

Putnam, R. 2020. *Bowling Alone: The Collapse and Revival of American Community.* New York: Simon & Schuster (paperback edition, 2000 original).

Rahman, K. S. and Gilman, H. R. 2019. *Civic Power: Rebuilding American Democracy in an Era of Crisis.* Cambridge: Cambridge University Press.

Ramsay, I. and Webster, M. 2017. 'Registered Charities and Governance Standard 5: An Evaluation'. *Australian Business Law Review* 45 (2): 127–158.

Riboldi, M., Fennis, L. and teer, M. 2022. *Nurturing Links Across Civil Society: Lessons from Australia's For-Purpose Sector's Response to COVID-19.* Sydney: Sydney Policy Lab, University of Sydney.

Siciliano, J. I. 1996. 'The Relationship of Board Member Diversity to Organizational Performance'. *Journal of Business Ethics* 15 (12): 1313–1320.

Skocpol, T. 2003. *Diminished Democracy: From Membership to Management in American Civic Life.* Norman: University of Oklahoma Press.

Zimmerman, B. and Dart, R. 1998. *Charities Doing Commercial Ventures: Societal and Organizational Implications.* Toronto: Canadian Policy Research Networks Inc and Trillium Foundation.

Sugin, L. 2007. 'Resisting the Corporatization of Nonprofit Governance: Transforming Obedience into Fidelity'. *Fordham Law Review* 76: 893–927.

Synge, M. 2023. *The University-Charity: Challenging Perceptions in Higher Education.* England: Mary Synge.

The British Academy. 2021. *Corporation Programme on 'Policy & Practice for Purposeful Business'.* London: The British Academy.

Treasury (Cth). 2011. *Scoping Study for a National Not-for-profit Regulator: Final Report.* Treasury.

Treasury (Cth). 2018. *Strengthening for Purpose: Australian Charities and Not-for-Profits Commission Legislation Review 2018.* Parkes: Treasury.

Zimmerman, B. and Dart, R. 1998. *Charities Doing Commercial Ventures: Societal and Organizational Implications.* Toronto: Canadian Policy Research Networks Inc and Trillium Foundation.

Chapter 11

CIVIC ENGAGEMENT AMONG THE AUSTRALIAN AFRICAN DIASPORA: NATIONAL AND TRANSNATIONAL ACTIVITY

Farida Fozdar, Sarah Prout Quicke, Dominic Dagbanja, David Mickler, Nothando Ngwenya, Chika Anyanwu, Janet Dzator, Karen Farquarson, Alan Gamlen and Kiros Hiruy[1]

Introduction

A key indicator of successful migrant settlement is often identified as participation in civic life, both in formal processes such as voting and lobbying politicians in liberal democracies, and informally in associational engagement and activity. Such engagement is also vital for a sense of national belonging and integration. According to Ager and Strang (2008, 170), civic rights are the foundation on which other settlement outcomes for migrants rest.

This chapter considers the forms of civic engagement, nationally and transnationally, of one of Australia's newest and most visible migrant diaspora communities, those from the African continent. It considers not only participation in Australian democracy but also the importance of civil society groups and transnational political engagements. We argue that civic responsibility, with a transnational orientation, is a feature of this migrant community, demonstrating a positive commitment to formal and informal democratic participation in both the host nation and the country of origin. This broader transnational political connection and commitment demands, we argue, a reconsideration of definitions of the Habermasian 'public sphere' as being bounded by the nation-state. However, we acknowledge that these 'transnational' connections are just that, enactments of a political (and economic) commitment based on *national* affiliation to home and host countries, as per Anderson's (1983) classic notion of 'imagined communities' which exist within the minds of co-nationals and manifest as 'long-distance nationalism' (see also Skrbis 2017). Thus we demonstrate Calhoun's (2007) argument that 'nations [still] matter', even for migrant populations. Rather than reporting evidence of

---

1. The authors are working on an ARC-funded project (DP220101642) investigating the political and economic agency of Africans in Australia.

cosmopolitan universalism in political engagement, even while personal identities begin to broaden as pan-African, African migrants' civic commitment is to two nation-states – Australia and their countries of origin.

We begin by considering migrants' civic engagement generally and in the Australian context and then briefly outline details of the African diaspora in Australia as background. We then make several observations about their civic or political engagement based on preliminary data from exploratory studies. These include consideration of formal citizenship, voting and political participation and other forms of civic engagement and community activity nationally and transnationally, together with questions of pan-African and diasporic local engagement. We conclude with some questions for further research.

Migrants and Civic Engagement

The ability to participate in civic life is often viewed as a key indicator of successful migrant integration. For example, in their now classic model of successful settlement and integration of refugees, Ager and Strang (2008, 166–91) argue that political rights are paramount. Their model presents as an inverse triangle, in some ways the inverse of Maslow's hierarchy of needs, of 10 domains of integration, with 'rights and citizenship' as the anchor domain (Figure 11.1) from which flow social relations and therefore opportunities in the more material and social elements of settlement.

These material aspects (the top layer), which are both markers of integration and the means of achieving it (employment, housing, education and health), rely upon the second layer of social connections, social bonds (connection within one's group), bridges (connections between groups) and links (with structures of the state), which are, in turn, facilitated by language, cultural knowledge, safety and stability (the next layer). But

Figure 11.1 Ager and Strang's 10 domains of migrant integration.

the foundation is rights and citizenship, which require specific legal and institutional structures to facilitate them – thus the means available at this foundational level are key.

These structures differ, of course, by country of settlement and visa category, even across liberal democracies. Ager and Strang (2008, 174) make the point that some countries, such as Germany, conceptualise citizenship as a quality of membership of a community of descent, making the settlement and integration of migrants difficult. Others, such as the UK and Australia (with some limitations), use an ethnic pluralist definition, enabling belonging to rest on shared rights such as human dignity, equality, freedom of cultural choice, justice, security and independence. We see here that a broad definition of citizenship, rather than a more limited formal legal one, is being used in Ager and Strang's conceptualisation of this foundation. But both are important in determining positive settlement outcomes. It is both the formal and informal aspects of civic engagement that we consider in this chapter.

Civic engagement requires agency. Davies (1991, 51) argues that one can think of agency as the ability of an individual to possess or access the freedom to 'have the right to speak and to be heard', as well as to act to achieve outcomes that align with their 'meanings and desires' as they navigate the social constraints within which their identity is positioned. Thus, people, as actors in the public sphere, are able to take action that achieves their desired results or outcomes. With Hakli and Kallio (2014, 181), we see political agency as the ways in which individuals and collectives actively engage in structured activity such as social movements and institutional political processes. But we also recognise that civic engagement may be more informal in terms of community connections and action and that it requires resources (time, money, skills), psychological engagement (political interest and information, sense of political efficacy and so forth) and social networks (Hoefer 2021, 68). This can be a challenge for migrants. We also recognise, as Hakli and Kallio (2014, 190) also argue, that political engagement is subject to, or at least informed by, the physical and social space that individuals occupy and navigate within, spaces that may be constrained for migrants.

One cannot talk about political agency without considering the concept of the public sphere, as developed by Jurgen Habermas, as the basis for democratic engagement. Habermas (1984, 1996) sees the public sphere as an 'intersubjectively shared space' wherein opinion is developed through communicative rationality, a process designed to reach understanding through reflexivity and respectful listening, formal inclusion, discursive equality and autonomy (Dahlberg 2005, 112). While these conditions are not easily met, they provide a framework for considering how migrants might begin to be included as well as take action themselves to ensure they are heard.

What is often omitted from discussions of Habermas is the scale and location of the 'public sphere'. There is a tendency to assume the nation-state is the unit of analysis, displaying the common fallacy of methodological nationalism (Beck 2007) that presumes the social (and therefore the political) is bounded by the nation-state, or at best is the unit understood as the logical structure for such analysis. On the contrary, for migrants, political engagement may extend beyond the host country to countries of origin and beyond, as we will see shortly.

Benedict Anderson's classic conceptualisation of the nation actually recognises this. He argues the nation exists as an 'imagined community' – 'imagined because the members of even the smallest nation will never know most of their fellow-members, meet them, or even hear of them, yet in the minds of each lives the image of their communion' (1983, 6–7). This communion is a 'deep, horizontal comradeship', which he notes, importantly, has elastic boundaries beyond the state. In the same way that the means of communication (the printing press) connected and created that imagination within the nation-state in the nineteenth and twentieth centuries, in the 40 years since Anderson was writing both the forms of communication and processes of *diaspora-isation* have expanded to enable strong transnational commitments among transmigrants across continents.

Thus, the phenomenon of long-distance nationalism, the political consciousness and engagement, as well as identity reproduction, that exists across international borders (Skrbis 2017) is increasingly visible. Indeed, Skrbis (2017, xiii) has argued that 'it is mistaken to see globalisation, transnationalisation and nationalist processes as contradictory. Rather, they should be seen as complementing each other' and existing simultaneously. While Skrbis was more interested in the effect of the long-distance nationalism of former Yugoslav (Slav and Croatian) migrants to Australia on internal nationalist struggles, there is also a developing role for transnational engagements that have a more developmental focus. We are interested in how this plays out in the democratic engagement of a relatively new and visible migrant community in relation to the host nation and their countries of origin.

Thus, we argue that Ager and Strang's model, Habermas' framework for communicative action in the public sphere and Anderson's insights on long-distance nationalism provide useful analytical tools to explore political engagement among migrants, particularly as they offer a foundation for successful settlement and integration, as well as ongoing commitment to political and economic processes in countries of origin. What that engagement looks like in practice is a matter for empirical investigation.

Migrants' Political Engagement in Australia

There have been a number of studies of political engagement of migrants within Australia. While older work has shown that migrants and ethnic minorities in Australia tend to vote for social-democratic parties (McAllister and Makkai 1991) as in other Western democracies (for the UK, see Saggar 2000); Bilodeau, McAllister and Kanji (2010) and Jiang (2016, 430) found that migrants participate at least as much and tend to vote in similar patterns to the rest of the Australian population, with non-English-speaking background (NESB) voters resembling Australian migrant voters of English-speaking backgrounds and Australian-born voters. Zhinger and Thomas (2012, 378) pointed out that the immigrant bloc is not a monolith, demonstrating differences in political participation patterns (measured by interest in politics and voting) among migrants to Australia by ethnicity and socioeconomic factors. Bilodeau, McAllister and Kanji (2010, 149–51) found that in Australia, migrants from authoritarian regimes tend to be less supportive of democracy yet participate at least as much as the rest of the population in electoral activities, noting both the persistence of, and change in, migrants' pre-migration political orientations.

Work by Kirpitchenko and Mansouri (2014), using the lens of social capital and active citizenship, emphasises the importance of young migrants' agency in negotiating, interpreting and appropriating the conditions of social inclusion, and as well as the importance of social networks and creative civic engagement in their ability to do so (Mansouri and Kirpitchenko 2016, 319–20). Another focus of Australian research has been on Muslim migrants, with a range of authors reporting active, self-driven participation in multicultural civic spaces, particularly among the young and a growing professional elite, as well as those who are more religious (Roose and Harris 2015; Peucker, Roose and Akbarzadeh 2014; Vergani et al. 2017), challenging stereotypes of disengaged religious minorities.

And participation appears related to access to government services. In a recent study of the civic engagement of migrants and its relationship with multicultural service provision in Australia, Mansouri and colleagues (2024) found access to services, rather than contributing to urban segregation and social exclusion, is significantly correlated with higher levels of civic engagement.

In a comprehensive study using the Australian Election Study data, Clive Bean (2012, 116) reports earlier work that shows Australians demonstrate political participation through voting and working cooperatively with others but are less likely to work for political parties or candidates than in some other countries. Significantly, he found migrants follow this pattern. He attributes this Australian pattern to the compulsory voting system, which requires less campaign engagement, given citizens are required to vote. Yet he also states that direct campaigning (such as trying to persuade others to vote for a particular party or candidate, supporting a party or candidate by attending a meeting or putting up a poster, attending political meetings or rallies or contributing money to a political party or election candidate) by migrants and non-migrants alike, while low, is equivalent to the prevalence of these activities in other countries.

However, Bean (2012, 121) does find that NESB migrants are less likely to discuss politics with others than either the Australian-born or migrants from an English-speaking background, yet perhaps contradictorily, are more likely to try to persuade others how to vote. He finds that, of all factors, being born in a non-English-speaking country is the most likely predictor of political participation (2012, 124). Bean reports that despite the influxes of migrants from a range of European and Asian countries that may not have strong democratic traditions, migrants show little or no sign of participatory disadvantage and, in fact, tend to participate more than the Australian-born in things such as campaign activities. He did find some sociodemographic groups were disadvantaged in their use of the internet for accessing election information. On more general civic engagement in communal activities (participating in protests, working with others who share a concern, contacting a politician about something), their interest in politics, trust in government and belief that their vote can make a difference, Bean finds migrants are similar to the wider Australian population, which reflects levels of engagement in other similar countries. So in short, nothing to see here – migrants to Australia are typical in their civic engagement compared to non-migrant Australians.

Yet there remains a perception that migrants may be excluded from civic participation due to a range of barriers. Indeed, a number of resources have been developed to encourage migrants to get involved in civic life. The Settlement Council of Australia (SCOA 2018), for example, developed a discussion paper on civic participation, defined as the ability 'to effectively engage in the Australian community and exercise their individual and collective rights under the law'. This is both a broad (it is unclear what 'effectively engage' means) and a narrow (limiting participation to the exercise of legal rights) definition. They found migrants from humanitarian backgrounds tend to engage in cultural activities, such as festivals or celebration of special days, followed by participation in school activities; but their engagement in formal processes of democratic action is lower. Not surprisingly, civic engagement improved over time. Barriers to civic participation identified include education and English language levels, employment, financial hardship and sense of belonging. The Federation of Ethnic Communities Councils has produced a toolkit for civic participation (FECCA 2022) to help migrants understand civic participation processes such as setting up an organisation, lobbying politicians, gaining support and fundraising, community leadership and advocacy. The resource also provides information on more formal institutional processes such as levels of government, the democratic system and so on. Thus service providers have sought to improve access to political representation for migrant communities in Australia.

We turn now to the emerging African migrant community in Australia to consider what is known about their democratic participation and the range of ways in which they connect locally and transnationally to pursue their interests.

African Australians' Civic Engagement in Australian Democracy

There has been little direct work on African migrants' experiences of rights and citizenship. Fozdar and Hartley (2013) found refugees from African backgrounds perceive belonging and unbelonging in ways that mirror the theoretical ethnic versus civic nationalism distinction found in Western conceptualisations of nationalism. Civic belonging is predominant in the ways African refugees talk about belonging in Australia and is experienced in terms of access to services and rights. This can be seen in the following quotes from their participants.

> *Interviewer:* Do you think you belong here in Australia?
> *Respondent:* Not really because I do not understand Australian people [...] in terms of communication as I can't express in front of them and let myself be understood.
> *Interviewer:* Where do you belong/not belong?
> *Respondent:* I know that I belong to Australia, because I receive all assistance as a citizen. *(Male, Congo)*

> *Interviewer:* Do you feel you belong here in Australia?
> *Respondent:* I don't feel welcome here sometimes, even though I wanted to be one of the Australians. But I'm hoping one day, I will feel Australia is my home too.
> *Interviewer:* Do you think that there is anything that could make you feel more like you belong here? If yes, what?

Respondent: I belong here because the security here is good, I don't have to worry about anything. I'm getting the services that are normally needed to have progress, such as education, health. I can grow to what I wanted, and my dreams can be true.
(Male, Sudan[2] (Dinka))

But the African migrants simultaneously aspire to 'ethnic' belonging. This is difficult, however, given their experiences of interpersonal and structural exclusion from/by mainstream Australian society, as described below.

Interviewer: Do you feel that you belong to Australia and the area you live in?
Respondent: Actually I can't doubt that Australia is a very convenient country and we have very good support from the government but I really have some concerns about the way of treating us. I feel like most of Australian people are racist; they judge you just because of your colour.
(Male, Ethiopia)

Interviewer: Where do you feel you belong: to Australia, your local area, somewhere else or a combination of places or nowhere?
Respondent: I feel like I'm still belonging to South Sudan. I wanted to belong here, but sometimes; I don't feel welcome in the society.
(Female, Sudan (Dinka))

Research into the effects of citizenship testing legislation introduced in the early 2000s, which critics suggest moved formal membership of the nation-state along the civic-ethnic continuum towards the ethnic end by testing values and historical cultural knowledge, found that access to formal citizenship has become difficult for some African migrants. Indeed, Ndhlovu (2011, 450) argues that Australia's citizenship regime targets black Africans particularly negatively despite citizenship being of fundamental importance to them.

For young refugees, including those of African backgrounds, Nunn et al. (2016, 382) found that citizenship is indeed seen as of great benefit, providing opportunities for mobility, transnational identities and attachments, protection and security. In an application of Ager and Strang's model to understand settlement and integration among Africans in Australia, Fozdar (2023) finds very little research on political engagement with, and articulation of, civic rights among these communities, and a bias towards studies of migrants from refugee backgrounds, making generalisation difficult.

2. Note that the country of origin is identified as Sudan rather than South Sudan because, at the time of interview, South Sudan did not yet exist.

Who Is the African Diaspora in Australia?

Before considering other dimensions of African Australians' civic engagement, it is necessary to outline the demographics of this emerging migrant population. Australia has seen a rapid increase in the number and diversity of African migrants over the past two decades, creating a range of transnational political, economic and cultural links and further diversifying contemporary multicultural Australian society away from its Eurocentric and 'White Australia' foundations. At the most recent (2021) Census, 3.2 per cent of the Australian population were either born in, or have at least one parent born in, Africa. Around 496,140 African-born people were estimated to be living in Australia at that time and a further 326,280 were born in Australia to at least one African-born parent (Prout Quicke 2023, 2). Interestingly, 70.5 per cent of the African-born population are from just five countries – South Africa (40.7 per cent), Egypt, Zimbabwe, Mauritius and Kenya – each of which have racially diverse populations, including those of European, Indian and Arab, as well as black African, backgrounds.

Three characteristics of the African diaspora, in particular, bear further comment here. First, despite the concentration of migrants from a small handful of countries, the African diaspora in Australia is highly diverse in terms of visa category (i.e. skilled, humanitarian, international student), historical experience, race and ethnicity, generation, age, religious identification and expression, culture, language and socioeconomic status (Prout Quicke 2023). These forms of diversity stratify the diaspora with regard to their ability to participate politically, economically and socially in Australian life.

Second, 78.6 per cent of African-born migrants have arrived in Australia since the late 1990s (Prout Quicke 2023, 4). Because most Africans are relatively recent arrivals and because they still represent a small share of all migrants, their experiences of settlement, integration and civic participation are both nascent and understudied – they have not been subject to the same degree of scholarly examination as some of Australia's more established migrant communities, such as those from Eastern Europe and Asia.

Third, negative publicity about African migrants has been a feature of Australian media and political rhetoric in the recent past, and this has been reinforced by existing research that has often focused on settlement problems among a small minority from particular countries and of refugee backgrounds, and the interpersonal and structural racism they face (Fozdar 2023). The effect of such dominant narratives can be to mask evidence of more positive settlement experiences, and broader and deeper processes of deliberate, innovative and active engagement with civic and democratic processes in Australia and beyond, among the African diaspora. It is to this that we now turn.

Formal Citizenship, Voting, and Formal and Informal Political Participation

Most African migrants in Australia have arrived in Australia since the introduction of a limited migration system focused on skilled migrants and since pathways to citizenship have narrowed. While some African countries have made it possible for their diaspora members to acquire dual citizenship and retain voting rights in their countries of origin, others have not. This can significantly affect both the nature of the diaspora's political engagement and their ability to move freely between home and host countries.

Despite these challenges, Census data reveal the African diaspora has disproportionate levels of citizenship and hence formal voting rights. Figure 11.2 presents a bar chart of the voting-age population in Australia by migrant and citizenship status. Migrants are disaggregated into two categories: those born in Africa and those born elsewhere overseas (other migrants). 'Voters' are migrants who have citizenship status in Australia, given that only Australian citizens can vote in Australian elections.

It shows, unsurprisingly, that the largest share (65 per cent) of the voting-age population are Australian-born citizens. A further 35 per cent were born overseas but have Australian citizenship. And over 1 in 10 (12.9 per cent) of the voting-age population are temporary migrants who are restricted by their visa status from voting in Australian elections. For our population of interest, while they make up a small overall share of the voting-age population (1.9 per cent), African migrants are more likely to be voting citizens than other migrants (77.1 per cent compared to 62.1 per cent). In other words, despite Ndhlovu's (2011) concerns outlined above, African migrants are securing Australian citizenship (and hence voting rights) at a higher rate than other migrants.

More recent data from the Scanlon Foundation Research Institute's Mapping Social Cohesion study, provided by our colleagues from the Australian National University who manage the study on behalf of and in collaboration with the Institute, tell a similar story of active social and political engagement, although they are slightly less active on some counts than the general population. Unpublished findings from the 2023 data show that, in the last three years, 42 per cent of African migrant respondents reported having signed a petition (compared to 50 per cent of the total sample) and 16 per cent

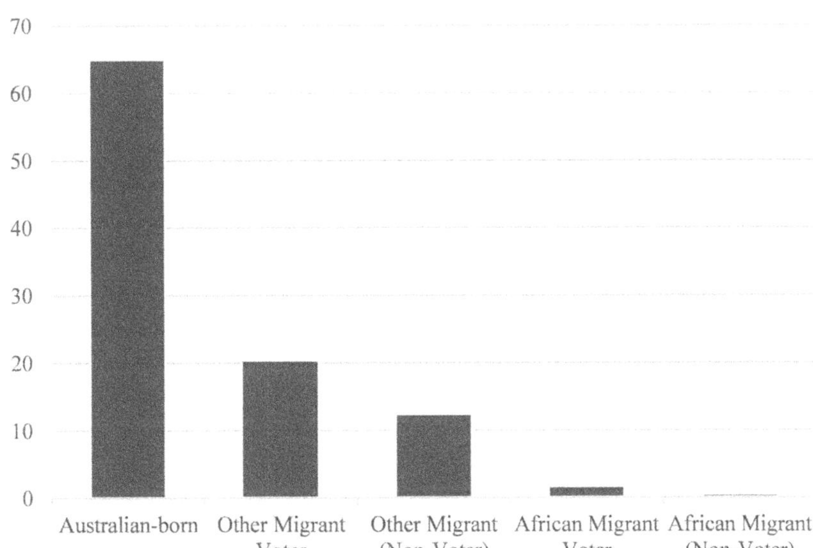

Figure 11.2 Voting-age population in Australia, 2021.

report having written or spoken to a Federal or State Member of Parliament (compared to 20 per cent of the total sample) (pers comm, 2023 survey data[3]).

African migrants are also increasingly entering politics formally in Australia. This includes African-born migrants of European descent such as Sussan Ley (Nigeria) and David Pocock (South Africa), as well as those of North African (Ann Aly, Egypt) and Sub-Saharan African descent. Lucy Gichuhi (born in Kenya), for example, was the first person of Black African descent to be elected to the Australian Parliament in 2017. Others have since followed at the state and territory level, including Ayor Makur Chuot (of South Sudanese descent), who in 2021 became the first MP of African descent to sit in the Western Australian Parliament.

African-born parliamentarians in Australia bring with them knowledge of, experience in, and connections to the African continent that are largely absent from the wider Australian political class. They also likely have additional layers of connection to African diasporic communities in Australia beyond their own immediate electoral constituencies and, as such, can better understand and are perhaps more willing to advocate for issues important to those communities within wider political debates, although how and the extent to which they do so is also mediated by their ideological, party and policy preferences. The visible differences between white and non-white African-born members of Australian parliaments also shape their ability to serve as political role models. The connections to Africa of those of European descent may not be immediately distinguishable or widely known. Yet for Black and other non-white Africans, their visibility among largely white Australian parliaments provides an indication to others that political careers in Australia are possible, even if challenging, for Black and other people of colour. This can also raise expectations by both diasporic communities and the mainstream around their assumed or automatic 'representation' of other Black Africans in Australia, which in turn may create both opportunities and burdens for those MPs.

In terms of direct engagement with the Australian government, results from a recent small exploratory Delphi study undertaken by some of the current authors (see Fozdar et al. 2022 for a description of the methodology) revealed that most participants expressed disappointment at the lack of interest shown by the Australian government in their communities and issues seen as important to them. Comments suggested a perception that there is no clear direction in how the Australian government is dialoguing with African migrants or governments on the continent, particularly regarding the engagement of the African diaspora in Australia on issues such as education and health, youth employment, skills exchange and reducing and regulating remittance costs. One participant suggested that African communities are sometimes 'used' by Australian politicians to 'spruik their multicultural credentials' through the media and

---

3. Permission to use this data and analysis has been provided by the researchers. The Scanlon survey data prior to 2022 is available from the Australian Data Archive (ADA | Australian Data Archive). Further information on the African sample can be found at O'Donnell, J. 2023. *Mapping Social Cohesion.* Scanlon Foundation Research Institute. https://scanloninstitute.org.au/mapping-social-cohesion-2023, in the chapter on 'Becoming Australian' (p. 77).

directly to communities, without genuine interest. Therefore, there was some cynicism about formal political engagement. The reduction in Australian Overseas Development Assistance to Africa over the last decade has also been received negatively as having 'widened the gap' between the two continents.

Of course, civic engagement in Australia's democracy extends well beyond formal practices of directly engaging politicians, voting and political representation, and here too, African migrants are actively participating. Table 11.1 summarises further unpublished results from the Scanlon Foundation's 2023 survey regarding some of these measures of civic engagement.

The findings show that on most measures, African migrants returned slightly lower levels than the total sample, though not markedly so (and mostly within the margin of error). The one area in which the African-born sub-sample returned higher results, and by the largest margin of any measure (apart from voting in an election, which is accounted for by their citizenship profile), was with respect to active participation in a civic or political group. This is significant, given this is a relatively 'young' population (in terms of age, length of residence and maturity of community) and coming from highly diverse political environments in countries of origin. Further research is required to understand more about the nature and diversity of their civic and political activity. However, early exploratory study findings point to diasporic advocacy and engagement, both nationally and transnationally, as a particularly significant form of political expression for African migrants.

Our colleagues at the Scanlon Foundation attempted to refine these quantitative results by analysing differences between the total population with African backgrounds, those of African background excluding South Africa (a blunt attempt to separate out the large white South African population – problematic admittedly, but an interesting exercise given differences of outcome in the Australian labour market) and the total

Table 11.1 Comparative Civic Engagement Measures.[a]

	African-born Respondents (%) (n = 211)	*Total Sample (%) (n = 7,454)*
Voted in an election in the last 3 years	69	79
Joined a boycott of a product or company	16	17
Attended a protest, march or demonstration	9	12
Gathered with others to resolve a local problem	11	13
Posted or shared something about politics online	21	25
Actively involved in any civic or political group	21	16

Source: Data from Scanlon Foundation Social Cohesion Survey (2023).

[a] Analysis should be treated with caution due to the small sample of 211 respondents (born or with one or more parents born in Africa). At the 95 per cent confidence level, it is likely the true estimate lies between 61 per cent and 75 per cent for the 69 per cent of all African Australian respondents who voted in an election in the last 3 years. The confidence intervals were calculated with Stata 18's inbuilt linearised variance estimator, see https://www.stata.com/manuals13/svysurvey.pdf. The linearised variance estimator is used (rather than a t-test) to take account of the survey weights. The Mapping Social Cohesion survey is weighted at a national level to ensure the results are representative of Australia by household composition, age, sex, education, geographic location and whether or not a language other than English is spoken at home.

sample (the Australian average). Raw numbers for each category are 211 for African background respondents, 114 excluding South African background and 7,454 for the total sample.

Their interest was in engagement with the formal political sphere and other civic actions. Thus they found 69 per cent (African background), 75 per cent (African background excluding South African) and 79 per cent (total sample) voted in an election in the last 3 years; 42 per cent, 47 per cent and 50 per cent respectively signed a petition; 16 per cent, 15 per cent and 20 per cent had written or spoken to a Federal or State Member of Parliament; 16 per cent, 21 per cent and 17 per cent had joined a boycott of a product or company; 9 per cent, 9 per cent and 12 per cent had attended a protest, march or demonstration; 11 per cent, 6 per cent and 13 per cent had gotten together with others to try to resolve a local problem; 21 per cent, 23 per cent and 25 per cent had posted or shared anything about politics online; and in the last 12 months, 21 per cent, 23 per cent and 16 per cent respectively had been actively involved in any civic or political groups. Thus, the non-South African population (a blunt proxy for Black) appears on most measures to be more active than the sample that includes South Africans, although both are marginally lower on most measures compared with the total sample. Of particular interest is that they score higher on the likelihood of involvement in civic or political groups.

A feature of the African communities in Australia, something often commented upon by service providers, is their self-organisation into more and less formal associations that engage in actions to support settling migrants and build capacity, leadership and community. This appears supported by the Scanlon data outlined above. As well as a number of ministerial reference groups that provide advice more formally on different portfolios, observation suggests a range of organisations that identify community needs and deliver on them, while providing opportunities for network- and capacity-building; that is, they serve an important role in the development of social and cultural capital. There is a wide range of kinds of associations and activities: leadership and empowerment courses, such as The Blue Nile Program, a short course offered by the University of Melbourne in collaboration with the African Australian Community organisation to African Australian entrepreneurs, working professionals and leaders of not-for-profit organisations; associations for professionals, such as African Professionals of Australia, which is a networking organisation; activities focused on women, including the African-Women Leadership, Empowerment and Development (A-Lead) Program offered in partnership between Curtin University and the Organisation of African Communities in WA, which seeks to build leadership capacity for women; and programmes for young people, such as the African Youth Initiative, which seeks to reconnect African youth to their communities, or the Edith Cowan University-led ‘Stop the Violence’ programme to reduce youth recidivism. These are just a few examples of this self-organised civic activity.

These examples are illustrative of an extensive and growing presence of Africans in the civic sphere in Australia, which is also evident online. A recent audit of websites associated with African Australian migrant activities and groups identified over a thousand sites from state and national associations, ethnic, religious and country of origin organisations, and individual one-off activities such as the Jambo festival in Western Australia (at which the major political parties have stalls, as well as offering a showcase of pan-African diaspora consciousness through a range of organisations, African goods and food stalls and networking opportunities). The existence of such a plethora of public-facing sites suggests high levels of civic engagement.

A feature of this population is the growing pan-African diaspora consciousness. This is evident in the many active African Australian community organisations and range of activities (Fozdar, Prout Quicke, and Mickler 2022), in which tribal, ethnic, religious and national affiliations are subservient (though not exclusive) to identification as African. It is also evident in the trend among younger Africans, particularly second generation, to identify as African rather than from countries of origin (Gebrekidan 2018). This suggests the African Union's (AU's) project to embed a diasporic consciousness in the global African population, described shortly, is bearing fruit. And as noted, despite diversity and divisions, there is significant transnational cultural, political and economic engagement (Fozdar et al. 2022).

Transnational Engagements

One element of political engagement that is missing from many analyses is transnational engagement. As noted, this was recognised by Anderson (1983) as long-distance nationalism. Early empirical work by Schiller, Basch and Blanc-Szanton (1992) recognised that migrants do not relinquish their ethnocultural identity from and engagement with countries of origin but maintain a range of contacts, connections and activities, referring to this phenomenon as transnational migration and the migrants involved as transmigrants. Transnational migration is 'the process by which immigrants forge and sustain simultaneous multi-stranded social relations that link together their societies of origin and settlement' (Schiller, Basch and Blanc-Szanton 1992, 48).

Such migrants maintain multiple interconnections across international borders, building identities configured in relation to more than one nation-state (Basch 1994, 6; Schiller, Basch and Blanc-Szanton 1992). As noted, these relationships include a range of political commitments. Thus, migrants contribute meaningfully to the socioeconomic development of both host and origin countries when they exercise community action, engage with state power, and participate in political decision-making (Lai and Hynie 2010; Putnam 2000; Sapkota 2023). For some migrant communities, political engagement may be more oriented towards home than host countries. For example, in a European context, Martiniello (2005) and Solomos and Back (1991) found African immigrants' campaigning and mobilisation efforts tend to be transcontinental rather than directed towards destination countries, with a focus on development and fighting injustices in their homelands. This research is somewhat dated, however.

While we do not yet have quantitative data to indicate the relative strength and frequency of such transcontinental engagements among African Australians, we can share qualitative data indicating the types of national and transnational political engagement of this emerging migrant population. In the Delphi study mentioned above, while participants were asked to reflect on the political engagement of the Australian African diaspora, most of the discussion focused less on formal political engagement and more on the work of community diaspora-focused organisations, both in Australia and transnationally in countries of origin. Such organisations and activities were generally described as ad hoc, rather than being part of a coordinated architecture designed to raise political consciousness and build diplomatic or other relations between Australia and African countries of origin (or the African continent as a whole).

However, some were seen to be the direct result of initiatives by African countries designed specifically to engage their diaspora for political and economic ends. This may partly be the result of the AU's designation of the African diaspora as the Sixth Region of Africa. The Declaration of the Global Diaspora Summit in 2012 recognised the need to build enduring partnerships between the African continent and the African diaspora through sustainable dialogue and effective engagements. The AU defined this diaspora as 'peoples of African origin living outside the continent, irrespective of their citizenship and nationality and who are willing to contribute to the development of the continent and the building of the African Union' (African Union 2006). This was an explicit call for not only economic engagement but political engagement, transnationally.

A recent AU Global African Diaspora Symposium in 2023, attended by one of the current authors, focused on identifying more concrete engagement strategies and partnerships with members of the African diaspora and their host countries to manifest this vision. The summit highlighted the importance of diaspora engagement both within their countries of residence and with the African continent, again focusing on building connections and influence both internally and externally. This reflects the growing recognition of the value of diaspora populations to countries and regions of origin, who are often used to leverage resources and influence. As argued by Gamlen (2019), dedicated institutions set up by countries of origin and tasked with building such relationships are found in over half the world's countries, being used by origin states in what he terms 'human geopolitics', to 'tap' migrants for resources, 'embrace' them for identity projects and as leverage to 'govern' them, with the latter function now dominating (Gamlen et al. 2019, 492). There is growing evidence of African countries engaging in such activity. While this describes the view from the perspective of the home nation or region, we are interested in the perspective of those in the diaspora itself.

However, our Delphi participants were clear that transnational political and economic activity was generally migrant-driven and family- or hometown-focused. Examples provided by participants include raising funds to send books to schools back home to raise levels of education and opportunity, pooling resources to purchase hospital equipment in regions that can't afford basic equipment, collaborating with NGOs to train street children to provide alternative life pathways, providing support for underprivileged youth and women, supporting empowerment programmes financially or through transnational mentoring and networking and providing other forms of social support, including in the context of COVID-19. The provision of remittances, while more obviously an example of economic engagement, also has a political element as they build a sense of diaspora identity, as well as supporting development agendas (Fozdar et al. 2022; Gamlen 2019).

Participants reported that maintaining links with home countries, including virtual (particularly social media) connections, regularly visiting, doing business, returning on retirement, sending children back for part of their education, as well as assisting with development financially and with expert advice and mentoring, all tend to generate a sense of collectivity while also maintaining awareness of, and interest in, local politics and development agendas. These practices, encouraged by the AU's framing, are seen as shaping a positive 'hybrid' identity. However, it must be noted that the connections, for example, with hometown activities and the provision of remittances, tend to be with localised areas of origin rather than being generalised beyond the local area or nation to the African region as a whole. They are thus further evidence of long-distance nationalism.

A range of collective and community activities were identified by Delphi participants as both examples of political engagement and as a means of encouraging a shared identity. Some groups have been formed to represent national or cultural communities and seek to preserve and promote country-specific cultures and offer a social network for members. Religious organisations offer not only support and social connections in Australia but also ongoing connection with home countries. Celebration of national or independence days, social transitions such as marriages and funerals, return visits and continuing international connections through community organisations, such as 'hometown associations', orient people to their places of origin, as the following quote illustrates:

> There are hometown associations that many of these diaspora belong to and meet regularly to discuss their own welfare issues as well as how to support development back home. Many sociocultural activities such as Independence Day, funerals and festivals are also celebrated in Australia and hence contribute to connect the diaspora to their origin countries and the African continent. (Delphi participant)

It was suggested by participants that second- and third-generation Africans may not feel as connected with their homelands or the region due to their integration in Australia, although more empirical evidence is required before such a conclusion can be reached. Likewise, this was suggested to hold for some who arrived as refugees, due to the political circumstances that led to their fleeing their home countries, making ongoing civic engagement impossible. However, for some who migrated as refugees in the early 2000s due to the Sudanese Civil War, many of whom had been politically active in the independence movement, the formation of an independent South Sudan in 2011 served as an opportunity for return, with an explicit agenda to rebuild and shape the new nation.

On the other hand, some Delphi participants also noted that a sense of pan-African identity is growing in Australia due to both feelings of internal solidarity and pan-African pride:

> Despite their diversity, Africans in Australia seem to have developed a sense of shared identity as a diaspora. It is common for people of African backgrounds, especially first generation Africans, meeting for the first time, to refer to each other as 'brothers' and

> 'sisters' and to connect over similarities in their languages, upbringing, cultural practices, and social norms. Many Africans also bond over discussions around governance, the state of the economy and the political environment back home. Community events that focus on bringing 'Africans' together solidify that sense of identity for Africans collectively and for African immigrants from the different countries. (Delphi participant)

This quote illustrates the difficulty of trying to extricate local, national and transnational connections. Shared culture and activities, plus an interest in the economic and political situation in countries and regions of origin, serve as a source of social capital and basis of identity.

Participants in the Delphi study identified a range of benefits associated with African diasporic transnational activity. Most related to improving outcomes in countries of origin, including holding home governments accountable to ensure economic and political development, lobbying the Australian government to invest in African enterprises and development objectives and so on. They also identified a series of challenges, particularly in relation to the potentially polarising, splintering and resource-intensive nature of engaging in political debates and advocacy relating to countries of origin.

These transnational connections briefly outlined demonstrate that political agency is being exercised transnationally, often through organised community groups and activities, but also through everyday conversations, engagements and identities. The intersubjectively shared space of the public sphere is definitionally enlarged to include not only Australia as the country of residence, but also the region, country or hometown of origin.

Conclusion

By way of summary, we have constructed a simple table of the sorts of activities mentioned by participants in the Delphi study, which suggests African Australian political engagement both in Australia and in countries of origin (Table 11.2).

Table 11.2 Political engagement of the Australian African diaspora as identified in a Delphi Study.

Activities in Australia	*Activities Related to Countries of Origin*
Voting	Holding home governments accountable
Product or company boycotts	Lobbying for investment in Africa
Resolving local problems	Involvement in ministerial reference groups
Posting and sharing something about politics online	Celebrating national/independence days
Active involvement in civic or political groups	Engaging in social transitions
Signing petitions	Activity related to hometown associations
Writing or speaking to a federal or state member of parliament	Remittances to support development
Attending protests, marches or demonstrations	Supporting empowerment programs
Running for local, state or federal office	Social support

This is not, of course, an exhaustive list, just the sorts of things mentioned by Delphi participants. It raises an interesting set of questions: are Africans in Australia engaged in similar ways and degrees as they are (or were) at home? What does the difference in engagement look like? Is engagement in Australia more formal and structured, compared to pan-African engagement which may present as more ad hoc and less structured? Or vice versa? How does each affect the other? Can both forms of engagement be seen as the same or held as having the same value, and how are these related to African or traditional 'Southern' understandings of political agency? And what are the drivers, enablers, barriers of each?

If we return to Ager and Strang's framework for successful settlement, which sees positive settlement outcomes as relying on the foundation of rights and citizenship, we have offered evidence that Africans in Australia value citizenship, participate in democratic processes and engage in a range of activities to build their own communities and capacity. They demonstrate their agency in a range of ways as described, with individual and collective structured activity including the formation of community organisations, developing and enacting social support and educational programs, as well as involvement with institutional political processes such as gaining citizenship and voting. We have seen how this civic engagement both relies on and builds resources, engagement (political efficacy and so forth) and social networks, as predicted by Hoefer (2021). African Australians' levels of engagement are influenced by the social and political context in which they find themselves. As Hakli and Kallio (2014) have argued, this includes the affordances of the citizenship regime (such as citizenship testing and dual citizenship rules), migration policies that allow ongoing travel, and the wider context of multiculturalism that (ostensibly) encourages diversity in representation and some level of resourcing for community organisations and humanitarian provisions. We have also seen evidence that they are critical citizens with somewhat cynical responses to Australian politicians' patchy overtures to engage with their communities or support their interests.

Perhaps most interesting are their ongoing connections to, and involvement with, the civic sphere in their region of origin, demonstrating Anderson's predicted long-distance nationalism in a range of ways that support their countries of origin economically and politically, and maintain their relationships and interests. Considering Habermas' conceptualisation of deliberative democratic engagement in the public sphere, we acknowledge there are some ways in which Africans in Australia may feel somewhat excluded from the public sphere of their host nation, but also that they are actively involved in creating their own civic organisations and other forms of representation to build community, connection and influence. Simultaneously, they are building and maintaining transnational strings of connection and influence that expand the public sphere beyond the nation-state, providing benefits at both ends. These appear focused on countries of origin, and even quite local concerns, suggesting that national (rather than cosmopolitan) consciousness is what drives this ongoing engagement, concern and activity.

Further work is necessary to tease out both ends of this relationship. More work is needed to understand the motivations behind and patterns of political engagement and disengagement, as well as the various personal and structural facilitators and barriers to this engagement. Given the perception that African migrants in Australia tend to be very active in the formation of associations and the development of community programs, a further area of research would be to understand African concepts of agency in general and political agency in particular. Key will be to adopt the normative aim of repositioning Africans as active and purposive political agents operating within dynamic social structures, thus offering 'a rejoinder to accounts of African actors which depict their actions as shaped solely by outside actors and discourses over which they have little or no control' (Beswick and Hammerstad 2013, 466). We hope this chapter has begun to contribute to this alternative narrative. A fuller picture of African contributions to both the formal political and informal civic sphere would offer empirical support for determining the relevance of Habermas' conceptualisation of public sphere engagement and whether these communities feel part of an intersubjectively shared space wherein they have a voice.

References

African Union. 2006. 'Decision on the Definition of the African Diaspora, Doc. EX.CL/164 (VII)'. https://archives.au.int/handle/123456789/4589.

Ager, A. and Strang, A. 2008. 'Understanding Integration: A Conceptual Framework'. *Journal of Refugee Studies* 21 (2): 166–191.

Anderson, B. 1983. *Imagined Communities: Reflections on the Origin and Spread of Nationalism*. London: Verso.

Basch, L., Glick-Schiller, N. and Szanton-Blanc, C. 1994. *Transnational Projects: A New Perspective*. Pennsylvania: Gordon and Breach Science Publishers.

Bean, C. 2012. 'Democratic Participation in a Globalised World: Immigrants in Australia in the Early 21st Century'. *Australian Journal of Political Science* 47 (1): 115–131.

Beck, U. 2007. 'The Cosmopolitan Condition: Why Methodological Nationalism Fails'. *Theory, Culture & Society* 24 (7–8): 286–290.

Beswick, D. and Hammerstad, A. 2013. 'African Agency in a Changing Security Environment: Sources, Opportunities and Challenges'. *Conflict, Security & Development* 13 (5): 471–486.

Bilodeau, A., McAllister, I. and Kanji, M. 2010. 'Adaptation to Democracy among Immigrants in Australia'. *International Political Science Review* 31 (2): 141–165.

Calhoun, C. 2007. *Nations Matter: Culture, History and the Cosmopolitan Dream*. London: Routledge.

Dahlberg, L. 2005. 'The Habermasian Public Sphere: Taking Difference Seriously?' *Theory and Society* 34 (2): 111–136.

Davies, B. 1991. 'The Concept of Agency: A Feminist Poststructuralist Analysis'. *Social Analysis: The International Journal of Social and Cultural Practice* 30: 42–53.

FECCA (Federation of Ethnic Communities Councils of Australia). 2022. 'Civic Participation Community Toolkit'. https://fecca.org.au/wp-content/uploads/2022/05/Western-Sydney-MRC-Civic-Participation-Community-Toolkit.pdf.

Fozdar, F. 2023. 'Belonging in the Land Down Under: Black Africans in Australia'. *International Migration* 61 (1): 23–38.

Fozdar, F. and Hartley, L. 2013. 'Refugee Resettlement in Australia: What We Know and Need to Know'. *Refugee Survey Quarterly* 32 (3): 23–51.

Fozdar, F., Mickler, D., Quicke, S. P., Setrana, M. B., Suleiman, M. D. and Dagbanja, D. N. 2022. 'Transnational Economic Engagements: The Africa-Australia Nexus'. In *Understanding Diaspora Development: Lessons from Australia and the Pacific*, edited by M. Phillips and L. Olliff, 61–85. Cham: Springer International Publishing.

Fozdar, F., Prout Quick, S. and Mickler, D. 2022. 'Are Africans in Australia a Diaspora?'. *Diaspora Studies* 15 (1): 87–117.

Gamlen, A. 2019. *Human Geopolitics: States, Emigrants, and the Rise of Diaspora Institutions*. Oxford: Oxford University Press.

Gamlen, A., Cummings, M. E. and Vaaler, P. M., 2019, 'Explaining the Rise of Diaspora Institutions', *Journal of Ethnic and Migration Studies* 45 (4): 492–516.

Gebrekidan, B. 2018. '"African-Australian" Identity in the Making: Analysing its Imagery and Explanatory Power in View of Young Africans in Australia'. *Australasian Review of African Studies* 39 (1): 110–129.

Habermas, J. 1984. *The Theory of Communicative Action, Volume One, Reason and the Rationalization of Society*. Translated from the German by T. McCarthy. Boston: Beacon Press.

Habermas, J. 1996. *Between Facts and Norms: Contributions to a Discourse Theory of Law and Democracy*, trans. William Rehg, 360–362. Cambridge: Polity Press.

Hakli, J. and Kallio, K. P. 2014. 'Subject, Action and Polis: Theorizing Political Agency'. *Progress in Human Geography* 38 (2): 181–200.

Hoefer, R. 2021. 'Applications of Theory to Social Policy: Civic Engagement Theory'. *Journal of Policy Practice and Research* 2 (2): 67–70.

Jiang, L. 2016. 'Valence Politics and Immigrant Voting in the 2013 Australian Election'. *Australian Journal of Political Science* 51 (3): 418–435.

Kirpitchenko, L. and Mansouri, F. 2014. 'Social Engagement among Migrant Youth: Attitudes and Meanings'. *Social Inclusion* 2 (2): 17–27.

Lai, Y. and Hynie, M. 2010. 'Community Engagement and Well-being of Immigrants: The Role of Knowledge'. *Canadian Issues*, Summer: 93–97.

Mansouri, F. and Kirpitchenko, L. 2016. 'Practices of Active Citizenship among Migrant Youth: Beyond Conventionalities'. *Social Identities* 22 (3): 307–323.

Mansouri, F., Vergani, M. and Weng, E. 2024. 'Parallel Lives or Active Citizens? Examining the Interplay between Multicultural Service Provision and Civic Engagement in Australia'. *Journal of Sociology* 60 (2). https://doi.org/10.1177/144078332312190.

Martiniello, M. 2005. *Political Participation, Mobilisation and Representation of Immigrants and their Offspring in Europe* (Vol. 1, No. 05). Malmö, Sweden: School of International Migration and Ethnic Relations, Malmö University.

McAllister, I. and Makkai, T. 1991. 'The Formation and Development of Party Loyalties: Patterns among Australian Immigrants'. *Journal of Sociology* 27: 195–217

Ndhlovu, F. 2011. 'Post-refugee African Australian' Perceptions about Being and Becoming Australian: Language, Discourse and Participation'. *African Identities* 9 (4): 435–453.

Nunn, C., McMichael, C., Gifford, S. M. and Correa-Velez, I. 2016. 'Mobility and Security: The Perceived Benefits of Citizenship for Resettled Young People from Refugee Backgrounds'. *Journal of Ethnic and Migration Studies* 42 (3): 382–399.

Peucker, M., Roose, J. M. and Akbarzadeh, S. 2014. 'Muslim Active Citizenship in Australia: Socioeconomic Challenges and the Emergence of a Muslim Elite'. *Australian Journal of Political Science* 49 (2): 282–299.

Prout Quicke, S. 2023. 'Africans in Australia: A Population Overview Working Paper no. 1'. https://sites.google.com/view/africanimpactinoz/resources/publications?authuser=0.

Putnam, R. D. 2000. *Bowling Alone: The Collapse and Revival of American Community*. New York: Brooking Institute Press.

Roose, J. M. and Harris, A. 2015. 'Muslim Citizenship in Everyday Australian Civic Spaces'. *Journal of Intercultural Studies* 36 (4): 468–486.

Saggar, S. 2000. *Race and Representation: Electoral Politics and Ethnic Pluralism in Britain*. New York: Manchester University Press.

Sapkota, S. 2023. 'Immigrants Participation in Australian Politics'. Doctoral dissertation.

Schiller, N. G., Basch, L. and Blanc-Szanton, C. 1992. 'Transnationalism: A New Analytic Framework for Understanding Migration'. *Annals of the New York Academy of Sciences* 645 (1): 1–24.

SCOA (Settlement Council of Australia). 2018, 'Civic Participation Settlement Council of Australia Discussion Paper' (October), SCoA-Policy-Focus_Civic-Participation.pdf.

Skrbiš, Z. 2017. *Long-distance Nationalism: Diasporas, Homelands and Identities.* Abingdon: Routledge.

Solomos, J. and Back, L. 1991. 'Black Political Mobilisation and the Struggle for Equality'. *The Sociological Review* 39 (2): 215–237.

Vergani, M., Johns, A., Lobo, M. and Mansouri, F. 2017. 'Examining Islamic Religiosity and Civic Engagement in Melbourne'. *Journal of Sociology* 53 (1): 63–78.

Zhinger, J. N. and Thomas, M. S. 2012. 'Patterns of Immigrant Political Behaviour in Australia: An Analysis of Immigrant Voting in Ethnic Context'. *Australian Journal of Political Science* 47 (3): 377–397.

Chapter 12

AUSTRALIAN DEMOCRACY AND THE CLIMATE CRISIS

Joo-Cheong Tham

There are three puzzles when it comes to Australian democracy and the climate crisis. First, Australia is a high-performing democracy and a climate laggard. According to International IDEA's Global State of Democracy Indices (GSoD), Australia is a high-performance democracy that scores 0.83 for Representative Government, 0.87 for Fundamental Rights, 0.87 for Checks on Government and 0.86 for Impartial Administration (International IDEA 2020). Democracies consistently out-perform authoritarian regimes in terms of climate change mitigation policies (Bättig and Bernauer 2009; Lindvall 2021, ch. 3). Yet, the 2022 Climate Change Performance Index places Australia sixth-last in its assessment of the climate action of 61 countries (Burck et al. 2021, 7).[1]

Second, Australia's climate inaction jars with its climate responsibility and vulnerability. Australia is among the highest per capita emitter of greenhouse gases internationally (Climate Analytics 2019) and among the most fossil-fuel dependent countries (Australia Institute 2019; Clean Energy Council 2022). The key climate risks already experienced by Australia are:

- an *increase in average temperature* by 1.44 degrees Celsius (since national records began in 1910), resulting in *more frequent extreme heat events* including *extreme fire weather*;
- *decline in rainfall and run-off* in southwest Australia, together with *increases* in parts of northern Australia;
- ocean *acidification and warming* contributing to more *frequent and longer marine heatwaves*; and
- *rising sea levels* (including more frequent extremes).

Australia is projected to experience continued increases in all of these risk areas in the coming decades (IPCC 2014; 2018; CSIRO 2020; Hoegh-Guldberg and Hughes 2021). In 2022, the *State of Environment Report 2021* found that 'the state and trend of environment of Australia are poor and deteriorating', with climate change 'continuing and . . .

1. Special thanks to Cate Read for exceptional research assistance and also to the peer reviewer of an earlier draft. This chapter draws upon 'Australia' in Tham (2023).

increasing the impacts of other pressures on our environment' (SoE 2021). Indigenous communities have been particularly affected. As the Lowitja Institute's report *Climate Change and Aboriginal and Torres Strait Islander Health* stated, '[c]limate change is compounding historical injustices and disrupts cultural and spiritual connections to Country that are central to health and wellbeing' (Lowitja Institute 2021).

Third, Australia's climate inaction has occurred despite strong public support for climate action. In the last federal election, 'global warming' was the third most important policy issue with nearly half of voters seeing it as 'extremely important' (Cameron et al. 2022, 9–10). In 2019 and 2023, hundreds of thousands of Australians joined the global student climate strikes calling for a ban on new fossil-fuel projects, 100 per cent renewable energy generation and exports by 2030, and a just transition and job creation for all fossil-fuel workers and communities (Cox 2019; Mayes and Talukdar 2023).

This chapter seeks to unravel these puzzles by examining two questions:

1. How can Australian democracy effectively address the climate crisis?
2. How can Australian democracy effectively address the threats it faces from the climate crisis?

It sets out the key circumstances of democratic debilitation hindering effective climate action in Australia (short-termism, capture by vested interests, self-referring decision-making) and the threats to democracy from the climate crisis (insecurity, instability, inequality, democratic back-sliding and the impact on free and fair elections).

It argues that in both respects, Australian democracy needs to be renewed on three fronts: it needs to forge a democratic planning state; it must embrace a solidaristic ethos; and it must work to achieve fair and inclusive politics.

Democratic Debilitation Hindering Effective Climate Action

The major tendencies debilitating Australian democracy in terms of effective climate action are short-termism, capture by vested interests and self-referring dynamics (Held and Fane Hervey 2009).

Short-termism

As to *short-termism*, Australia's former treasurer referred to the climate crisis as requiring 'significant structural change' (Frydenberg 2021). The Grattan Institute has said that '[g]etting to net zero will be arguably the biggest economic transformation Australia has seen outside of wartime' (Wood, Reeve and Ha 2021, 17). As chair of the Net Zero Economy Agency, Greg Combet likened getting to net zero to the post-war reconstruction (Morton 2024c). Yet, there are no meaningful plans for jobs and industries in a climate-safe economy.

The federal ALP Albanese government was elected in May 2022 with a plan to 'create jobs, cut power bills and reduce emissions by boosting renewable energy' through its *Powering Australia* policy (Australian Labor Party 2021). Since its election, the Albanese government has increased Australia's climate ambition by changing Australia's Nationally Determined Contribution (NDC) under the Paris Agreement to commit Australia to reducing its greenhouse gas emissions to 43 per cent below 2005 levels by 2030 (in contrast to the previous government's commitment of 26 to 28 per cent), while reaffirming the commitment to net zero emissions by 2050 (Australian Government 2022). These targets have been enacted into law through the *Climate Change Act 2022* (Cth), together with a ratchet mechanism based on recommendations from the Climate Change Authority.

Although Australia's climate ambition has improved, it is still consistent with 2°C increase in global temperatures, the upper end of the Paris Agreement's temperature targets (Climate Analytics 2022). This change has only improved Australia's overall Climate Action Tracker rating from 'Highly Insufficient' (Climate Action Tracker 2022) to 'Insufficient' (Climate Action Tracker 2023). Others have argued that to be consistent with the lower end of the Paris Agreement's temperature targets (namely, 1.5 °C), Australia's emissions must be reduced by 75 per cent by 2030, with net zero emissions reached by 2035 (Climate Council 2022).

The *Climate Change Act* has also been criticised for failing to provide a long-term road map for decarbonising the economy (Jotzo 2022). Crucially, there is no plan for phasing out fossil-fuel industries. The *Climate Change Act* is silent on phasing out such fuels; and indeed, the Albanese government has argued that a ban on coal production will not reduce emissions, as other countries will continue to engage in such production (Brown 2022).

Unsurprisingly, then, many fossil-fuel projects are under development (Ogge, Quicke and Campbell 2021), despite the fact that the changing economics of energy production will lead to further closures of coal-fired plants. The Australian Energy Market Operator projects that most of Australia's 20-odd coal plants will close over the next two decades (AEMO 2020). Without credible plans to address such closures, the stranded assets are likely to lead to stranded communities.

At the time of writing, 2024 has witnessed contradictory movements in addressing short-termism. On the positive side, the ALP Albanese government has proposed a Net Zero Economic Authority has been established under the ALP Albanese government to 'promote orderly and positive economic transformation' (*Net Zero Economic Authority Act 2024* (Cth); Gorman 2024), as well as a $22.7 billion *Future Made in Australia* package that seeks to maximise 'the economic and industrial benefits of the move to net zero' by realising 'Australia's potential to become a renewable energy superpower' (Budget 2024). On the negative side, the Opposition Coalition has indicated that it will repeal the 2030 emissions target legislated in the *Climate Change Act*, prompting criticisms of breaching the Paris Agreement (Morton 2024a).

The short-term orientation stems in part from discourses of security that focus on the immediate future rather than the longer term (McDonald 2015). Part of the difficulty is also what Wilkinson has dubbed the 'no regrets' policy prevailing in both major parties (the Coalition and the ALP) since the Coalition Howard Government's tenure (1996–2007); namely, the principle that climate action should not result in costs to Australia's economy in the short term, especially concerning its fossil-fuel industries

(Wilkinson 2020). The prioritisation attached to avoiding negative impacts on fossil-fuel industries is no coincidence and raises another circumstance of democratic debilitation – *capture by vested interests.*

Capture by Vested Interests

There are indications of a fossil-fuel policy hegemony in Australia (Wright, Nyberg and Bowden 2021); one that was, perhaps, vividly illustrated by the former prime minister, Scott Morrison, brandishing a lump of coal provided by the Minerals Council of Australia in the Commonwealth Parliament in 2017 (Murphy 2017). Some have pointed to the nexus between the fossil-fuel industry and the media (Holmes and Star 2018), while others have highlighted the historical and contemporary connections between the coal industry and the Australian state (Baer 2016). Professor Ross Garnaut, who wrote two comprehensive reports on climate change, has observed in relation to Australia that '[e]missions-intensive industries have invested heavily to influence climate change policy since the early days of discussion of these issues' (Garnaut 2009, 15).

The investment in influence by these industries is notable in the following ways:

- The resources industry is the largest sector making financial contributions to both major party groupings (Crowe 2021).
- The success of the $22 million advertising campaign by mining companies against the Rudd Government's resource super-profits tax is part of political folklore – to the extent that '[i]t's now become routine for industry groups to threaten a "mining tax style campaign" every time they don't get their way with government' (Knott 2011; Davis 2011).
- Employees and lobbyists of industry have included former ALP ministers, former National party leaders and former Liberal Party ministers (see e.g. Davies 2015; Henderson and Bradfield 2016).

Power of this nature has a profound impact and enlivens the notion of 'policy capture' (OECD 2017). Wilkinson's book *The Carbon Club* provides a meticulous account of how a network of climate-science sceptics, politicians and business leaders brought about decades of climate inaction in Australia (Wilkinson 2020). Under the Howard Government, climate change policy was effectively determined by fossil-fuel lobbyists (many of whom were former senior public servants), who likened themselves to organised crime through a self-styled label – the greenhouse mafia (Hamilton 2007, ch. 1). And perhaps the most singular fact – fossil-fuel companies have played an instrumental role in ousting two out of the five prime ministers in office since 2007 – namely, Kevin Rudd (Davis 2011) and Malcolm Turnbull (Alberici 2018).

The capture by the fossil-fuel industry is undemocratic for not only who it unduly empowers but who it disempowers. Among those disenfranchised are Indigenous communities. Australia is a settler-colonial state with its First Nations constituting the oldest living culture in the world. The Indigenous Estate – land where First Nations people hold rights and interests – amounts to 40 per cent of the continent, often in areas of high conservation value (Gammage 2012).

In an understated way, the 2022 IPCC report coverage of Australasia refers to '[r]ecognition of the role of Aboriginal and Torres Strait Islander Peoples in identifying solutions to the impacts of climate change [as] slowly emerging [citation omitted], having been largely excluded from meaningful representation from the conception of climate change dialogue through to debate and decision-making' [citation omitted] (IPCC 2022, ch. 11). Others have argued that Indigenous communities are 'the first to be impacted and the last to be heard' (Moggridge et al. 2022).

The profound climate impact on Australia's First Nations people was poignantly illustrated by the unprecedented international legal action brought by a group of eight Torres Strait Islanders (known as the 'Torres Strait 8') to the UN Human Rights Committee. The Committee found that the Australian government had violated the plaintiffs' rights under the International Covenant on Civil and Political Rights due to inadequate climate action – specifically, Article 17 (right to be free from arbitrary interference with privacy, family and home) and Article 27 (right to culture) (UN Human Rights Committee 2022).

Self-referring Decision-making

The third driver of democratic debilitation, *self-referring decision-making*, arises from democratic mechanisms (particularly elections) underpinned by accountability to constituents of a nation state and to current voters (a section of the present generation). To this, we can also add the politics of self-interest, both sectional and individual.

The 'climate wars', reignited by the Opposition Coalition's proposal to repeal 2030 emissions targets (Morton 2024b), have contributed to the ousting of three prime ministers since 2007 (Crowley 2021). The climate wars have also distorted different interests to the point that they have become irreconcilable, thereby providing a platform for political polarisation and the exploitation of division for electoral gain (Eckersley 2015). Such polarisation is reflected in the importance ascribed to emissions reductions by voters, which sharply divides along lines of political party preference (Colvin and Jotzo 2021). It has also resulted in divisiveness and conflict, much of which was unnecessary and false trade-offs between:

- protecting jobs as opposed to protecting the environment;
- regions and cities; and
- blue-collar and white-collar workers (Fitzgibbon 2021).

Weak Multilateralism

These self-referring dynamics are connected to the fourth cause of democratic debilitation, *weak multilateralism*. Rather than emerging as a global climate leader, Australia has been criticised by former UN secretary-general, Ban Ki-Moon, for not pulling its weight on climate action (Thorpe 2021), and by current UN secretary-general, Antonio

Guterres, as a 'holdout' on meaningful 2030 targets (O'Malley 2022). At the 2021 Glasgow COP, Australia refused to join more than 40 countries – including several fossil-fuel dependent nations, such as South Korea and Indonesia – to end the use of coal power (Morton 2021).

In a welcome sign, *Powering Australia*, ALP Albanese's plan for action, commits the government to '[r]estoring Australia's reputation with trading partners and allies by meeting international commitments made by Australia, and advancing climate diplomacy'. The plan also includes a bid to co-host a future Conference of the Parties in Australia with Pacific nations. However, whether these efforts will be fully successful are somewhat moot, given the government's inadequate climate ambition (Harris 2022).

Threats to Australian Democracy from the Climate Crisis

The threats to Australian democracy arising from the climate crisis come foremost as 3'I's: insecurity, instability, inequality. Insecurity will result from climate disruptions, climate action and their impact on lives, livelihoods (jobs), homes, food and water supply. In Australia, climate change will heighten the risks of food shortages and price increases (Quiggin 2007; Bartos 2022). According to Lindvall, food insecurity will fuel public discontent, nationalism and authoritarian populism, and emerge as the 'one single consequence of the climate crisis that represents the biggest threat to democracy in the future' (Lindvall 2020).

A Senate Committee report on the *Implications of Climate Change for Australia's National Security* identified four categories of climate risk that impact on Australia's national security (Foreign Affairs, Defence and Trade References Committee 2018, ch. 2):

1. extreme weather and physical effects;
2. health and wellbeing;
3. the economy; and
4. threats to Australia's region.

As to threats to Australia's region, the Climate Council has warned of the risks to Australia from conflicts over water, as well as increased displacement and forced migration from countries in the region facing significant sea level rises, specifically the Pacific Island nations, Bangladesh, China, Vietnam, India and Indonesia (Durrant, Bradshaw and Pearce 2021; Spratt and Dunlop 2019). The *Powering Australia* plan recognises these risks by '[t]reating climate change as a security threat' and having committed to 'an urgent climate risk assessment' by the director-general of National Intelligence and the Secretary of Defence (Australian Labor Party 2021, 50).

Insecurity and instability intertwine with inequality because climate risks fall unevenly. It has been said that '[c]limate change has the potential to significantly accelerate inequality' in Australia (Flanagan 2018), with concern voiced for low-income workers and families (Brotherhood of St Laurence 2024). Fossil-fuel dependent communities in regional Australia will clearly be disproportionately affected by the shift away from fossil fuels. The climate crisis also threatens to deepen health inequities by creating a 'multiplier effect', notably through extreme weather events (Friel 2014).

The 3'I's do not only arise from climate change but also climate action (mitigation and adaptation). According to the Intergovernmental Panel on Climate Change (IPCC), 'rapid, far-reaching and unprecedented changes in all aspects of society' are required to effectively address the climate crisis (IPCC 2018). According to an International Labour Organization (ILO) research paper, the impact of the climate crisis is 'akin to an industrial revolution' given the extensive industry and job restructuring it will entail (Montt, Fraga and Harsdorff 2018). The ALP government acknowledges that '[t]he net zero transformation will be one of the most significant economic shifts since the Industrial Revolution' (Explanatory Memorandum 2024, 5). Given what Michael Mann has dubbed 'the procrastination penalty of climate inaction' (Vidal 2019; see also Mann 2009), this transformation will need to occur at a rapid pace. Unless effectively managed, such a transformation will inevitably result in insecurity and instability for workers and businesses; it also threatens to deepen inequality unless there is sufficient protection for those adversely affected (see 'A Solidaristic Ethos' below).

Indigenous communities are at particular risk in the climate crisis. The 2014 IPCC report explained that Indigenous people in Australia 'have higher than average exposure to climate change because of a heavy reliance on climate-sensitive primary industries and strong social connections to the natural environment, and face particular constraints to adaptation' (IPCC 2014, 1375). These factors interact with, what the 2022 IPCC report characterises as, the 'ongoing impacts of colonisation' (including lower levels of income, school outcomes and employment opportunities, set against higher levels of poverty and ill-health, as compared with non-Indigenous Australians) (IPCC 2022, ch. 11).

The Lowitja Institute report highlights that rising sea levels are submerging the Torres Strait Islands (Lowitja Institute 2021). This is the context in which the 'Torres Strait 8' made their claim to being 'refugees in their own country' (UN News 2022). The Lowitja Institute report also warns of the broader threat of forced climate migration, with Indigenous people moving from climate-affected Traditional Country to urban areas and thus becoming displaced from land, culture and spiritual connections.

The 3'I's will invariably affect Australia's democracy. Political participation and equality will be impacted, particularly in communities affected by climate change and action. States of emergency risk significant shifts of power to the executive branch of government (from the legislature) and the militarisation of responses to extreme weather events, such as bush fires (McDonald 2021).

Calls to go on a 'war' footing and fight the climate crisis like World War III serve only to exacerbate these risks (McInerney and Garrett 2020; Blair, Treagust and McCulloch 2020). Comparing the climate crisis to war resonates because both involve urgent and existential threats, and both require large-scale societal transformation and mobilisation. Yet, war as a metaphor fails because there is no enemy to be defeated: it is not the climate that is to be defeated, as it is part of our living world; nor is it other nations, as global cooperation is essential to address this planetary challenge.

In fact, the metaphor of war is positively dangerous. It not only conjures strong authoritarian tendencies and distorts the nature of the crisis to be addressed. It also paves the way for militarisation of the crisis with the use of armed and security forces, and a reliance on coercive measures, and inevitably, the concomitant reduction of protections for freedoms and liberties, as well as demonisation of the 'other' through distinctions between 'friends' and 'enemies', and 'us' and 'them'.

Finally, there is the impact of climate crisis on free and fair elections. In a report on the future conduct of elections during times of emergency, the Commonwealth Joint Standing Committee on Electoral Matters (JSCEM) acknowledged the impact of severe climate events on the conduct of elections. The report specifically noted the likely effects on voter participation by vulnerable communities, disruption in election campaigning and, more generally, trust in the electoral process by disrupting the conduct of elections (JSCEM 2021, pt 3).

Renewing Australian Democracy to Address the Climate Crisis

Australian democracy needs to be renewed in response to the climate crisis (Huntley 2019; Garnaut 2021; Megalogenis 2021). The debilitation it will suffer, and the threats that it faces from the climate crisis, can be addressed by embracing a planning state, a solidaristic ethos and the commitment to fair and inclusive politics.

A Planning State

In its 2021 report, *Achieving a Net Zero Economy*, the Business Council of Australia stated that

> To achieve a net zero economy by 2050, the nation needs an unprecedented level of coordination, with bipartisan support, to align and accelerate investment signals, enhance regulation and provide much needed policy certainty for business and communities. (BCA 2021, 5)

There are elements here of what Giddens has called for to counter short-termism – specifically, a Planning State (Giddens 2011). This is where nation states take the lead on responsibility in:

- *planning*: in terms of both mitigation and adaptation;
- *regulation of the economy*: including instituting the 'polluters pay' principle and establishing the economic framework for a low-carbon economy;
- *coordination and integration*: between government, the private sector, citizens, as well as different levels of government; and
- *holistic risk mitigation*: addressing the risks of the climate crisis, together with other risks experienced by contemporary societies (including through social protection).

Of these elements, holistic risk mitigation is critical and relatively neglected (IPCC 2014, 1376).

The necessity and centrality of the State in addressing the climate crisis is not difficult to comprehend, with both the 2006 Stern Review on *The Economics of Climate Change* and, in Australia, the 2008 *Garnaut Climate Change Review* recognising that climate change is 'the greatest and widest-ranging market failure ever seen' (Stern 2006, I; Garnaut 2008).

The Australian States provide some insight towards an effective planning State, with elements identified by Giddens present in various State climate policies (NSW Government 2022; Government of South Australia 2024; see also Giddens 2011). At the federal level, the ALP government is making movements in the right direction with its Net Zero Economy Authority Act. This Act aims to 'promote orderly and positive economic transformation as the world decarbonises' and establishes a Net Zero Economy Authority whose functions include 'promot[ing] coordination and consistency in the design and implementation of Australian government policies, programs and plans . . . to facilitate the achievement of Australia's greenhouse gas emissions reduction targets and [to] support Australia's transition to a net zero emissions economy' (Net Zero Economy Authority Act 2024, ss 3(a), 16(1)(a)(i)).

Elements of a democratic planning state are also present in the climate change Bill proposed by the independent federal parliamentarian, Zali Steggall. The Bill emphasises that planning in the climate crisis is a democratic enterprise, with one of its key principles being to promote 'community engagement and self-determination' (Climate Change (National Framework for Adaptation and Mitigation) Bill 2020 (Cth), cl. 15). This is consistent with the thinking of the International Energy Agency (IEA) that '[c] itizens must be active participants in the entire process, making them feel part of the transition and not simply subject to it' (IEA 2021, 4).

The vital importance of democratic planning in the climate crisis should not be downplayed. The crisis is a societal and existential challenge that implicates a complex range of issues – not just technical aspects but also social, economic, political and environmental dimensions. Thus, it is imperative that we harness our collective wisdom to address the crisis.

Of central importance here is ensuring that First Nations are adequately represented in decision-making, as required by the United Nations Declaration on the Rights of Indigenous Peoples (2007). Critical here is the call by the *Uluru Statement from the Heart* (2017) to address the 'torment of our powerlessness' through 'a First Nations Voice enshrined in the Constitution' and 'a Makarrata Commission to supervise a process of agreement-making between governments and First Nations and truth-telling about our history' (Uluru Statement from the Heart 2017).

Self-determination of First Nations is of particular significance to the Indigenous Estate, not only because of its scale (around 40 per cent of Australia's land mass) but also because of its importance to climate mitigation including capture capture and renewable energy (wind and solar) (O'Neill 2021). Effective Indigenous representation also enables vital learning to be transmitted from the oldest living cultures, particularly in respect of developing an understanding of societal wellbeing that goes beyond the gross domestic product and other economic considerations. As the Lowitja Institute report highlights:

> Central to all Aboriginal and Torres Strait Islander cultures is the holistic nature of health and wellbeing. Good health is dependent on respectful and reciprocal relationships to Country, culture, spirituality, community and family. It is a cultural responsibility to look after and respect oneself (connection to body, mind and emotions), each other (family, kinship, community) and the environment (connection to Country). (Lowitja Institute 2021, 13)

This broader conception of societal wellbeing is consistent with the Albanese government's plan – following initiatives in Canada and New Zealand – to introduce a 'well-being' budget that includes measures relating to climate change (Chalmers 2022). It also profoundly connects to Indigenous sovereignty. As the *Uluru Statement from the Heart* (2017) says, '[t]his sovereignty is a spiritual notion: the ancestral tie between the land, or "mother nature", and the Aboriginal and Torres Strait Islander peoples' (Uluru Statement from the Heart 2017).

A Solidaristic Ethos

The politics of self-interest arising from self-referring mechanisms must be countered by a solidaristic ethos, which can also be utilised to address the risks from insecurity, instability and inequality. It is vital to recognise that solidarity is a democratic principle. As International IDEA has explained, solidarity 'refers to the ties in a society that bind different people to one another, expressing social bonds rather than autonomous individual ties' (IDEA 2020). Viewed from this perspective, voters are not just protectors of their own interest but also trustees for the public interest (broadly conceived).

This stems from a fundamental truth – democracies are, by nature, communities. They are not random collections of individuals, but rather, a 'we' that considers itself 'a people'. Democracy is the process of *collective* self-determination. It is through solidarity that fuller meaning is given to the third (neglected) principle of the French Revolution – fraternity. And, as the Dalai Lama has stressed, fraternity should be at the heart of our response to the climate crisis (The Dalai Lama and Stril-Rever 2018).

The social bonds that underpin democratic solidarity have triple significance: they furnish the rationale for such solidarity; they define solidaristic action as collective action (particularly through the state); and they provide the object of such action, the sustenance and enhancement of such bonds. In the climate crisis, such solidarity should be broad and inclusive, encompassing inter-generational and intragenerational solidarity, as well as solidarity within and among nations, and with nature (Tham 2023, ch. 1).

In Australia, voice and social protection are two implications of promoting democratic solidarity in the climate crisis. Communities that are particularly affected by climate change and climate action – front-line communities – should have a meaningful voice. This includes First Nations people; communities in regional Australia suffering from drought, water scarcity and bushfires; and fossil-fuel dependent communities. The *Climate Change Act* gestures to these communities by emphasising particular regard to the impact on rural and regional Australia. More explicitly, if established, the Net Zero Economy Authority will have as one of its functions 'to support Indigenous persons to participate in, and benefit from, Australia's transition to a net zero emissions economy' (Net Zero Economy Authority Act 2024, s 16(1)(d)).

One way to enhance the voice of these 'frontline' communities is through citizens' assemblies in areas particularly affected by climate change and action. While these would occur at a different level to the national climate citizens' assemblies held in several countries (Curato, Smith and Willis 2024; Duvac-Paoli 2022), local assemblies have the potential to foreground the views of marginalised groups in a meaningful way (Buklijas 2022). They may also avoid the ill fate of the 2010 proposal by the Gillard ALP government for a national climate citizens' assembly given their more specific focus (Leslie 2010).

In the world of work, where there will be extensive industry and job restructuring, it means putting in place mechanisms for social dialogue, which will be integral to a just transition (see Chapter 1). The ALP's 2021 policy platform affirmed the Paris Agreement's 'requirement for just transition planning involving local communities, unions, and industry' (ALP National Platform 2021, [23]) – referred to in Zali Steggall's Bill as a 'fair employment transition' (Climate Change (National Framework for Adaptation and Mitigation) Bill 2020, cl. 14). Similarly, the ALP's 2023 National Platform affirms its support for the Paris Agreement and its objective of 'taking into account the imperatives of a just transition of the workforce and the creation of decent work and quality jobs' (ALP National Platform 2023, [40(a)]).

A just transition in the climate crisis that – to quote from the UN Sustainable Development Goals – 'leaves no one behind' (UN Sustainable Development Group n.d.) emphasises the role of social protection, which is another pillar of the ILO's Decent Work Agenda (see Chapter 1). Protection of this nature in Australia will require dedicated plans for communities particularly affected by the climate crisis. The Business Council of Australia (BCA) has called for a low carbon regional road map (BCA 2021). The Australian Council of Trade Unions (ACTU) has advocated for plans to provide an orderly closure of coal-fired power stations (ACTU n.d.), as has the Australia Institute (Stanford 2020), including for specific plans to phase out thermal coal (Quiggin 2020).

An agreement between the ACTU and the BCA has called for 'an independent and properly resourced National Energy Transition Authority to manage an orderly and fair transition process for workers in emissions intensive industries and their communities, particularly in regional areas, that has governance of governments, industry, community and unions' (BCA 2022). This idea has been adopted in the ALP government's Net Zero Economy Authority Act which seeks to 'ensure Australia's regions and workers are supported in relation to, and benefit from, Australia's transition to a net zero emissions economy' (Net Zero Economy Authority Bill Act, s 3(c)). A key element of the Bill is an Energy Industry Jobs Plan that will establish processes where employers affected by the closures of coal-fired and gas-fired power stations can be subject to a series of obligations to assist affected workers (including career advice, training and paid time off to look for a job) (Net Zero Economy Authority Act 2024, pt 5).

At the State level, the Queensland Government has, together with energy companies and unions, agreed upon the *Queensland Energy Workers' Charter* which establishes a Job Security Guarantee for affected workers in government-owned energy corporations, including the guarantee of a job for such workers within these corporations, and financial support for them to transition to new careers (Queensland Government 2022).

More general measures should be contemplated, including those suggested by Garnaut in his book *Reset*, in which he argues for employment security in the form of a national commitment to full employment and income security through a universal basic income, together with proposals for a job guarantee (Garnaut 2021; 2022; Mitchell n.d.). Former ALP deputy opposition leader, Jenny Macklin, has called for an emissions and employment accord that embraces a policy of full employment, nation-building plans and an increased social wage (Macklin 2019).

Arguably, a positive-sum orientation is integral to a solidaristic ethos on the climate crisis. This entails framing issues in a way that promotes 'win-win' situations to address the climate crisis alongside other policy goals, as well as the needs of current and future generations, the various groups within the current generation and especially those particularly affected by climate change and climate action. An orientation of this nature would provide a launch pad for finding policies that encourage synergies between the complex dimensions of the climate crisis, such as through the creation of 'green' jobs for those employed in fossil-fuel industries (ILO n.d.). The ALP government's 2024 *Future Made in Australia* agenda is in a similar vein with its $22.7 billion package aimed at 'creating new jobs and opportunities for every part of our country by maximising the economic and industrial benefits of the move to net zero' (Budget 2024).

There is much to be learnt from Indigenous communities regarding the notion of a solidaristic ethos in terms of broadening the understanding of societal wellbeing. In his book *Sand Talk: How Indigenous Thinking Can Save the World*, Indigenous thinker Tyson Yunkaporta outlines how an Indigenous knowledge perspective can be helpful in curbing self-interested (narcissistic) behaviour and dealing with the sustainability crisis (Yunkaporta 2019).

Fair and Inclusive Politics

Fair and inclusive politics include democratic planning, a voice for 'frontline communities' and social dialogue. Regarding Indigenous communities, Indigenous writer Tony Birch (2017) has emphasised how dialogue between Indigenous communities and non-Indigenous people must be equitable and reciprocal, and based on an unflinching recognition of colonialisation and its continuing impact; others have similarly called for the '[d]ecolonising [of] solidarity' (Land 2015). Equally, these dialogues should be based on a recognition of Indigenous sovereignty, as called for by the Uluru Statement from the Heart (that 'this ancient sovereignty can shine through as a fuller expression of Australia's nationhood'). Treaties with First Nations are critical and treaty processes are underway in Queensland, Victoria, South Australia and the Northern Territory. This points to the need for a national treaty with Australia, one of the few settler-colonial states without a national treaty (ATNS n.d).

Fair and inclusive politics extends to two other aspects. The central role of the State underlines the importance of public integrity measures. The ALP's *Powering Australia* involves a substantial amount of public funds with much of this money dispensed through the exercise of discretion, whether by ministers, government departments and/or public agencies. There is clearly a risk here of misuse of public funds.

Second, the toxic influence of money in Australian politics needs to be eradicated through robust regulation of lobbying and political funding. While the prospect of robust regulation of federal lobbying seems distant (Tham 2024a), this is not the case with political finance laws. In November 2024, the federal ALP government proposed the Electoral Legislation Amendment (Electoral Reform) Bill. The Bill includes significant changes to the two pillars of current federal laws (disclosure and public funding) while adding another two (caps on gifts and caps on electoral expenditure). It is the most ambitious reform of federal political finance laws attempted since the current regime was established four decades ago.

The Bill will reduce the influence of big money in politics, but it does not go far enough in curbing large donations and excessive spending. Its scorecard on promoting fair elections is mixed: it will make elections fairer in key respects, but also unduly favour the major parties, political parties with wealthy candidates and those with investment income (Tham 2024b).

In face of fierce opposition from Clive Palmer, the Teal MPs and the main funder, Climate 200, the ALP government had planned to rush the passage of the Bill in the last parliamentary sitting of 2024 on the basis of an in-principle agreement with the Liberal Party Opposition. It has not, however, managed to introducing more effective disclosure obligations and spending caps (Karp 2022) to secure full agreement from the Opposition at the time of writing (December 2024) and is now reported to seeking support from the cross-bench over the 2025 summer.

Conclusion

We return to the three puzzles posed in the introduction. We see that the disjuncture between Australia's democratic performance and climate action can be better grasped through a more nuanced understanding of their relationship, one that goes beyond broad indicators – however useful they are – to the concrete practices of Australian democracy. These practices, specifically captured by vested interests and short-termism, also helps us to comprehend the stark gap between Australia's climate action and its climate responsibility and vulnerability: the 'public interest' has been distorted by fossil-fuel companies and narrowed to a short time-horizon. The influence of these companies together with the polarising dynamics of the 'climate wars' explains why popular support for climate action has not translated to high levels of climate action – it is blocked by the policy capture of fossil-fuel interests and splintered in the 'climate wars'. The climate crisis is at once a crisis for Australian democracy. Not only are the practices of Australian democracy a climate culprit but Australian democracy is also endangered in an existential way through the threats from the climate crisis (insecurity, instability, inequality, democratic back-sliding and the undermining of free and fair elections). The climate crisis should, however, be grasped fully as a 'crisis', as a turning point and moment of truth, with extreme danger and also significant opportunity for humanity generally, and democracy more specifically (Diamond 2019). Australian democracy can more effectively address the climate crisis by broadening and deepening: forging a *democratic* planning state; embracing a *democratic* solidaristic ethos; and ensuring *political equality* through fair and inclusive politics. The stakes perhaps could not be higher. The climate crisis is clearly not a short-term crisis but a 'long emergency' (Wiseman 2021) – the climate crisis will be a defining, perhaps *the* defining, challenge for and to democracy for decades to come. As Figueres and Rivett-Carnac (2021) have argued, '[i]f democracy is to survive and thrive into the twenty-first century, climate change is the one big test that it cannot fail'.

References

ACTU (Australian Council of Trade Unions). [n.d.]. 'The Need for a Just Transition'. https://www.actu.org.au/climate-change/the-need-for-a-just-transition/.

AEMO (Australian Energy Market Operator). 2020. '2020 Integrated System Plan (ISP)'. https://aemo.com.au/en/energy-systems/major-publications/integrated-system-plan-isp/2020-integrated-system-plan-isp.

Alberici, Emma. 2018. 'Alex Turnbull: Coal Miners Exerting "Undue Influence" on Liberal Party, Says Son of Former PM Malcolm Turnbull'. *ABC News*, 28 August. https://www.abc.net.au/news/2018-08-28/alex-turnbull-says-coal-miners-have-undue-influence-on-liberals/10170908.

ALP National Platform. 2021. 'Adopted at the 2021 Special Platform Conference'. https://alp.org.au/media/2594/2021-alp-national-platform-final-endorsed-platform.pdf.

ALP National Platform. 2023. 'Determined by the 49th National Conference'. https://www.alp.org.au/about/national-platform.

ATNS (Agreements Treaties and Negotiated Settlements). [n.d.]. 'Treaties with Indigenous Peoples'. https://www.atns.net.au/treaties-landing.

Australia: State of the Environment (SoE) 2021. 2021. https://soe.dcceew.gov.au/overview/key-findings.

Australia Institute. 2019. 'High Carbon from a Land Down Under: Quantifying CO_2 from Australia's Fossil Fuel Mining and Exports'. https://australiainstitute.org.au/wp-content/uploads/2020/12/P667-High-Carbon-from-a-Land-Down-Under-WEB_0_0.pdf.

Australian Government. 2022. 'Australia's Nationally Determined Contribution'. https://unfccc.int/sites/default/files/NDC/2022-06/Australias%20NDC%20June%202022%20Update%20%283%29.pdf.

Australian Labor Party. 2021. 'Powering Australia'. https://www.alp.org.au/policies/powering-australia.

Baer, Hans A. 2016. 'The Nexus of the Coal Industry and the State in Australia: Historical Dimensions and Contemporary Challenges'. *Energy Policy* 99: 194–202.

Bartos, Stephen. 2022. *Fork in the Road: Impacts of Climate Change on Our Food Supply.* Farmers for Climate Action. https://farmersforclimateaction.org.au/portfolio/fork-in-the-road-impacts-of-climate-change-on-our-food-supply/.

Bättig, M. B. and Bernauer, T. 2009. 'National Institutions and Global Public Goods: Are Democracies more Cooperative in Climate Change Policy?' *International Organization* 63/2: 281–308.

BCA (Business Council of Australia). 2021. 'Achieving a Net Zero Economy'. https://www.bca.com.au/achieving_a_net_zero_economy.

BCA (Business Council of Australia). 2022. 'ACTU and BCA Shared Principles and Policy Suggestions'. *Media Release*, 31 August. https://www.bca.com.au/actu_and_bca_shared_principles_and_policy_suggestions.

Birch, Tony. 2017. 'Climate Change, Recognition and Social Place-Making'. *Sydney Review of Books*, 3 March. https://sydneyreviewofbooks.com/essay/climate-change-recognition-and-caring-for-country/.

Blair, David, Treagust, David Franklin and McCulloch, Malcolm. 2020. 'We Must Fight Climate Change Like It's World War III – Here are 4 Potent Weapons to Deploy'. *The Conversation*, 16 March. https://theconversation.com/we-must-fight-climate-change-like-its-world-war-iii-here-are-4-potent-weapons-to-deploy-131052.

Brotherhood of St Lawrence. 2024. 'Equity and Climate Change'. https://www.bsl.org.au/about/advocacy/equity-and-climate-change/.

Brown, Greg. 2022. 'Albanese: Coal Ban Won't Cut Emissions'. *The Australian*, 21 July. https://www.theaustralian.com.au/ [subscription required].

Budget 2024–25. 2024. 'Investing in a Future Made in Australia'. https://budget.gov.au/content/03-future-made.htm.

Buklijas, Tatjana. 2022. 'Citizen Assemblies Offer Hope for Democracy and Climate Change Challenges'. *Newsroom*, 29 September. https://newsroom.co.nz/2022/09/29/citizen-assemblies-offer-hope-for-democracy-and-climate-change-challenges/.

Burck Jan et al. 2021. 'Climate Change Performance Index (CCPI) 2022', 9 November. https://ccpi.org/download/climate-change-performance-index-2022/.

Cameron, Sarah et al. 2022. *The 2022 Australian Federal Election: Results from the Australian Election Study*. Australian National University. https://australianelectionstudy.org/wp-content/uploads/The-2022-Australian-Federal-Election-Results-from-the-Australian-Election-Study.pdf.

Chalmers, Jim. 2022. 'Economic Challenges, Opportunities and Wellbeing on Both Sides of the Tasman'. Address to the Australia New Zealand Leadership Forum, 8 July. https://ministers.treasury.gov.au/ministers/jim-chalmers-2022/speeches/address-australia-new-zealand-leadership-forum-sydney.

Clean Energy Council. 2022. 'Clean Energy Australia Report 2022'. https://apo.org.au/node/317318.

Climate Action Tracker. 2022. 'Australia', 23 May. https://climateactiontracker.org/countries/australia/2022-05-23/.

Climate Action Tracker. 2023. 'Australia', 11 December. https://climateactiontracker.org/countries/australia/.

Climate Analytics. 2019. 'Australia on Track to Become One of the World's Major Climate Polluters', 8 July. https://climateanalytics.org/press-releases/australia-on-track-to-become-one-of-the-worlds-major-climate-polluters.

Climate Analytics. 2022. 'Australian Election 2022 Political Party and Independent Climate Goals: Analysis', 6 May. https://climateanalytics.org/publications/australian-election-2022-political-party-and-independent-climate-goals-analysis.

Climate Council. 2022. 'Where Do Australia's Major Parties Stand on Climate Action? Australia Political Party Platform Analysis – 2022 Federal Election'. https://www.climatecouncil.org.au/resources/australias-major-parties-climate-action-policy-2022/.

Colvin, Rebecca M. and Jotzo, Frank. 'Australian Voters' Attitudes to Climate Action and their Social-Political Determinants'. *PLoS One* 16 (3). https://doi.org/10.1371/journal.pone.0248268.

Cox, Lisa. 2019. 'Climate Strike in Australia: Everything You Need to Know about Friday's Protest'. *The Guardian*, 19 September. https://www.theguardian.com/environment/2019/sep/14/going-to-the-streets-again-what-you-need-to-know-about-fridays-climate-strike.

Crowe, David. 2021. '"Highly Problematic for Public Trust": Australian Political Donations Revealed'. *The Sydney Morning Herald*, 18 January. https://www.smh.com.au/politics/federal/highly-problematic-for-public-trust-australian-political-donations-revealed-20210117-p56up0.html.

Crowley, Kate. 2021. 'Climate Wars, Carbon Taxes and Toppled Leaders: The 30-Year History of Australia's Climate Response, In Brief'. *The Conversation*, 15 October. https://theconversation.com/climate-wars-carbon-taxes-and-toppled-leaders-the-30-year-history-of-australias-climate-response-in-brief-169545.

CSIRO. 2020. 'State of the Climate 2020'. https://www.csiro.au/en/research/environmental-impacts/climate-change/state-of-the-climate.

Curato, Nicole, Smith, Graham and Willis, Rebecca. 2024. *Deliberative Democracy and Climate Change: Exploring the Potential of Climate Assemblies in the Global South*. International IDEA. https://www.idea.int/publications/catalogue/deliberative-democracy-and-climate-change-exploring-potential-climate.

The Dalai Lama and Stril-Rever, S. 2018. *A Call for Revolution: An Appeal to the Young People of the World*. London: Rider.

Davies, Annie. 2015. 'CSG Industry Hires Well-Connected Staffers'. *The Sydney Morning Herald*, 25 May. https://www.smh.com.au/national/nsw/csg-industry-hires-wellconnected-staffers-20150515-gh2rg3.html.

Davis, Mark. 2011. 'A Snip at $22m to Get Rid of PM'. *The Sydney Morning Herald*, 2 February. https://www.smh.com.au/business/a-snip-at-22m-to-get-rid-of-pm-20110201-1acgj.html.

Diamond, J. M., 2019. *Upheaval: Turning Points for Nations in Crisis*. New York. Little, Brown and Company.

Durrant, Cheryl, Bradshaw, Simon and Pearce, Alix. 2021. *Rising to the Challenge: Addressing Climate and Security in Our Region*. Climate Council. https://www.climatecouncil.org.au/resources/climate-security-region/.

Duvac-Paoli, Leslie-Anne. 2022. 'Re-Imagining the Making of Climate Law and Policy in Citizens' Assemblies'. *Transnational Environmental Law* 11 (2): 235–261.

Eckersley, Robyn. 2015. 'Australian Democracy and Climate Politics for the Long Term'. *Meanjin* 74 (3): 140–145.

Explanatory Memorandum. 2024. 'Net Zero Economy Authority Bill 2024'. https://www.aph.gov.au/Parliamentary_Business/Bills_Legislation/Bills_Search_Results/Result?bId=r7177.

Figueres, Christine and Rivett-Carnac, Tom. 2021. *The Future We Choose: The Stubborn Optimist's Guide to the Climate Crisis*. London. Manilla Press.

Fitzgibbon, Joel. 2021. 'Why Labor Must Not Abandon the Miners'. *Australian Financial Review*, 24 May. https://www.afr.com/politics/federal/why-labor-must-not-abandon-the-miners-20210523-p57ufe [subscription required].

Flanagan, Frances (Convenor). 2018. 'Living in a Warming World: Part 2'. *University of Sydney* (Video), 4 June. https://www.sydney.edu.au/engage/events-sponsorships/sydney-ideas/2018/why-we-need-to-think-about-inequality-and-climate-change.html.

Foreign Affairs, Defence and Trade References Committee. 2018. *Implications of Climate Change for Australia's National Security*. Parliament of Australia. https://www.aph.gov.au/Parliamentary_Business/Committees/Senate/Foreign_Affairs_Defence_and_Trade/Nationalsecurity/Final_Report.

Friel, Sharon. 2014. 'Climate Change Will Widen the Social and Health Gap'. *The Conversation*, 15 August. https://theconversation.com/climate-change-will-widen-the-social-and-health-gap-30105.

Frydenberg, Josh. 2021. 'Capital Markets and the Transition to a Low Emissions Future'. Address to the Australian Industry Group, 24 September. https://ministers.treasury.gov.au/ministers/josh-frydenberg-2018/speeches/address-australian-industry-group-melbourne.

Gammage, Bill. 2012. *The Biggest Estate on Earth: How Aborigines Made Australia*. Crows Nest: Allen & Unwin.

Garnaut, Ross. 2008. 'The Garnaut Climate Change Review: Final Report'. https://apo.org.au/node/3028.

Garnaut, Ross. 2009. 'Climate Change: The Public Interest and Private Interests in Australian Policy'. 2009 Annual Hawke Lecture, 4 November. https://cpb-ap-se2.wpmucdn.com/blogs.unimelb.edu.au/dist/a/142/files/2016/01/2009-Hawke-Lecture-Ross-Garnaut-287yxpi.pdf.

Garnaut, Ross. 2021. *Reset: Restoring Australia After the Pandemic Recession*. Carlton: La Trobe University Press.

Garnaut, Ross. 2022. 'Jobs and Skill Dinner Speech'. Parliament House, 1 September. https://cdn.theconversation.com/static_files/files/2279/Ross_Garnaut_JOBS_AND_SKILL_DINNER_SPEECH_1_September_2022.pdf.

Giddens, Anthony. 2011. *The Politics of Climate Change*, 2nd edn. Cambridge: Polity.

Gorman, Patrick. 2024. 'Net Zero Economy Authority Bill 2024. Senate'. *Parliamentary Debates*, 27 March. https://parlinfo.aph.gov.au/parlInfo/search/display/display.w3p;query=Id%3A%22chamber%2Fhansardr%2F27626%2F0051%22.

Government of South Australia, 2024. 'Government Action on Climate Change'. Department for Environment and Water. https://www.environment.sa.gov.au/topics/climate-change/government-action-on-climate-change.

Hamilton, Clive. 2007. *Scorcher: The Dirty Politics of Climate Change*. Melbourne: Black Inc. Agenda.

Harris, Rob. '"In the Spotlight": Climate Boss Warns Australia Needs to Lift its Climate Ambitions'. *The Sydney Morning Herald*, 24 July. https://www.smh.com.au/world/europe/in-the-spotlight-climate-boss-warns-australia-needs-to-lift-its-climate-ambitions-20220723-p5b3xn.html.

Held, David and Hervey, Angus Fane. 2009. 'Democracy, Climate Change and Global Governance: Democratic Agency and the Policy Menu Ahead'. Policy Network Paper. https://www.researchgate.net/publication/253384972_Democracy_Climate_Change_and_Global_Governance/link/00b7d529782f53fa52000000/download?_tp=eyJjb250ZXh0Ijp7ImZpcnN0UGFnZSI6InB1YmxpY2F0aW9uIiwicGFnZSI6InB1YmxpY2F0aW9uIn19.

Henderson, Anna and Bradfield, Elly. 2016. 'Former Resources Minister Ian Macfarlane Says New Mining Job Complies with Code of Conduct'. *ABC News*, 26 September. https://www.abc.net.au/news/2016-09-26/ian-macfarlane-appointed-to-run-queensland-mining-lobby/7876942.

Hoegh-Guldberg, Ove and Hughes, Lesley. 2021. 'Seriously Ugly: Here's How Australia Will Look If the World Heats By 3°C this Century'. *The Conversation*, 31 March. https://theconversation.com/seriously-ugly-heres-how-australia-will-look-if-the-world-heats-by-3-c-this-century-157875.

Holmes, David and Star, Cassandra. 2018. 'Climate Change Communication in Australia: The Politics, Mainstream Media and Fossil Fuel Industry Nexus'. In *Handbook of Climate Change Communication: Vol 1—Theory of Climate Change Communication*, edited by Walter Leal Filho et al., 151–170. Cham, Switzerland: Springer.

Huntley, Rebecca. 2019. 'Renewing Democracy in a Time of Environmental Crisis'. *Pursuit* (Podcast), 18 November. https://pursuit.unimelb.edu.au/podcasts/renewing-democracy-in-a-time-of-environmental-crisis.

IEA (International Energy Agency). 2021. 'Net Zero by 2050: A Roadmap for the Global Energy Sector'. https://www.iea.org/reports/net-zero-by-2050.

ILO (International Labour Organization). [n.d.]. 'Green Jobs'. https://libguides.ilo.org/green-jobs-en.

International IDEA. 2020. 'The Global State of Democracy Indices: Australia'. https://www.idea.int/gsod-indices/countries-regions-profile?rsc=%5B900%5D.

IPCC. 2014. 'Australasia'. In *AR5 Climate Change 2014: Impacts, Adaptation, and Vulnerability. Part B: Regional Aspects. Contribution of Working Group II to the Fifth Assessment Report of the Intergovernmental Panel on Climate Change.* https://www.ipcc.ch/report/ar5/wg2/.

IPCC. 2018. *Global Warming of 1.5°C: An IPCC Special Report on the Impacts of Global Warming of 1.5°C Above Pre-Industrial Levels and Related Global Greenhouse Gas Emission Pathways, In the Context of Strengthening the Global Response to the Threat of Climate Change, Sustainable Development, and Efforts to Eradicate Poverty.* https://www.ipcc.ch/sr15/.

IPCC. 2022. *Climate Change 2022: Impacts, Adaptation and Vulnerability. Working Group II Contribution to the Sixth Assessment Report of the Intergovernmental Panel on Climate Change.* https://www.ipcc.ch/report/ar6/wg2/.

Joint Standing Committee on Electoral Matters. 2021. *Report of the Inquiry on the Future Conduct of Elections Operating During Times of Emergency Situations.* Parliament of Australia. https://www.aph.gov.au/Parliamentary_Business/Committees/Joint/Electoral_Matters/Emergencysituation/Report.

Jotzo, Frank. 2022. 'Labor's Climate Change Bill Is Set to Become Law – But 3 Important Measures are Missing'. *The Conversation*, 8 September. https://theconversation.com/labors-climate-change-bill-is-set-to-become-law-but-3-important-measures-are-missing-190102.

Knott, Matthew. 2011. 'The Power Index: Lobbyists, Mining Magnate Hooke at #5'. *Crikey*, 28 November. https://www.crikey.com.au/2011/11/28/the-power-index-lobbyists-mining-magnate-hooke-at-5/.

Land, Clare. 2015. *Decolonising Solidarity: Dilemmas and Directions for Supporters of Indigenous Struggles.* London: Zed Books.

Leslie, Tim. 2010. 'Gillard to Ask the People on Climate Change'. *ABC News*, 22 July. https://www.abc.net.au/news/2010-07-22/gillard-to-ask-the-people-on-climate-change/916006.

Lindvall, Daniel. 2020. 'Upphettning: Demokratin i klimatkrisens tid' [Heating: Democracy in the Times of the Climate Crises]. In *Sustainable Democracy: Discussing the Nexus Between Democracy, Youth and Climate Change* (Video), 19 November. Agora: Portal for Parliamentary Development. https://www.agora-parl.org/events-and-lectures/sustainable-democracy-discussing-nexus-between-democracy-youth-and-climate.

Lindvall, Daniel. 2021. 'Democracy and the Challenge of Climate Change' (International IDEA DiscussionPaper 3/2021, 20 October 2021), (accessed 7 September 2022).

Lowitja Institute. 2021. 'Climate Change and Aboriginal and Torres Strait Islander Health'. Discussion Paper. https://www.lowitja.org.au/resource/climate-change-and-aboriginal-and-torres-strait-islander-health/.

Macklin, Jenny. 2019. 'The Case for an Emissions and Employment Accord'. Speech, 21 November. https://assets.bsl.org.au/assets/aa_documents/Macklin_Sambell_Oration_2019.pdf?mtime=20200811132256.

Mann, Michael E. 2009. 'Do Global Warming and Climate Change Represent a Serious Threat to Our Welfare and Environment?' *Social Philosophy and Policy* 26 (2): 193–230.

Mayes, Eve and Talukdar, Ruchira. 2023. 'As School Students Strike for Climate Once More, Here's How the Movement and Its Tactics have Changed'. *The Conversation*, 16 November. https://theconversation.com/as-school-students-strike-for-climate-once-more-heres-how-the-movement-and-its-tactics-have-changed-217663.

McDonald, Matt. 2015. 'Climate Security and Economic Security: The Limits to Climate Change Action in Australia?' *International Politics* 52 (4): 484–501.

McDonald, Matt. 2021. 'After the Fires? Climate Change and Security in Australia'. *Australian Journal of Political Science* 56 (1): 1–18.

McInerney, Marie and Garrett, Peter. 2020. 'Peter Garrett Calls for Australia to Go onto a "War" Footing on Climate Change'. *Croakey Health Media*, 18 February. https://www.croakey.org/peter-garrett-calls-for-australia-to-go-onto-a-war-footing-on-climate-change/.

Megalogenis, George. 2021. *Exit Strategy: Politics After the Pandemic*. Quarterly Essay. Carlton: Black Inc.

Mitchell, Bill. [n.d.]. 'Full Employment via a Job Guarantee'. Blog. http://www.billmitchell.org/Job_Guarantee.php.

Moggridge, Bradley J. et al. 2022. 'IPCC Reports Still Exclude Indigenous Voices. Come Join Us at Our Sacred Fires to Find Answers to Climate Change'. *The Conversation*, 4 March. https://theconversation.com/ipcc-reports-still-exclude-indigenous-voices-come-join-us-at-our-sacred-fires-to-find-answers-to-climate-change-178045.

Montt, Guillermo, Fraga, Federico and Harsdorff, Marek. 2018. 'The Future of Work in a Changing Natural Environment: Climate Change, Degradation and Sustainability'. Research Paper. International Labour Organization. https://www.ilo.org/publications/future-work-changing-natural-environment-climate-change-degradation-and.

Morton, Adam. 2021. 'Australian Government Refuses to Join 40 Nations Phasing Out Coal, Saying It Won't "Wipe Out Industries"'. *The Guardian*, 5 November. https://www.theguardian.com/environment/2021/nov/05/australia-refuses-to-join-40-nations-phasing-out-coal-as-angus-taylor-says-coalition-wont-wipe-out-industries.

Morton, Adam. 2024a. 'Peter Dutton Accused of Trying to "Rip Up" Australia's Commitment to Paris Climate Agreement'. *The Guardian*, 8 June. https://www.theguardian.com/environment/article/2024/jun/08/peter-dutton-accused-of-trying-to-rip-up-australias-commitment-to-paris-climate-agreement.

Morton, Adam. 2024b. 'Peter Dutton has Reignited Australia's Climate Wars. We Factcheck the Major Claims'. *The Guardian*, 13 June. https://www.theguardian.com/environment/article/2024/jun/13/peter-dutton-has-reignited-australias-climate-wars-whats-he-saying-and-whats-the-reality.

Morton, Adam. 2024c. 'Australia Faces Postwar-Style Reconstruction to Reach Net Zero Target, Greg Combet Says'. *The Guardian*, 2 April. https://www.theguardian.com/australia-news/2024/apr/02/australia-faces-postwar-style-reconstruction-to-reach-net-zero-target-says-combet.

Murphy, Katharine. 2017. 'Scott Morrison Brings Coal to Question Time: What Fresh Idiocy is This?' *The Guardian*, 9 February. https://www.theguardian.com/australia-news/2017/feb/09/scott-morrison-brings-coal-to-question-time-what-fresh-idiocy-is-this.

NSW Government. 2022. 'NSW Climate Change Policy Framework'. https://www.energy.nsw.gov.au/sites/default/files/2022-08/nsw-climate-change-policy-framework-160618.pdf.

OECD. 2017. 'Preventing Policy Capture: Integrity in Public Decision Making'. https://www.oecd.org/gov/preventing-policy-capture-9789264065239-en.htm.

Ogge, Mark, Quicke, Audrey and Campbell, Rod. 2021. 'Undermining Climate Action: The Australian Way'. Discussion Paper. *The Australia Institute*, 3 November. https://australiainstitute.org.au/report/undermining-climate-action/.

O'Malley, Nick. 2022. 'UN Boss: "Madness" to Back Fossil Fuels as Global Energy Crunch Bites'. *The Sydney Morning Herald*, 21 March. https://www.smh.com.au/environment/climate-change/un-boss-madness-to-back-fossil-fuels-as-global-energy-crunch-bites-20220321-p5a6j9.html.

O'Neill, L. et al., 2021. 'Renewable Energy Development on the Indigenous Estate: Free, Prior and Informed Consent and Best Practice in Agreement-Making in Australia' 81 *Energy Research & Social Science*: 102252.

Queensland Government. 2022. 'Queensland Energy Workers' Charter'. https://www.epw.qld.gov.au/__data/assets/pdf_file/0010/33031/queensland-energy-plan-workers-charter.pdf.

Quiggin, John. 2007. 'Drought, Climate Change and Food Prices in Australia'. https://d3n8a8pro7vhmx.cloudfront.net/auscon/pages/1345/attachments/original/1474000113/Climate_change_and_food_prices_in_Australia.pdf.

Quiggin, John. 2020. 'Getting Off Coal: Economic and Social Policies to Manage the Phase-Out of Thermal Coal in Australia'. Discussion Paper. *The Australia Institute.* https://australiainstitute.org.au/report/getting-off-coal-economic-and-social-policies-to-manage-the-phase-out-of-thermal-coal-in-australia/.

Spratt, David and Dunlop, Ian. 2019. 'The Third Degree: Evidence and Implications for Australia of Existential Climate-Related Security Risk'. Discussion Paper. *National Centre for Climate Restoration*, 27 July. https://apo.org.au/node/271446.

Stanford, Jim. 2020. 'Employment Aspects of the Transition from Fossil Fuels in Australia'. *The Australia Institute.* https://apo.org.au/node/310142.

Stern, Nicholas H. 2006. *The Stern Review Report on the Economics of Climate Change.* H.M. Treasury. https://webarchive.nationalarchives.gov.uk/ukgwa/20100407172811/https:/www.hm-treasury.gov.uk/stern_review_report.htm.

Tham, Joo-Cheong. 2023. *Climate Change and Democracy: Insights from Asia and the Pacific.* International IDEA. https://www.idea.int/publications/catalogue/climate-change-and-democracy-insights-asia-and-pacific.

Tham, Joo-Cheong. 2024a. 'Senate Report on Lobbying Passes the Buck on Improving Transparency or Legislation'. *The Conversation,* 8 May 2024.https://theconversation.com/senate-report-on-lobbying-passes-the-buck-on-improving-transparency-or-legislation-229510 Tham, Joo-Cheong. 2024b. 'Political Finance Law Reforms will Reduce Big Money in Politics but Rich Donors will be the Ultimate Winners'. *The Conversation,* 19 November 2024). https://theconversation.com/political-finance-law-reforms-will-reduce-big-money-in-politics-but-will-rich-donors-be-the-ultimate-winners-243906

Thorpe, Andrew. 2021. 'Australia Not Pulling Its Weight on Climate: Former UN Secretary-General Ban Ki-Moon'. *The Canberra Times*, 19 August. https://www.canberratimes.com.au/story/7392600/australia-not-pulling-its-weight-on-climate-former-un-secretary-general/.

Uluru Statement from the Heart. 2017. https://ulurustatement.org/the-statement/view-the-statement/.

United Nations Declaration on the Rights of Indigenous Peoples. 2007. A/RES/61/295. https://www.un.org/en/genocideprevention/documents/atrocity-crimes/Doc.18_declaration%20rights%20indigenous%20peoples.pdf (accessed 13 September).

UN Human Rights Committee. 2022. 'Views Adopted by the Committee under Article 5(4) of the Optional Protocol, Concerning Communication No. 3624/2019'. CCPR/C/135/D/3624/2019. 21 July. https://tbinternet.ohchr.org/_layouts/15/treatybodyexternal/Download.aspx?symbolno=CCPR%2fC%2f135%2fD%2f3624%2f2019&Lang=en.

UN News. 2022. 'First Person: Torres Strait Islanders Fight the Loss of their Ancestral Home'. *United Nations*, 23 April. https://news.un.org/en/story/2022/04/1116552.

UN Sustainable Development Group. [n.d.]. 'Leave No One Behind'. https://unsdg.un.org/2030-agenda/universal-values/leave-no-one-behind.

Vidal, John. 2019. 'The Lost Decade: How We Awoke to Climate Change Only to Squander Every Chance to Act'. *HuffPost,* 30 December. https://www.huffpost.com/entry/lost-decade-climate-change-action-2020_n_5df7af92e4b0ae01a1e459d2.

Wilkinson, Marian. 2020. *The Carbon Club: How a Network of Influential Climate Sceptics, Politicians and Business Leaders Fought to Control Australia's Climate Policy.* Crows Nest: Allen & Unwin.

Wiseman, John. 2021. *Hope and Courage in the Climate Crisis: Wisdom and Action in the Long Emergency.* Cham, Switzerland. Palgrave Macmillan.

Wood, Tony, Reeve, Alison and Ha, James. 2021. *Towards Net Zero: A Practical Plan for Australia's Governments.* Grattan Institute. https://grattan.edu.au/report/towards-net-zero-a-practical-plan-for-australias-governments/.

Wright, Christopher, Nyberg, Daniel and Bowden, Vanessa. 2021. 'Beyond the Discourse of Denial: The Reproduction of Fossil Fuel Hegemony in Australia'. *Energy Research & Social Science* 77. https://doi.org/10.1016/j.erss.2021.102094.

Yunkaporta, Tyson. 2019. *Sand Talk: How Indigenous Thinking Can Save the World.* Melbourne: Text Publishing.

Legislation

Climate Change Act 2022 (Cth)
Climate Change (National Framework for Adaptation and Mitigation) Bill 2020 (Cth)
Net Zero Economy Authority Bill 2024 (Cth)

INDEX

Note: Page references in *italics* refers to figures and **bold** refers to tables

www.ingramcontent.com/pod-product-compliance
Ingram Content Group UK Ltd.
Pitfield, Milton Keynes, MK11 3LW, UK
UKHW041536250325
456655UK00002B/2

9 781839 993534